The
Black American
Experience

From Reconstruction
to the Present

The Black American Experience

From Reconstruction
to the Present

Arvarh E. Strickland

Jerome R. Reich

HBJ HARCOURT BRACE JOVANOVICH, INC.

New York   Chicago   San Francisco   Atlanta   Dallas

ABOUT THE AUTHORS:

Arvarh E. Strickland has taught history and the social sciences in secondary schools in Mississippi. He also served as high school principal and then as Supervisor of Schools in Madison County, Mississippi.

Dr. Strickland is professor of history at the University of Missouri at Columbia, where he teaches courses in both Afro-American history and American history. He also has taught history at Tuskegee Institute in Alabama and at Chicago State University. He served on the Committee of Examiners which developed the Afro-American history examination for Educational Testing Service's college level examination program. In 1973, he was one of five historians appointed to a special advisory committee on the publication of the papers of black Americans. This committee is advisory to the National Historical Publications Commission.

Dr. Strickland received his Ph.D. in history from the University of Illinois. He has written a *History of the Chicago Urban League* and is co-author of the American history textbook *Building the United States*. He has contributed articles and book reviews to the *Missouri Historical Review, Encyclopaedia Britannica*, the *Journal of Negro History*, the *Journal of American History*, and other professional journals.

Jerome R. Reich has taught history and social studies in secondary and elementary classrooms in the Chicago public school system for nearly twenty years. Dr. Reich also served as principal in several Chicago schools from 1955 to 1965. Most of his teaching and administrative career has been in inner-city schools.

At present Dr. Reich is professor of history at Chicago State University. He also has taught education courses and supervised student teachers in history and the social sciences.

Dr. Reich received his Ph.D. in history from the University of Chicago. He has written a study of Leisler's Rebellion and has contributed articles to the *Journal of Negro History, Social Education*, and the *Illinois Schools Journal*. He is co-author of several widely used school textbooks, *Building the American Nation, Building the United States*, and *Building the Modern World*.

ACKNOWLEDGMENTS: For permission to reprint copyrighted material, grateful acknowledgment is made to the following sources:

Kraus-Thomson Organization Limited: Six lines of poetry by W. E. B. Du Bois from *The Negro Caravan*, edited by Sterling A. Brown, Arthur P. Davis and Ulysses Lee. Excerpt from *Dusk of Dawn: An Essay Toward an Autobiography of a Race Concept* by W. E. B. Du Bois.
Twayne Publishers, Inc.: Four lines from "White Houses" and two lines from "If We Must Die" by Claude McKay, from *Selected Poems of Claude McKay*, copyright 1953 by Bookman Associates.

ISBN 0-15-371052-7

Printed in the United States of America

CONTENTS

UNIT THREE **BLACK AMERICANS AND PROGRESSIVISM**

UNIT FOUR **THE UNCERTAIN YEARS OF THE 1920'S**

UNIT FIVE **FROM DEPRESSION TO WORLD WAR II**

UNIT SIX THE POSTWAR YEARS, 1945 TO THE 1970'S

UNIT ONE

THE YEARS OF BETRAYAL

Chapter 1

Black Americans and Populism

Black political participation in the South did not end with the return of white rule in the years after Reconstruction. The deep-rooted divisions among white Southerners allowed blacks to have a limited role in Southern politics. The basic split among white Southerners was due to the conflicting interests of the large planters and the small farmers.

The small farmers challenged the control exercised by the large planters. The small farmers, who formed independent parties and later joined the Populist movement, wanted the support of black voters. However, planters, or large land owners, were able to prevent any effective cooperation between blacks and white farmers. On the one hand, the planters were able to allow certain political rights to Southern blacks without feeling any threat to their power. On the other hand, they appealed to the race prejudice of the white farmers. The planters also controlled the political machinery of the state and local governments, and they used it in their fight to defeat Populism.

THE WHITE SOUTH WAS NOT "SOLID"

The white South was never as "solid" as some people suggested. Divisions between the planters and the upcountry farmers played an important role in the political fate of Afro-Americans after Reconstruction. The white farmers occupied land not suited to plantation-type agriculture. Their land was less fertile than the bottom land owned by the planters. The farmers often had trouble making a living from the small patches of barren, rocky land they cultivated. The planters, on the other hand, controlled large amounts of fertile land. They employed many black sharecroppers and farm day laborers. They used this land and labor to produce large crops for the world market. In fact, the planters had more in common with the commercial, banking, and industrial groups of the North than with the self-sufficient, small white farmers of the South.

The difference between planters and farmers had existed for a long time. Before the Civil War, the two groups had divided politically into the Whig and the Democratic Parties. Even though the planters, like the farmers, became Democrats after the war, the conflict between the two groups continued. They united for a while to overthrow the Republican-controlled state governments set up during Reconstruction. But after that their economic and social differences caused problems within the Democratic Party. They disagreed on the question of inflation. By favoring easy credit and the issuing of more paper money, the farmers favored inflation. The planters wanted to end inflation, tighten credit, and sharply limit the supply of paper money in order to stop inflation and have a stable currency. The planters also favored the practice of leasing prisoners to work on plantations, and some planters became rich by using such cheap prison labor. The white farmers' crops were forced to compete with products grown by planters who used this cheap labor.

A major conflict also arose over state debts. These debts were largely the result of state money paid to aid railroad building during Reconstruction. Southern farmers wanted to reduce these debts so that their taxes would be lower. The farmers wanted the state governments to repudiate the debt caused by railroad building—that is, to have the state refuse to pay it. Such a policy was considered dishonest by the planters and businessmen in the Democratic Party. During the hard times caused by the depression of 1873, the farmers increased their demand that something be done to reduce taxes. But the planters controlled the Democratic Party, and they blocked efforts to reduce the state debts by repudiation.

FARMERS FORMED THEIR OWN PARTIES

Southern farmers finally realized that the only way they could get anything done was to leave the Democratic Party. As early as 1874, independent farmer-supported candidates began to run for office. Within a few years, independent candidates were challenging conservative Democratic candidates in South Carolina, Arkansas, and Tennessee. These independent farmer groups now were called "radicals." And they became even more unhappy with the national Democratic Party after 1878, when the party declared that it favored "hard money." This meant that the Democrats were against paper money and inflation.

By 1880, many Southern radicals were supporting third parties. The Greenback-Labor Party was one of the first groups to receive their support. In Virginia and Tennessee, the state debt issue was especially important. The farmers' candidates ran as "Readjusters" and "Low-Tax Democrats." The radicals had some success in Virginia. They won a majority in the legislature in 1879. Two years later, their candidate was elected governor of the state.

The Readjusters made a number of changes in Virginia. They reduced the state debt by about one third. Taxes on land were reduced, and taxes on corporations were increased. Railroads now had to pay taxes, and their activities were regulated. One important law made it legal for labor unions to organize. Another bill ended whipping as punishment for crime. The Readjusters also improved the public schools in Virginia. Under the conservatives, many of the schools had been in danger of closing because of a lack of money. The radicals increased funds for school support, paid teachers their back salaries, and opened new schools.

In other states, the radicals were not as successful as they were in Virginia, and they were able to win only a few offices. In most states, the planters and the business leaders were too firmly in control for the farmers to make much progress. And the planters showed that they were determined to use any means necessary to maintain their control.

BOTH SIDES WANTED BLACK VOTES

The only way the radicals could gain success in most Southern states was to cooperate with local Republicans. Leaders of the two groups often agreed not to run candidates for the same offices. Then the radicals and the Republicans would work together against the Democrats. Such agreements, or fusion tickets, made possible the election of radicals and Republicans to office. The national Republican Party,

4

as the party of business and industry, stood for everything that the radical farmers opposed. In addition, the Republican Party in the South was composed largely of blacks. The strongest racial hatred had always existed between blacks and the group of white farmers who supported the independent parties.

The cooperation between the radicals and the Republicans left the radicals open to attack by the conservative Democrats. The Democrats accused the radicals of trying to bring back Republican control and black rule in the South. The Democrats even supported some of the Republican black candidates, because they wanted blacks in a few state offices so that they could use the threat of black rule to stir up hatred against the radicals. The Democrats believed that if most Southern whites regarded the Republican Party as the party of blacks, whites would vote against both the Republicans and the radicals.

At the same time, the conservative Democrats needed black votes. Since they controlled most of the Southern governments' election machinery, they were often able to use this power to win elections. The Democrats used black votes to help defeat the radicals. They used several means to control the black vote. Violence and intimidation were common means. Many planters still regarded blacks as their responsibility and gave them a certain amount of protection. They knew that their sharecroppers and tenants were economically dependent upon them. Many planters were even willing for blacks to have certain political and economic rights, so long as these rights were no threat to planter control. From time to time, the conservative Democrats rewarded a loyal black with a minor political office.

PLANTERS USED THE RACE ISSUE AND FRAUD

The use of the race issue finally caused the radicals' defeat. By appealing to racial prejudice, the conservative Democrats were able to destroy the alliance between the radicals and the Republicans. Many white Southerners worked against their own economic and social interests because of their support of white supremacy. In Virginia, for example, the Readjusters were defeated in 1883 following a race riot in Danville. Whites flocked to the polls and returned the conservative Democrats to power.

Where racism did not work, the conservatives used fraud. Ballot boxes were stuffed with illegal Democratic votes in some places. In others, boxes with large numbers of radical votes were destroyed. Newspapers in Mississippi reported that "boxes containing anti-Dem-

During the 1880's and 1890's, both the Populists and the Democrats tried to gain the political support of black Southerners, especially those in farming areas.

ocratic majorities had been eaten by mules or horses." In this way, the radical farmers were defeated. Then, in the early 1890's, the farmers renewed the fight by joining the Populist movement.

THE POPULISTS NEEDED BLACK SUPPORT

Populism was similar to the earlier radical political movement among the upcountry white farmers of the South. The new Populist movement was strong in the same Southern counties where the independent radical parties had been strong. But Populism was a nationwide political effort. Farmers in many parts of the nation supported the Populist Party because they felt that farming interests were being sacrificed to the interests of business and industry. The Populist Party was supported by farmers' alliances that had been forming in many states during the 1880's. At first, the alliances were mainly small groups of local farmers organized to help each other. By the 1890's, they were more strongly organized and began to make their power felt in state and national politics. In the South, there were two separate organizations. The Southern Alliance accepted only white farmers as members. Black farmers joined the Colored Farmers' Alliance.

When Populism began in the early 1890's, the black vote was still important in the South. In spite of threats, fraud, and violence, many blacks still were able to vote. Where black votes made a difference, white candidates made appeals for black support. In trying to gain power, the Populists worked to attract black voters to their cause.

Tom Watson, a Georgia Populist leader, urged lower-class whites to join with blacks to win elections. Later, Watson became one of the most bigoted of Southern leaders. But at this time, he told both white and black Southerners: "You are kept apart that you may be separately fleeced of your earnings. You are made to hate each other because upon that hatred is rested the keystone of the arch of financial despotism which enslaves you." A Northern Populist, Ignatius Donnelly, said in 1892 that the Populists proposed to "wipe the Mason-Dixon line out of our geographies" and "to wipe the color line off all our politics."

SOME BLACKS RESPONDED TO THE POPULIST APPEAL

Black voting and political activity increased as the Populists grew stronger. Political participation among blacks had declined somewhat during the 1880's, but the Populists helped to reverse this trend. They fought to regain the vote for black people in places where they had lost it. In other places, they helped to add more black voters to those eligible to vote. In 1896, for example, Republicans and Populists took over the town of Washington in Louisiana, and they forced the Democratic election officials there to register black voters.

Blacks were brought into the structure of the Populist Party. By 1890, blacks in Kansas, for example, felt deserted by the Republican Party. The Republicans were no longer supporting black candidates for office nor supporting measures to protect the rights of black people. Benjamin F. Foster, a militant black leader, spoke out against the Republicans. When the Populist Party was formed in Kansas, Foster joined it and urged other blacks to follow his lead. Foster was selected as Populist candidate for state auditor in 1890. The following year, he was a delegate to the Populist convention at Cincinnati, Ohio.

It was common practice to elect black members to the state executive committees of the Populist Party. The Texas state executive committee had two black members in 1892. Conventions in other states followed this example. Tom Watson nominated a black Georgian as a member of that state's Populist executive committee. In Arkansas, the Populist convention approved a resolution offered by a black delegate which declared: "That it is the object of the Peoples' [Populist] Party to elevate the downtrodden sons and daughters of industry in all matters before the people, irrespective of race or color."

Blacks were also active on Populist campaign committees. The ten-member campaign committee in Greene County, Georgia, included five blacks. This participation sometimes led to trouble. H. S. Doyle, a black minister who had campaigned for Watson, was threatened with lynching in 1892. Watson called upon his supporters for help. For two nights, Doyle was given protection by 2,000 armed white farmers.

BLACKS WERE ELECTED TO POLITICAL OFFICE

It was common for blacks to serve in Southern state governments. Blacks held office in the city government of Richmond, Virginia, until 1896. In Georgia, North Carolina, and other states, blacks were elected to the state legislatures throughout the 1890's. Black Republican leaders remained powerful in state affairs. Chief among these were W. H. Deas in South Carolina, W. A. Pledger in Georgia, Norris Wright Cuney in Texas, and James J. Hill, John R. Lynch, and Blanche K. Bruce in Mississippi.

Several Southern states continued to send blacks to Congress during these years. A number of those who had been elected during Reconstruction continued to be elected. In some states, new men were elected with Populist support. Virginia had a black Congressman until 1891. South Carolina sent black Representatives to Congress until the early 1890's. Henry P. Cheatham of South Carolina was the only black elected to Congress in 1891. He was replaced by George W. Murray in 1893. Murray was reelected in 1895. In North Carolina, George H. White served as a Representative until his term ended in 1901.

REPUBLICANS AND POPULISTS IN NORTH CAROLINA

Cooperation between Republicans and Populists continued in North Carolina until nearly the end of the 1890's. Important political changes took place in North Carolina as a result of this long period of fusion politics. The few black Democrats in the state were pressured by both whites and blacks. Before 1892, white Democrats opposed having blacks in the party. Blacks, on the other hand, considered those who deserted the Republican Party as disloyal to black people.

With the rise of Populist support in the state, the Democrats became concerned. The Democrats lost members to the new party. As early as 1890, some Democrats feared that a fusion, or combined, ticket of Republican and Populist candidates would defeat the Democrats. After 1892, the Democrats actively sought black votes, but their efforts failed in most cases. In 1894, the fusion ticket won, and Democratic state control ended.

A North Carolina election law passed in 1895 led to more black office holders at the local level. Under this law, the state legislature no longer appointed certain local officials; these officials now were elected by the local people. Many local governments were in the hands of the Democrats. In counties with large black populations, black officials were elected to some offices.

Black office holders appointed to office in Southern states also increased. In 1895, the North Carolina legislature appointed 300 black magistrates. Black sheriffs were elected in several counties. In New Bern and Wilmington, there were black policemen and aldermen. By 1898, there were 1,000 black office holders in North Carolina.

POPULISTS WERE SPLIT BY RACIAL PREJUDICE

The alliance between blacks and the Populists was an uneasy one. For many reasons, most blacks never trusted the Populists. Many of the white Populists were openly prejudiced. Moreover, the Populist Party never supported major issues that were of interest to blacks. The money question was of limited interest to landless black sharecroppers. At the same time, the Populists opposed federal help to blacks in protecting their constitutional rights. The Colored Farmers' Alliance, for example, supported federal bills to protect black voters and to provide aid to education. The Southern Alliance, composed of white farmers, opposed these bills.

Racial prejudice was largely responsible for keeping the farmers' alliance movement split along sectional and racial lines. The Southern Alliance would not merge with the Northern Alliance because the Northern group opposed a separate organization for black members. Nor would the Southern Alliance agree on a compromise providing for separate local organizations. The black and white alliances in the South came into strong disagreement in 1891 over a strike of cotton pickers. The Colored Alliance tried to organize black cotton pickers and to back a strike for decent wages. The leaders of the Southern Alliance urged planters to leave the cotton in the fields rather than agree to this demand.

CONSERVATIVE DEMOCRATS FOUGHT THE POPULISTS

The Democrats used every tactic they could to break up the alliance between Southern blacks and whites. The conservative Democrats convinced themselves that conditions in the South were the same in the 1890's as they had been during Reconstruction. Again, they tried to picture themselves as the saviors of the South. During the Reconstruction years, they had used fraud, terror, and even murder to achieve what they wanted. Now, in the 1890's, they tried to use these methods to defeat the Populist movement.

This time the result was different. The majority of those who lost political power during the 1890's were Southern whites. As one Populist editor pointed out: "It is no excuse to say that the iniquities are practiced to 'preserve white civilization.' In the first place it was white men who were robbed of their votes, and white men who were defrauded out of office." At the very same time the Democrats were criticizing the Populists for using the black vote, the Democrats were using it themselves. The conservative Democrats used fraud and terror to obtain large numbers of black votes in counties with large black populations. These conservative Democratic majorities in the black counties helped overcome Populist majorities in the white counties.

But the role of independent black voters in the defeat of Populism also needs to be recognized. Black citizens often decided to vote for the Democrats as a lesser evil than the Populists. To claim that Democratic votes by blacks were the result of fraud and intimidation alone ignores the fact that blacks were sensitive to Populist racism.

The Southern Populists remained supporters of white supremacy. They opposed measures they felt might lead to social or political equality for blacks. Populist candidates often were more openly racist in their campaigns than were the conservatives. In such cases, blacks often voted for the Democrats. For example, Georgia blacks turned against the Populists and voted Democratic in 1895. A black ward in Augusta gave Populist leader Tom Watson only nine votes, while casting 989 for his opponent.

Chapter 2

Becoming Second-Class Citizens

The United States Supreme Court, following the lead of Northern opinion and the Republican Party leaders, began to turn its back on black Americans. The election of 1876 had made it clear that the North had lost interest in protecting the rights of the former slaves. The idealism and crusading spirit of earlier years were soon replaced by a less humane spirit that accompanied America's new era of great industrial growth.

In keeping with these changing conditions, the Supreme Court helped to legalize second-class citizenship for Afro-Americans. During the years from 1876 to 1914, the Supreme Court removed most of the protection blacks had received from the laws and amendments to the Constitution enacted during the Reconstruction period.

THE CIVIL RIGHTS ACT OF 1866 WAS PASSED
Congress passed its first civil rights act in April, 1866. This law made blacks citizens and gave them the rights that go with citizenship. The

act made it unlawful for states and territories to deprive citizens of their rights because of "race and color" or "any previous condition of slavery or involuntary servitude." Anyone who used a law to discriminate against any American citizen because of race, color, or previous condition of servitude could be punished under the Civil Rights Act of 1866. As further protection for blacks, this law provided that if state and local courts failed to protect the rights guaranteed by the Civil Rights Act, cases could be brought into federal district courts. In addition, the President was given the power to use the "land or naval forces of the United States, or the militia" to enforce the act.

THE FOURTEENTH AND FIFTEENTH
AMENDMENTS WERE ADDED

Congress took steps to strengthen the provisions of the Civil Rights Act of 1866 by having them added as amendments to the United States Constitution. It is more difficult to secure an amendment to the Constitution than it is to pass a bill in Congress. It is also more difficult to repeal an amendment than it is to change or repeal a law of Congress. Therefore, Congress sought to add the Fourteenth and Fifteenth Amendments to the Constitution so that it would be impossible for a conservative majority in Congress in future years to repeal the Civil Rights Act. Those who favored equal rights for black people worked hard to make these rights a part of the Constitution.

The Fourteenth Amendment, drawn up by Congress, was ratified by the states in 1868. Blacks received little immediate protection from the provisions of this amendment, but it had important long-range effects. The most important part of the amendment is the first section, which says that no state may "abridge the privileges and immunities of citizens of the United States; nor . . . deprive any person of life, liberty, or property without due process of law; nor deny to any person . . . the equal protection of the laws." These parts of the amendment—often referred to as the "privileges and immunities" clause, the "due process" clause, and the "equal protection" clause—became the Constitutional foundation for major breakthroughs in civil rights that were to occur in later years.

The Fifteenth Amendment, ratified by the states in 1870, granted blacks the right to vote. The Fifteenth Amendment provided: "The right of citizens of the United States to vote shall not be denied or abridged by the United States or by any State on account of race, color, or previous condition of servitude."

In proposing this amendment, Congress acted to overcome the refusal of Southern states in their constitutions and laws to permit black people to vote. The Republicans in Congress were also aware of the importance of black voters in keeping the Republican Party in power. Their importance had been made clear in the Presidential election of 1868. General Ulysses S. Grant received a popular-vote majority of only 300,000 votes. His majority would not have been possible without the votes of 700,000 Southern black voters.

CONGRESS PASSED SEVERAL MORE CIVIL RIGHTS ACTS

Between 1866 and 1875, Congress passed seven civil rights acts. Soon after the first act in 1866, two less important laws also were passed. The Civil Rights Act of May 21, 1866, made it a crime for any citizen of the United States to sell any black person into servitude either in the United States or in a foreign country. The Civil Rights Act of March 2, 1867, made it unlawful to hold a person in servitude because of debt.

After the Fourteenth and Fifteenth Amendments were approved by the states and became part of the Constitution, Congress passed a series of acts, or laws, to enforce their provisions. These civil rights acts were called "force acts" by Southerners. The first such act, the Enforcement Act of May 31, 1870, had almost the same provisions as the Civil Rights Act of 1866. But the new act was written primarily to support the provisions of the Fourteenth Amendment and to punish efforts to deny blacks the right to vote granted them by the Fifteenth Amendment. An act passed in February, 1871, also dealt with the right to vote. It placed the supervision of elections in the hands of federal officials.

The Ku Klux Act of April 20, 1871, was another law to protect rights guaranteed by the Fourteenth Amendment. It was aimed at the Ku Klux Klan and other terrorist organizations. This law placed penalties on those who deprived "any person or any class of persons of the equal protection of the laws, or of equal privileges or immunities under the laws."

The Civil Rights Act of March 1, 1875, was the last such act passed by Congress during Reconstruction. The 1875 act was the most far-reaching law of all. It went beyond the protection of political rights contained in the Civil Rights Act of 1866. It guaranteed all citizens "the full and equal enjoyment of the accommodations, advantages, facilities, and privileges of inns, public conveyances on land or water, theatres, and other places of public amusement." Persons guilty of discriminating against blacks in these areas could be sued for damages. The act also made it unlawful to exclude citizens from service on juries because of their race or color.

THE SUPREME COURT WEAKENED CIVIL RIGHTS

Even before Congress had completed this framework for the protection of black rights, the Supreme Court began to tear it down. Numerous decisions weakened the rights guaranteed to black Americans by the Constitutional amendments and the civil rights laws. In fact, the Supreme Court helped to prepare the way for segregation and disfranchisement, or loss of the right to vote.

In rulings on the Fourteenth and Fifteenth Amendments, the Court weakened them in several ways. It ruled that the amendments applied only to the actions of states or state officials, not to the actions of private individuals. It declared that if the wording of a law contained no obvious discrimination, the Court would not review the law to see if it worked greater hardships on black citizens than on whites. It placed more importance on the police power of the states than it did on civil rights. Thus, the rights of individuals and guarantees of equal treatment were often set aside when the states claimed that they were acting under their police powers. The Court also ruled there was a difference between "discrimination" and "racial distinction." It ruled that the Constitution and laws often did not permit discrimination, but that racial distinction, such as "separate but equal" schools, was not forbidden by the Constitution.

THE SUPREME COURT WEAKENED
THE FOURTEENTH AMENDMENT

The first great blow struck against the Fourteenth Amendment came from the Supreme Court's rulings in the *Slaughter House Cases* of 1873. These cases involved neither the civil rights of Afro-Americans nor racial discrimination. They concerned a monopoly granted by the Louisiana legislature. In 1869, Louisiana gave one company the exclusive right to slaughter animals for meat in the New Orleans area. This monopoly was justified on the grounds that the state was using its police power to protect the health and safety of its citizens.

Legal action against the monopoly was brought by an association of butchers. They said that the law granting one company exclusive right to engage in slaughtering violated the Thirteenth Amendment because it put many butchers out of work and caused involuntary servitude. They also said that the law conflicted with the privileges and immunities, due process, and equal protection clauses of the Fourteenth Amendment.

When the *Slaughter House Cases* came to the Supreme Court, the Court ruled against the butchers by a 5 to 4 decision. The Court ruled that the Louisiana law did not violate the Thirteenth Amendment. Placing restrictions on the free use of property, the Court said, did not result in involuntary servitude. In its ruling on the Fourteenth Amendment, the Court made that amendment almost useless as a guarantee of the rights of black Americans. The important first section of the amendment was so weakened that it became ineffective. The Court held that state and federal citizenship were separate and distinct. The Fourteenth Amendment had made it illegal for states to interfere with privileges and immunities that persons enjoyed as citizens of the United States. However, the Court now ruled that only a few privileges and immunities came with federal citizenship. Most civil rights were part of state citizenship, and the states were responsible for guaranteeing these rights. Therefore, the Court concluded, the rights enjoyed by citizens of a state were not covered in the Fourteenth Amendment, and the federal government was not responsible for protecting these rights.

OTHER SUPREME COURT RULINGS
WEAKENED CIVIL RIGHTS

In the case of the *United States v. Cruikshank*, the Supreme Court showed how much its ruling in the *Slaughter Houses Cases* had weakened the protection of black Americans' civil rights. The *Cruikshank Case*, which was decided in 1876, involved the Enforcement Act of 1870. A group of more than a hundred white Louisianans went to a meeting held by black citizens to discuss a Louisiana election. The whites broke up the meeting and, in doing so, killed two black men, Levi Nelson and Alexander Tillman. Three of the whites involved were arrested and brought to trial in a federal district court in Louisiana. The three were found guilty of violating the Enforcement Act by breaking up the meeting and by conspiring to prevent the blacks at the meeting from voting.

The United States Supreme Court reversed the ruling of the federal district court. Using the distinction it had made between federal and state citizenship in the *Slaughter House Cases,* the Court ruled that no federal crime had been committed. Persons could be accused of a federal crime only if their action—in this case breaking up the meeting—had something to do with national citizenship. Since the meeting was held to discuss a Louisiana election, the Court said the black citizens who attended it were not protected by the Fourteenth Amendment and federal laws.

In the *United States v. Reese,* also decided in 1876, the Supreme Court helped to make possible the legal disfranchisement of blacks in the South. This case grew out of a violation of the Enforcement Act of 1870. In deciding the case, the Court declared that parts of the Enforcement Act were unconstitutional. The Fifteenth Amendment, the Court ruled, did not guarantee nor grant the right to vote to anyone. The amendment prevented the federal government and the states from "giving preference . . . to one citizen of the United States over another, on account of race, color, or previous condition of servitude." This ruling opened the way to legal disfranchisement of black voters by measures which did not mention race, such as literacy tests and poll taxes.

THE SUPREME COURT UPHELD SEGREGATION IN TRAVEL

The operator of a steamboat on the Mississippi River between New Orleans and Vicksburg refused Mrs. DeCuir, a black woman, the use of cabin space because of her color. Mrs. DeCuir brought suit against the operator under a law passed by the Reconstruction legislature of Louisiana. The law prohibited discrimination on public transportation. Louisiana courts, including the state supreme court, ruled in favor of Mrs. DeCuir. Then the operator of the Mississippi steamboat decided to appeal the decisions that had been handed down by the Louisiana courts. Therefore, his lawyers took the case to the United States Supreme Court.

In the case of *Hall v. DeCuir,* the Supreme Court in 1878 overruled the state supreme court and declared the Louisiana anti-discrimination law to be unconstitutional. The Court said that the law conflicted with the federal government's exclusive right to regulate interstate commerce and travel. Furthermore, the Court said, a law prohibiting discrimination in transportation would cause embarrassment to those carrying interstate passengers. Such a law, declared the Court, was a direct burden on interstate commerce.

CIVIL RIGHTS CASES OF 1883
LIMITED FEDERAL ACTIONS

The high point of the Supreme Court's weakening of the Reconstruction civil rights laws and amendments came in the *Civil Rights Cases of 1883*. In that year, five cases reached the Court that involved violations of the Civil Rights Act of March 1, 1875. Four cases arose because black persons had been refused hotel rooms and seats at theaters in San Francisco, in New York City, and in the states of Kansas and Missouri. The fifth case was a civil suit brought by a black woman and her husband because the woman was refused admission to the ladies' car on a train in Tennessee. The couple sued the railway company for $500 damages.

The Supreme Court's ruling on these cases destroyed any remaining hope black Americans may have had that the Reconstruction amendments and laws granted them political and social equality. Justice Bradley, speaking for eight of the nine members of the Court, ruled on the meaning of the amendments in a way that was clearly different from the meaning Congress had intended when it proposed the amendments.

The Court's decision in the *Civil Rights Cases of 1883* was that the Thirteenth Amendment did not give Congress the power to pass "direct and primary" laws dealing with civil rights. The Court asked if "the denial to any person of admission to the accommodations and privileges of an inn, a public conveyance [transportation], or a theatre, does subject that person to any form of servitude, or tend to fasten upon him any badge of slavery?" The Court answered that it did not, and therefore that the power to pass the Civil Rights Act of 1875 was not given to Congress by the Thirteenth Amendment.

As to the Fourteenth Amendment, the Court declared that this amendment only forbade state actions. "Individual invasion [denial] of individual rights," the court ruled, "is not the subject-matter of the amendment." The only power given to Congress by the amendment was to correct any action taken by the states "which impairs [harms] the privileges and immunities of citizens of the United States, or which injures them in life, liberty, or property without due process of law, or which denies to any of them the equal protection of the laws." This meant that Congress was not free to pass federal laws granting or defining rights.

Justice John Marshall Harlan alone opposed the Supreme Court's decision in the *Civil Rights Cases*. However, his dissent became the majority view many years later. In disagreeing with the Court's opinion of the meaning of the Thirteenth Amendment, Justice Harlan said that slavery as an institution "rested wholly upon the inferiority, as a race, of those held in bondage." Therefore, true freedom had to guarantee the former slaves all of the civil rights enjoyed by "freemen of other races." Congress had the power to pass measures, even "direct and primary" laws, to keep blacks from being deprived because of their race of any civil rights enjoyed by others. These laws, Harlan said, could apply both to individuals and private corporations that serve the public as well as to the actions of state governments and state officials.

Harlan's view of the meaning of the Fourteenth Amendment was similar. He held that, under this amendment, Congress had the power to pass laws to protect blacks from discrimination in enjoying the civil rights enjoyed by whites in the same state. In addition, he said that those whose businesses involved public accommodations were agents of the state. Such individuals and corporations had duties to the public, and were therefore subject to government regulation. If a person was deprived of his civil rights by such agents of the state, it was the same as being deprived of these rights by the state itself. Otherwise, blacks, in seeking to enjoy their civil rights, could be denied their rights by corporations and individuals acting under powers granted by the states.

THE SUPREME COURT PROTECTED SOME NATIONAL RIGHTS

The Supreme Court provided some protection for national rights as it defined them. A case dealing with such rights reached the Court in 1884. A member of the Ku Klux Klan named Yarbrough and other Klansmen had been found guilty of conspiring to threaten Barry Saunders, a black man, during a Congressional election. Specifically, the Klansmen were convicted of violating the Enforcement Act of 1870. Yarbrough appealed to the Supreme Court on the grounds that Congress did not have the power to oversee elections.

This viewpoint was not supported by the Supreme Court. The Court held in *Ex parte Yarbrough* that the government could not exist without the power to "protect the elections on which its existence depends from violence and corruption." The Court found sufficient grounds for this opinion in Article 1, Section 4, of the Constitution.

But the Supreme Court stopped short of providing general protection of the right to vote. In *Williams v. Mississippi,* the Court upheld the taking away of blacks' voting rights by the Mississippi Constitution of 1890. The case concerned a black man named Williams, who had been indicted and convicted of murder by all-white juries. Williams' attorney argued that his client did not get a fair trial because black citizens in that state were unable to serve on juries. Only voters could serve on Mississippi juries and, since Mississippi blacks were disfranchised, Williams had not been tried by a jury made up of his peers.

The Court ruled that the Mississippi constitution and laws did not "on their face discriminate between the races." Therefore, the method of selecting jurors was not necessarily improper. The Court refused to consider any other issue raised by the laws. It upheld the conviction of Williams. In doing so, it approved Mississippi's disfranchising policies and the exclusion of blacks from juries.

THE COURT CONSIDERED FEWER CIVIL RIGHTS CASES

Few cases dealing with civil rights reached the Supreme Court between 1883 and 1914. This was not surprising, for the Court had made the Fourteenth and Fifteenth Amendments all but useless as a protection to black Americans against discrimination. The "privileges and immunities" clause of the Fourteenth Amendment was a dead letter after the *Slaughter House* and *Cruikshank Cases*. The "due process" clause was now being used mainly by corporations as protection against regulation by states, not as it was intended to be used. As a final blow, the Court had further weakened federal protection of black rights by making the "equal protection" clause of the Fourteenth Amendment meaningless.

In 1890, the case of *Louisville, New Orleans, and Texas Railway v. Mississippi,* the Supreme Court approved a law requiring segregation of passengers on public transportation systems. The Mississippi case involved a law requiring separate accommodations for black and white passengers on all trains. The law contained no distinction between intrastate and interstate trains. The Supreme Court ruled that this law did not conflict with the exclusive right of Congress to regulate interstate commerce, or commerce between states. It accepted the state supreme court's view that the law applied only to intrastate trains, or travel within a state. Nor did the Court find that such a law requiring segregation was a direct burden on interstate commerce. Earlier, in the case of *Hall v. DeCuir* the Court had found that laws forbidding discrimination were an undue burden. John Marshall Harlan, in his dissent, pointed out this contradiction to his fellow justices on the Supreme Court.

PLESSY V. FERGUSON MARKED A TURNING POINT

The "separate-but-equal" doctrine was handed down by the Supreme Court in 1896 in the case of *Plessy v. Ferguson*. This case involved state action to deny black citizens equal protection of the laws. Louisiana had passed a law in 1890 requiring all train companies to provide separate accommodations for blacks and whites. Homer Adolph Plessy, who was one-eighth black and seven-eights white, was arrested when he refused to ride in the "colored" coach of a railroad train. Plessy was on an intrastate trip, that is, traveling within just one state, from New Orleans to Covington, Louisiana.

Plessy went to court to stop the segregation law from being enforced on the grounds that it violated the Thirteenth and Fourteenth Amendments. Ferguson, against whom Plessy brought suit, was a Louisiana judge who had been chosen to try Plessy for violating the law. The Louisiana supreme court turned down a plea to stop Ferguson from hearing the case. In the meantime, Albion W. Tourgée, an upstate New York lawyer who had spent some time in the South during Reconstruction, was employed by a group of black leaders to represent Plessy.

When this case reached the United States Supreme Court, the Court handed down its "separate-but-equal" doctrine and paved the way for segregation. The decision said that the Fourteenth Amendment "in the nature of things . . . could not have been intended to abolish distinctions based on color, or to enforce social, as distinguished from political, equality, or a commingling of the two races upon terms unsatisfactory to either."

This was a new argument by the Supreme Court. Even in the *Slaughter House Cases,* the Court had said that the primary purpose of the Reconstruction amendments was the "freedom of the slave race, the security and firm establishment of that freedom, and the protection of the newly made freeman and citizen from the oppressions of those who had formerly exercised unlimited dominion over him." In *Plessy v. Ferguson,* however, the Court ruled that state laws requiring separate accommodations did not violate the equal protection clause if the separate accommodations were "substantially equal." Again, Justice Harlan alone wrote a dissenting opinion.

THE PERIOD OF JIM CROW BEGAN

The Supreme Court decisions handed down after the 1870's gave more proof that the federal government had ended its efforts to protect the

Under the Jim Crow system of racial segregation in the South, blacks had to accept separate drinking fountains, separate restrooms, and separate facilities in all public places.

rights of black Americans. When it became clear that the rights of blacks had been left to be dealt with by states, a generation of repression began. Between 1883 and 1914, blacks were forced to accept second-class citizenship and were kept in this low status by a combination of customs, laws, and violence that became known as "Jim Crow" policies.

In the Southern and border states, discriminatory laws and practices were enforced. States changed their constitutions to remove black citizens from state and local political life. Schools, theaters, restaurants, trains, buses, and other transportation, as well as places of public accommodation, were segregated by law. This Jim Crow system brought with it patterns of behavior that were expected of each group. Blacks were forced to act as inferior persons, to "stay in their place," by the police power of the state and by the terror and brutality of white mobs. Lynchings in the South and race riots in the North became common during the years 1883 to 1914.

Chapter 3

Losing the Vote

Between 1890 and 1910, black citizens in all Southern states were disfranchised. That is, they lost their right to vote. Mississippi led the way by revising its constitution to keep blacks from voting. Other states followed Mississippi's example. Literacy clauses, poll taxes, white primaries, and other means were used to end black voting.

WHY WERE BLACKS DISFRANCHISED?
A number of reasons have been given to explain the movement to rob Southern black citizens of their votes. One historian believed that this simply was a way of removing blacks from their position as the balance of power in the South. With the Populists and the Democrats divided, each side was forced to appeal to black voters for support. Both sides wanted to end so important a role for Afro-Americans. But both sides were unable to agree on how to disfranchise blacks. The Populists were afraid that, in getting rid of black voters, a large number of poor whites

might also lose their votes. This was sure to happen if fair means were used to disfranchise citizens.

Another explanation goes deeper than destruction of the black balance of power. According to this view, black Americans were to be treated as scapegoats in order to bring the white factions in the South together. Blacks already had been abandoned by the North and used as scapegoats to unite the nation as a whole after Reconstruction. Now the divided South needed something to bring it together. The only thing powerful enough to do this was racism—the "magical formula of white supremacy." White radicals and conservatives, white Populists and Democrats, all were able to unite under this banner. The chief victims were the black Americans.

To carry out the policy of white supremacy, it was necessary to remove blacks completely as a political force. This step called for disfranchisement, or denial of voting rights. The whites gave two reasons for this step. First, they claimed that without the need to seek black support, white Southerners would have no cause for conflict with each other. Second, they claimed that without blacks, corruption would disappear from Southern politics. In other words, if there were no black voters, violence and fraud would not be necessary in Southern elections. One observer saw the weakness of this argument. He pointed out that blacks were being disfranchised "to prevent the Democratic election officials from stealing their votes." Such action, he felt, would be "to punish the man who had been injured." But Southern whites were blinded by the formula of white supremacy. They did not want to see the weakness of such reasoning.

MISSISSIPPI LED THE EFFORT TO END BLACK VOTING

A movement to disfranchise blacks by changing state constitutions began in Mississippi in 1890 and spread through much of the South. At first, conservative political leaders of Mississippi opposed the calling of a constitutional convention. Greatest support for a convention came from radical farmers' groups. Gradually, conservative political leaders began to change their minds. With solid farmer support and help from several powerful conservatives, a bill calling a convention was passed by the Mississippi legislature.

But Mississippi voters were not enthusiastic about the convention. Under the Reconstruction constitution of 1868, few Mississippians were denied the right to vote. Just about every adult male, black and white, enjoyed this right. In 1890, there were about 262,000 persons qualified to vote in the state. Only 40,000 of them took part in the election of delegates to the convention. Hinds County, the largest county in the state, had 8,500 voters, but only 540 of them voted. Sharkey County had 1,600 qualified voters, but only four voters took part in the election of delegates.

Democrats ran the convention. Out of the 134 delegates who were elected, 130 were Democrats. Only one called himself a regular Republican. He was Isaiah T. Montgomery, the only black delegate elected. A Democrat contested the seating of Montgomery. It was reported that Montgomery kept his seat by agreeing to support the conservative Democratic group in the convention.

It became clear early in the convention that the majority wanted to revise the constitution in order to insure white supremacy. The key to this aim was to end black voting. A number of schemes to do this were presented. Some delegates favored an educational qualification for voters. This meant that people who were unable to read and write could not vote. Other delegates wanted to require voters to pay a special tax called a "poll tax" before they could vote. A few called for limiting the right to vote to those who owned property worth a certain amount.

White farmers were afraid of some of these plans. Delegates from the white counties, where the poorer farmers lived, opposed educational qualifications. Delegates from the black counties, where white planters were in control, favored educational and property qualifications. The white radicals were afraid that too many whites would lose their votes under either of these plans.

MISSISSIPPI REVISED ITS CONSTITUTION

In devising ways to discriminate against black voters, the Mississippi convention had to get around federal laws and the United States Constitution. The Fourteenth Amendment to the Constitution was supposed to protect the rights of the freedmen. One of its provisions was that all citizens must have equal rights under the laws. That is, a state could not pass laws that discriminated against some of its citizens. The Fifteenth Amendment said that citizens could not be denied the right to vote because of "race, color, or previous condition of servitude." Thus, it required careful planning at the Mississippi convention to come up with a scheme that would end black voting without violating the Constitution.

Another federal law made the work of the convention even more difficult. In the law that Congress had passed in 1870 to readmit Mississippi into the Union, there was a provision dealing with voting. According to this law, the state could not limit the suffrage, or those who might vote, in any way beyond limitations contained in the state constitution of 1868. Suffrage provisions in that constitution were very liberal. Almost any adult male who lived in the state for six months and in the county for one month was eligible to vote. Under these provisions, Mississippi had a majority of black voters numbering about 42,000.

The judiciary committee of the Mississippi convention ruled on the 1870 federal law. The committee said that Congress did not have the power to pass such a law. States alone had the power to say who was and who was not eligible to vote. Thus, Mississippi, as a sovereign state, had the power to fix the rules for voting in spite of the 1870 law. But, the committee pointed out that any new voting regulations would have to "apply alike to both races."

The convention included in the Mississippi constitution several provisions aimed at disfranchising blacks. A longer period of residence was required because it was believed that blacks moved more often than whites. Now a person had to live in the state two years in order to vote and in the county one year. Voters had to register four months before the election. They had to present evidence at the time of the election that they had paid all their taxes for the past two years. Taxes had to be paid in full by February 1 of the year in which a person wanted to vote. Crimes that were thought to be committed more often by blacks than by whites were also used to restrict voting.

A poll tax of two dollars was required of all voters. This tax was supposed to be paid by all male residents between the ages of 21 and 60. The money from this tax was to be used for schools. Voters needed poll-tax receipts for two years in order to vote. Members of the convention did not think that blacks would keep the receipts that long, even if they paid the tax. But the crucial point was the amount of the tax. Two dollars was a great deal of money to a poor sharecropper or farm worker. In the 1890's, a poor person might have to work four days to earn two dollars.

All of these provisions might restrict black voting, but the key provision of the Mississippi constitution of 1890 was the "understanding clause," or literacy test. Under this provision, every voter had to be able to read any section of the state constitution, or "be able to understand the same when read to him." It was generally agreed that whites who were not able to read or understand the constitution were

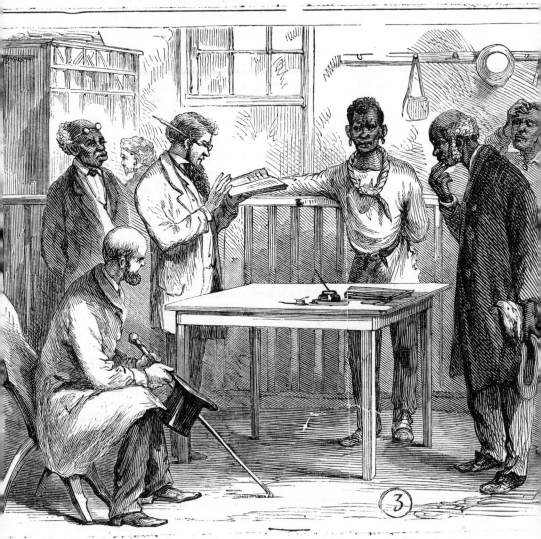

The right to vote was taken away from most black Southerners by literacy tests, poll taxes, and other unfair state laws on voting.

to be passed by the officials registering voters. It also was agreed that no black person was to be allowed to pass the test.

Nothing in any provision of the constitution said that it was intended to disfranchise blacks. In theory, all of the new regulations applied equally to blacks and whites. But in practice the situation was different. The convention had tried to legislate against what it thought were the "peculiar racial characteristics" of black people. The Supreme Court of the United States understood what the convention had done. Still, the Court did not declare the poll tax or the literacy clause unconstitutional.

POLITICAL LIFE IN MISSISSIPPI CHANGED

The revised state constitution brought important changes to political life in Mississippi after 1890. The most obvious change was the sharp decrease in black voters and great loss of Republican strength. In 1876, for example, the Republican Party had polled 52,000 votes in spite of a campaign of terror to keep blacks away from the polls. But in 1892, only 1,500 votes were cast for the Republican ticket. Black political participation ended, or nearly did. Only in counties with large black majorities did blacks continue to be active for several years more. Some of the counties along the Mississippi River continued to have fusion tickets. Blacks from these counties were elected to the state legislature until early in the 1900's. However, even where blacks were no longer a direct political influence, they remained a strong indirect influence. The actions of white politicians and voters were greatly influenced by the presence of the blacks.

The revised Mississippi constitution of 1890 had an adverse effect on many white voters. Even though the voting laws were aimed at blacks only, thousands of whites also lost the right to vote because of the new laws. This condition grew worse as the years passed. White voters were probably most affected by the poll tax. Many poor whites were no more able to pay the two-dollar poll tax than were many poor blacks.

ISAIAH MONTGOMERY WAS CALLED A TRAITOR

Many blacks were shocked by views expressed by Isaiah Montgomery during the Mississippi convention. No one expected that a single black member would have much effect on the work of the convention. But many blacks expected that Montgomery would speak out for black rights. Instead, he spoke out in favor of disfranchising blacks. In a speech, Montgomery favored using literacy tests and property qualifications to reduce the black vote below the level of the white vote. He argued that this outcome would be to the advantage of black Mississippians. They would be encouraged to obtain education and property in order to be able to vote. Thus, Montgomery claimed, the loss of the vote would only be temporary. Gradually, as blacks met the requirements, they would again become voters. In 1890, few black people were ready to accept such reasoning. Throughout the country, Montgomery was called "traitor" and "Judas." T. Thomas Fortune, a black editor, said of Montgomery's remarks: "No flippant fool could have inflicted such a wound upon our cause as Mr. Montgomery has done in this address."

SOUTH CAROLINA FOLLOWED MISSISSIPPI'S EXAMPLE

In South Carolina, farmers also led the fight to end black voting. Under the leadership of Benjamin R. Tillman, these farmers took control of the South Carolina Democratic Party in 1890. They elected a majority to the legislature in 1892. Two years later, the Tillman Democrats proposed that a state constitutional convention be called. By a small majority, they agreed to hold a convention.

The convention met on September 10, 1895. Benjamin R. Tillman was the leading figure at the convention. It was clear that the purpose of the convention was to follow the lead of Mississippi and disfranchise black voters. South Carolina, too, wanted to end black voting but without disfranchising whites and without openly violating the Fourteenth and Fifteenth Amendments. Tillman had the votes to accomplish this purpose. The convention was composed of 122 Tillman Democrats, 42 conservative Democrats, and 6 Republicans. The 6 Republicans were blacks, but there were no black members in the other groups.

The six black members at the convention were Robert Smalls, Thomas E. Miller, William J. Whipper, James Wigg, Isaiah R. Reed, and Robert B. Anderson. These men fought to keep any provision to disfranchise voters from discriminating against blacks. They realized that a far greater percentage of blacks than whites would be disfranchised by any property or literacy requirement.

A new constitutional article on voting was written by a committee headed by Tillman. To be eligible to vote, a citizen had to live in South Carolina for two years, in the county for one year, and in the election district for four months. As in Mississippi, this provision was written because landless blacks tended to move from place to place rather often. A poll tax also was required. This tax had to be paid six months before an election.

All voters also had to register every ten years. Requirements for registration were written in such a way as to make it possible for officials to discriminate against black citizens. Anyone wanting to register to vote had to be able to read and write any section of the state constitution. Or, instead of this, the registration official had the power to ask applicants to show that they owned, and had paid taxes on, property worth $300 or more. In order to permit the immediate registration of illiterate whites, until January 1, 1898, all males of voting age were allowed to register if they were able either to read a clause of the constitution or to understand a clause of the constitution when it was read to them by the registration official. As in Mississippi, it was agreed that no white would fail this test and that no black would pass it.

The black delegates spoke against the new voting article with great skill. Robert Smalls, pointing out that even a fair literacy test was all that was needed to insure a white voter majority, asked that all other requirements be dropped. Thomas E. Miller warned that poor whites also might lose their votes by these provisions intended to disfranchise blacks. This loss woud be a special danger, he added, if those controlling the state government wished to run it in the interests of wealthy planters or rich businessmen at the expense of poor farmers and workers, whether white or black.

But the black delegates' opposition was in vain. After Tillman spoke in favor of the proposal, the suffrage article passed the convention by a vote of 77 to 41. It was clear that the majority of delegates had one principal aim in mind—to end voting by blacks. They were not greatly concerned about fair elections. As one white delegate said: "We are perfectly disgusted with hearing about fair elections. Talk all around, but make it fair and you'll see what'll happen."

The revised constitution accomplished its purpose. Illiterate white citizens registered to vote and continued to participate in politics. The black citizens of South Carolina were disfranchised. Office-holding by blacks came to an end. No blacks were elected to Congress, and after 1902 no black officials served in state or local government offices.

OTHER SOUTHERN STATES SET UP NEW VOTING LAWS

The movement to disfranchise black voters spread throughout the South. In addition to Mississippi and South Carolina, six other states used new constitutional provisions to disfranchise black voters. These states were Louisiana, North Carolina, Alabama, Virginia, Georgia, and Oklahoma. Other states—Tennessee, Florida, Arkansas, and Texas—used poll tax laws and other laws to end black voting.

Two important questions that each state constitutional convention had to answer were whom to disfranchise and how to disfranchise them. The radical white farmers wanted to disfranchise blacks only, but conservative white planters and businessmen were not opposed to disfranchising white radicals at the same time. Generally, however, these white groups agreed that blacks were to be the targets of the disfranchising articles. In Alabama, Virginia, North Carolina, and Georgia, the Democratic Party pledged not to disfranchise any white citizens.

Lower-class whites were still worried they might lose their votes under the new literacy provisions. Delegates to the Louisiana convention were afraid that the requirement of understanding the constitution, even if used like the one in the Mississippi constitution, might eliminate too many white voters. The Louisiana convention, therefore, used the "grandfather clause" to give whites another way of getting around the literacy requirements. Under the "grandfather clause," anyone who had voted before January 1, 1867, and his sons and grandsons, could vote in all future elections without meeting any other requirements. This clause helped lower-class white voters, but it did not help black voters because Southern blacks lacked the right to vote in 1867. Many of the other Southern states also adopted grandfather clauses.

WHITE PRIMARIES WERE USED AGAINST BLACKS

In addition to laws and constitutional provisions, all of the former Confederate states used the white primary to help disfranchise blacks. Under the primary system, candidates for political offices were selected by the voters rather than by conventions. Because the Democratic Party was so strong in the South, the Democratic candidates chosen in the primaries were usually the only candidates in the general election. The idea behind the white primary was that political parties were private organizations. Therefore, they had the power to deny membership to black voters. Because only members of the party could vote in the primaries, blacks were unable to participate.

In the Democratic white primary, a small number of white voters selected nominees for offices from among a few white candidates. Thus, because there usually was no other candidate in the general election, a small group of white primary voters actually elected the nominees to office. This undemocratic system soon led to a general lack of concern about politics in the South. As a result, it became easy for political bosses to control Southern politics.

UNIT TWO

ACCOMMO-
DATION
AND
PROTEST

Chapter 4

Booker T. Washington and Accommodation

The years from the 1880's until World War I have been called "a period of accommodation" in race relations in the United States. During this period, Booker T. Washington was considered the principal leader and spokesman for black Americans.

BLACKS TURNED TO SELF-HELP

As political activity became much more difficult for black Americans, many black leaders came to feel that economic progress was the key to success. Throughout the country, black Americans began to stress self-help and racial unity. They began to act on the belief that since whites had lost interest in black progress, black people would have to unite and help themselves. Most of those who held this view were concerned mainly with economic self-help.

Those who preached self-help urged Afro-Americans to "buy black" in order to help black businesses grow. Black barbers, artisans, and shopkeepers needed black customers to make up for the loss of white support in the late 1800's and early 1900's. Such business activity also was believed to be a way for black Americans to enter the mainstream of American life. Believers in the self-help ideas felt that if blacks became prosperous and adopted black middle-class values, black people would earn the respect and acceptance of whites. This achievement would help to destroy prejudice and solve the so-called race problem. This set of ideas, which became known as the philosophy of accommodation, gave many black Americans a way of surviving within a segregated society.

Those who preached self-help did not necessarily accept the system of segregation and discrimination that was a part of America's racial caste system. This philosophy also contained within it the seeds of protest. For in order to foster group unity, it was necessary to develop group pride and self-respect.

Clearly, this was a complex set of beliefs that might lead black Americans in many directions. And no one person could speak for the millions of black Americans who believed in racial unity and self-help. Nevertheless, one man did come to be the main spokesman for the philosophy of accommodation. That man was Booker T. Washington.

BOOKER T. WASHINGTON WAS BORN A SLAVE

Booker T. Washington was born in Franklin County, Virginia, in 1856. Booker, his mother, a brother, and a sister were slaves on a small backcountry plantation owned by James Burroughs. Booker's mother, Jane Burroughs, was married to Washington Ferguson, a slave on a nearby plantation. Ferguson was the father of Booker's sister, but Booker never learned who his father was. He only knew that he was a white man from a plantation in the area.

Booker's mother was the plantation cook, and the cabin she lived in with her children served as the kitchen. This was the home that Booker T. Washington knew as a child. He never forgot its large fireplace that furnished welcome warmth in the winter or the almost unbearable heat in the summer. He also remembered the pallets of rags on which he and the other children slept on the earthen floor.

The end of the Civil War brought freedom to Booker and his family. Jane Burroughs took her children to live with her husband, Washington Ferguson. Ferguson had escaped from slavery during the Civil War and made his way to Malden, West Virginia. There he worked as a packer in the salt mines. When the war ended, Ferguson sent for his family. Life was hard for Booker in Malden. Although he was only 9 years old when he went to live with his stepfather, Booker and his 13-year-old brother joined Ferguson in working in the mines.

BOOKER WORKED HARD AS A BOY

Quite early, Booker showed a desire for education. He began his education by learning from a copy of Webster's spelling book that his mother got for him. The little he learned only made him want to know more. Therefore, it was a great day for Booker and other blacks in Malden when they were able to hire a teacher to start a school.

At first, Booker's stepfather did not permit him to attend the school. Ferguson said that the boy's earnings in the mines were too important to the family to allow him to stop work. Finally, however, he agreed that Booker might go to school if he worked in the mines for five hours before school and for two more hours after school. But, the family was so poor that they were not able to get along without all of Booker's earnings. So young Booker was able to stay in school for only a short time.

In school, Booker adopted the name by which he would be known for the rest of his life. Until he entered school, he had been known simply as Booker. But at school he found that other children had at least two names. So when he was asked his name, he answered Booker Washington. Later, he added Taliaferro as a middle name. This was the name his mother had given him at birth as a second name. Another thing Booker acquired while in school was the beginning of a point of view on education. He came to believe that education must be useful. Education, he believed, must enable a person to live a better life. But his own life for some time remained one of hard work in the mines.

After his short time in school, Booker returned to mining work full time. From 1865 to 1871, he worked either in the salt mines or in the nearby coal mines. He finally was able to leave the mines in 1871, when he became houseboy to the wife of the mine owner. Booker later credited Mrs. Lewis Ruffner, his employer, with helping him to develop habits of thrift, cleanliness, and hard work. Mrs. Ruffner also encouraged him to continue his education, and permitted him to spend the afternoon in school.

BOOKER ATTENDED HAMPTON INSTITUTE

Booker's great ambition was to go to Hampton Institute in order to continue his education. This dream finally began to be realized in 1872, when he set out across the mountains on his way to Hampton in Virginia. He left with the blessings and help of his family and many in the community. Still, his small savings and the small amount of money others gave him were not enough to pay his transportation to the school. When his money ran out, he tried to walk the rest of the way. He arrived in Richmond, Virginia, weak from lack of food. Booker decided to stay in Richmond a while and work. In this way, he was able to earn enough to pay his way to Hampton.

The story of Booker T. Washington's arrival and acceptance at Hampton has almost become a legend. When he reached the school in the autumn of 1872, he was suffering from the hardships of his trip. He was not an impressive candidate for admission as he stood before the assistant principal, Mary Mackie. His only suit showed the results of its constant wear since he left West Virginia. Nevertheless, Mary Mackie had him clean a room as a kind of entrance examination. And Washington was admitted to Hampton and obtained a job as janitor by making good use of the lessons in cleanliness he had learned from Mrs. Ruffner.

The person who had the greatest influence on Washington while he was at Hampton was General Samuel C. Armstrong, the principal. Armstrong had served in the Civil War, and came South after the war to help the freedmen. The American Missionary Association gave him the job of starting Hampton in 1868. It was Armstrong who shaped the educational ideas of the school. His own ideas about education were probably influenced by the Manual Labor School at Hilo, Hawaii. He thought the type of education he knew at Hilo was well suited for the freedmen.

Armstrong remained a hero to Washington throughout his life. Although he learned much about academic and practical subjects during his three years as a student, his contact with the general was equally important. Washington learned well, from Armstrong's teachings and personal example, about character, service, and the practical value of education.

WASHINGTON BECAME A TEACHER
At the end of his three-year course of study in 1875, Washington returned to Malden, West Virginia, to teach. He served the community well as a teacher, social worker, and respected leader. A number of his students went to Hampton. Then after three years in Malden, Washington decided to continue his education at Wayland Seminary in

Booker T. Washington's ideas urging black self-help through education and job training were interpreted in different ways by whites and by black Americans.

Washington, D.C. The emphasis on liberal arts studies at Wayland did not impress Washington. At Wayland, he became convinced that academic subjects should not be separate studies from vocational, or job related, courses. Washington also was disappointed by the urban black community in the nation's capital. He came to feel quite strongly that rural life or life on the farm was the best for his race. After eight months at Wayland, Washington returned to West Virginia. At this point, he still did not know what his life's work would be. He thought about becoming a lawyer and perhaps entering politics. Therefore, he began to study law under an attorney in Charleston, West Virginia.

This phase of his life ended when General Armstrong invited Washington to become a teacher at Hampton. His Hampton work experience was to be very important in his future career at Tuskegee. First, Washington was put in charge of a group of Indian students who had been admitted to Hampton as an experiment. He handled this job so well that he was given another challenging assignment during his second year at Hampton. This time, he helped to develop a night program for students who had to work during the day to earn money to attend school. This was one of the first work-study programs.

THE OPPORTUNITY CAME TO FOUND TUSKEGEE

In 1881, General Armstrong recommended Booker T. Washington as the man who could best help the people of Tuskegee, Alabama, to start a new school. The blacks of Tuskegee had obtained $2,000 from the Alabama legislature to start this school. Washington welcomed the opportunity to put into practice the things he had learned at Hampton.

When he reached Tuskegee, Washington had a chance to build. First, he traveled through the countryside, getting to know the people and selecting students. He picked thirty young people as his first student body. Lewis Adams, a black leader in Tuskegee and a member of the school's board, helped Washington obtain the use of the African Methodist Episcopal Zion Church and of a rundown building near the church. This was the first campus of Tuskegee Institute.

From these humble beginnings, Booker T. Washington built an institution that by 1915 had an endowment of $2 million. Black people supported his work and gave whatever they could to get the school started. An often-told story was that of the 70-year-old black woman who proudly came to present six eggs to help in the education of the black youth at Tuskegee. Southern whites, too, became more favorable, and Northern philanthropists supported Tuskegee and its founder.

TUSKEGEE EMPHASIZED JOB SKILLS TRAINING

The key to Washington's success was his message of industrial education. He constantly preached the importance of an education which taught students useful skills. Those who received such an education were to go back to their communities and make useful contributions. Tuskegee itself became an example of how such job skills could be put to use. The school's buildings were built from bricks made by the students, and student labor was used in constructing them. Students made the furniture used in the buildings, and they grew the food they ate at the school. Tuskegee graduates soon began moving into different parts of the South, bringing with them the message of industrial education, or training in job skills. Some of them started other schools modeled after Tuskegee.

WASHINGTON BELIEVED IN ACCOMMODATION

Washington's views on racial advancement were shaped by his times. With the strong pressures from whites to make blacks second-class citizens, Washington felt that little could be achieved by agitation and militancy. Racism had become too strong and idealism too weak for these methods to work. Washington believed that blacks must accommodate themselves to this situation.

He favored blacks' withdrawing from politics as a way of reducing tensions. The energy that once had gone into politics now should be turned to strengthening black communities. Economic success was the way to do this. Washington believed that when enough skilled craftsmen, successful businessmen, and competent professional people were found in black communities, black Americans would gain first-class citizenship.

WHITES HAILED WASHINGTON AS A BLACK LEADER

Washington was invited to speak at the opening of the Atlanta Cotton States and International Exposition on September 18, 1895. As a result of this speech, many white Americans came to look upon him as the leader and spokesman of black Americans. The accommodation doctrine set forth by Washington came to be called the "Atlanta Compromise." In Atlanta, Washington spoke to Southern whites, Northern whites, and to blacks at the same time. He wanted to bring all of these groups together and to secure at least the "better class" of Southern whites as allies for his race.

Washington's speech was based on the gospel of wealth. He urged blacks to stay in the South, where they had a better chance to get jobs and to succeed in business. Speaking to the white Southerners, he urged them to help uplift the black population because this would increase the economic well-being of all the South. In another appeal to white business and industrial interests, he said that he opposed unions and strikes because they harmed the workers.

He combined this economic appeal with his ideas of accommodation. Washington endorsed the white Southerners' view that Northerners should leave the race problem to the South for solution. "My faith," he said, "is that reforms in the South are to come from within." He assured the whites in the audience that blacks were more interested in industrial education and opportunities for jobs and economic advancement than in politics and political rights. He agreed that it was desirable to place some limits on the right to vote. He said that property and literacy, or reading, tests were proper ways of doing this.

Washington insisted that black Americans must not forget that most blacks had to live by working with their hands. Therefore, blacks would prosper only in "proportion as we learn to dignify and glorify common labour and put brains and skill into the common occupations of life." He reminded blacks that they had to begin at the bottom and work up. And as they did so, they should not allow their grievances to make them forget their opportunities. "The opportunity to earn a dollar in a factory just now," he said, "is worth infinitely more than the opportunity to spend a dollar in an opera-house."

JIM CROW WAS ACCEPTED

Washington's advice to blacks to accept their low status with dignity was aimed as much at whites in the audience as the blacks. Washington wanted to calm the fears of whites on the subject of "social equality," while assuring them of the loyalty and friendship of blacks. He denied that blacks had any interest in mixing socially with whites. "In all things that are purely social," he assured them, "we can be as separate as the fingers, yet one as the hand in all matters essential to mutual progress."

All in all, the Atlanta speech was aimed at quieting white fears and setting forth a philosophy of gradual progress for blacks. Washington spent little time talking about racial prejudice and the discrimination suffered by blacks. Instead he held up Southern whites as black people's friends. In fact, he blamed blacks themselves for much of the discrimination that existed. He said that blacks helped cause white prejudice by remaining poor and uneducated. Thus, blacks themselves must change their own lives before discrimination would end. This heavy burden for achieving better lives was placed on black people. Washington said that black Americans must pull themselves up by their own boot straps. Whites might help, but blacks must come up from slavery by themselves.

The best way for blacks to achieve first-class citizenship, Washington believed, was to become successful and prosperous and to live moral lives. Agricultural and industrial training was best suited to achieve these ends for the masses of black people, he claimed. For this reason, his program stressed farming, raising animals, and training in the hand crafts.

WASHINGTON'S PROGRAM HAD WEAKNESSES

Washington's program had a number of basic shortcomings. Clearly, when viewed in terms of the racial climate of those times his philosophy had a certain realism. But it was out of step with other realities of the period. The United States was fast becoming an urban nation. The great progress in business and industry after the Civil War marked the start of a rapid development of the nation's economy. On the other hand, Washington's ideas were drawn from the past, a past that was very different from the rapidly changing years in which he lived.

The education provided at Tuskegee reflected the past more than the future. The skills required for the new industrial age were being taught in technical and engineering schools, such as Carnegie Technological Institute. Tuskegee and the industrial schools that grew out of it still taught crafts which were more suited to America's economy before the Machine Age.

WASHINGTON WAS A COMPLEX MAN

Those who have closely studied the life and works of Booker T. Washington agree that he was a very complex person. For one thing, Washington presented his ideas in such a way that whites were able to read their own meaning into them. At the same time, blacks were reading entirely different meanings into them. The goal that Washington worked for was the complete acceptance of blacks into American society. His philosophy of accommodation was, he believed, the best way to accomplish this. Whites wanted to think that Washington meant that blacks would stay on the bottom of society for many, many generations.

But Washington did more than just preach accommodation. Historian August Meier has pointed out that some of Washington's private actions often conflicted with his public activities. Although he criticized academic education, his own children received a good liberal arts education. Nor did Washington follow his own public teachings and accept the separate-but-equal doctrine. He was accepted in the leading white social circles of the North. He was a friend of white business and industrial leaders, such as H. H. Rogers of Standard Oil, William H. Baldwin, Jr., of the Southern Railroad Company, and railroad owner Collis P. Huntington. Washington visited Rogers aboard his yacht several times, and he was a guest of Andrew Carnegie at Skibo Castle.

The same contradiction was found in Washington's politics. While advising blacks to turn away from politics, Washington became one of the most powerful black political leaders in history. He served as adviser on racial matters to Presidents Theodore Roosevelt and William Taft. All of the blacks appointed to office by Roosevelt and Taft were recommended by Washington. In some cases, his advice was even asked on Southern white appointees.

Washington was also an adviser to leading philanthropists. Black schools needed his approval to receive money from John D. Rockefeller, Andrew Carnegie, and other contributors to black education. Any institution or individual who came into disfavor with Washington found it hard to succeed.

Nevertheless, Washington worked hard to make and hold friends among influential blacks. He flattered some by inviting them to Tuskegee, where they were entertained well. He won over newspaper editors by placing advertisements in their papers and by giving money to keep struggling papers going. Washington even became part owner of the New York *Age.*

Behind the scenes, Washington also worked to destroy the Jim Crow system. He supported the fight against segregation on railroads. At one time, he furnished the money to pay a lobbyist to help defeat a bill in Congress discriminating against blacks. He feared that if this measure passed, it might lead to segregated trains in the North. Washington also spent thousands of dollars on legal cases opposing disfranchisement. A number of the cases that he financed reached the United States Supreme Court.

Without doubt, Washington exercised more power and influence over the black community than anyone else had ever done. Much of his authority resulted from his political power and his influence over sources of money. But Washington also influenced the day-to-day lives of blacks in other ways. The Tuskegee Negro Conferences had great impact on the rural people of the South. Black farm owners and tenants met at Tuskegee to discuss the problems they faced. Many tenants were inspired through these meetings to become farm owners. Schools throughout the South held meetings patterned after the Tuskegee conference.

In 1900, Washington organized the National Negro Business League. He remained president of the League until his death in 1915. This organization tried to deal with the problems faced by black businessmen. It preached racial unity and racial progress by gaining wealth and accepting middle-class values.

Chapter 5

Du Bois and the Niagara Movement

During the years of Booker T. Washington and the widespread influence of his ideas of accommodation, black protest activities did not stop. The man who made the strongest effort to express black discontent during these years was William Edward Burghardt Du Bois.

DU BOIS GREW UP IN NEW ENGLAND

The life of W. E. B. Du Bois is a unique and inspiring story of how this well-educated, intelligent black man dealt with the problem of being black in America. Du Bois was born in 1868, and first realized the difference his being black would make during his early boyhood. He grew up in the town of Great Barrington, Massachusetts, where for some time he remained unaware of the social divisions based on a person's race. But one day at school, a new girl showed that she disliked him, without any reason for acting this way. This made him realize that he was different from the other students. He learned, as he described it, that he was like the others "in heart and life and longing, but shut out from their world by a vast veil."

After he became aware of this difference, Du Bois began to change. He began to try to do better than his schoolmates in everything. On examinations, in races, or in fights, he showed that he was able to do better than they. But in time, this no longer satisfied him. And he now realized that opportunity for success was open to even the least able white student while it was closed to him. His goal became to succeed in spite of this handicap. In Great Barrington, Du Bois had experienced racism only in a mild form. He learned how it felt to be almost alone in a society that did not fully accept him. But it was not until he went South that he learned the real meaning of caste.

DU BOIS ATTENDED FISK UNIVERSITY
Although he wanted to go to Harvard University, Du Bois enrolled at Fisk University in Nashville, Tennessee. His family did not have the money to send him to college, and he was unable to get the necessary financial help to go to Harvard. But four churches in Connecticut gave him a scholarship to attend Fisk. When he arrived in Nashville in 1885, he entered a new world. He became a part of the black world of the South. He soon discovered the real meaning of caste. Describing this new life, he wrote: "I suddenly came to a region where the world was split into white and black halves, and where the darker half was held by race prejudice and legal bonds, as well as by deep ignorance and dire poverty."

Still, he was impressed by this new world. Southern blacks were not just a "little lost group," like the blacks in New England. The black population of the South was large enough to have some power. It was "a world in size," and it had the potential for accomplishing many things. Du Bois eagerly became a part of this world. "A new loyalty and allegiance replaced my Americanism: henceforward I was a Negro," he wrote.

THE SOUTH HELPED SHAPE DU BOIS' PERSONALITY
The conditions in the South during the 1880's had an important effect on Du Bois. Although he buried himself in his studies at Fisk, he was keenly aware of social conditions. He had very deep feelings about segregated travel, segregated housing, and the spirit of violence in the South. Each lynching, he said, "was a scar upon my soul."

To earn money to help meet his expenses, Du Bois went into the rural areas of Tennessee during the summers to teach. These summers taught him much about life in the South. In these rural areas, he met the black tenant farmer and the farm owner, and he learned what life was really like "within the veil." He wrote about the summers he spent teaching in his book *The Souls of Black Folk,* published in 1903. He recalled his first school, which had been a storage room for corn before it became a classroom. He remembered the children who came to him hungry for knowledge. He also recalled how the families he knew struggled against ignorance and poverty.

As he came to know these black families, Du Bois saw that they had many of the same longings that he had. In sharing their joys and their grief, he became aware of their discontent. He came to feel the unhappiness and discontent among the young. He understood how much the black tenants wanted to own their own land. And he also understood how lack of opportunity caused young people to develop attitudes of "listless indifference, or shiftlessness, or reckless bravado."

But in spite of his deep racial feelings and his understanding of the people he worked with, he could not completely enter their world. He seemed to remain outside looking into their world of ignorance and poverty. Although he felt a kinship with that world, his intellectual concerns and his life at Fisk University separated him from it. Nevertheless, that world of rural Tennessee taught him the meaning of being black and how to maintain his self-respect in a hostile society.

HE CONTINUED HIS EDUCATION

When he graduated from Fisk in 1888, Du Bois received a scholarship to attend Harvard. He remained somewhat alone during his years at Harvard, however. He said that he "asked nothing of Harvard but the tutelage of teachers and the freedom of the library." He made no attempt to become a part of the general life of the university. He carried on his social life outside the university among the blacks of Boston and other communities. But he was greatly impressed and influenced by his study under William James, Albert Bushnell Hart, George Santayana, and other members of Harvard's faculty. In later years, Du Bois looked back on his Harvard years with almost unmixed joy.

When he graduated from Harvard, The Slater Fund, a foundation which supported black education, made it possible for Du Bois to study for two years at the University of Berlin. These two years in Europe were significant years in his life. After the rather lonely years at Harvard, he was now fully accepted. Du Bois credited his experiences in Europe with altering his racial outlook. The friendships he enjoyed in Europe caused him to lose some of his racial feelings. He had expected prejudice and continued loneliness, but instead he found friendship. In Europe, he learned to know life. He became acquainted with "wine, women, and song," and hate became less important in his life.

It was also in Germany that he obtained the inspiration for his scientific study of Afro-Americans. The nineteenth century was the age of science, and the scientific spirit was all-important at Berlin. Du Bois left Berlin with a firm faith in scientific research as the way to progress. He believed that the races could be brought together in America through scientific research into the problems related to race. The results of investigating the race problem by using the scientific method would be used to bring changes in race relations.

HE BECAME A TEACHER AND RESEARCHER

Du Bois returned to the United States with his strong faith in scientific social progress and began seventeen years of teaching and research. His first teaching job was at Wilberforce University in Ohio. There he taught Greek, Latin, German, and English, and he asked for a chance to teach sociology. Du Bois spent two years at Wilberforce, but the emphasis on religion at the school and interference by church officials made Wilberforce a rather unpleasant place for him.

He eagerly accepted an offer from the University of Pennsylvania to become an assistant instructor there. He was given a salary of $600 a year to study the black community in Philadelphia. This was his first real opportunity to do scientific research. When he finished this study, he received an offer from Atlanta University in Georgia to take charge of the Atlanta studies on the Negro. Du Bois spent the years from 1897 to 1910 in teaching and research at Atlanta.

HE WROTE MANY SCHOLARLY BOOKS

Many scholarly books resulted from Du Bois' research during these years. The first of Du Bois' works to be published was his Harvard doctoral thesis, *The Suppression of the African Slave Trade to the United States of America, 1638–1870*, which was published in 1896. This work also became the first volume in the Harvard *Historical Studies*. In 1899, *The Philadelphia Negro* was published. This work grew out of his study conducted at the University of Pennsylvania. The results of his research also appeared in articles in the *American Historical Review* and in Census Bureau and Department of Labor publications.

Sixteen sociological studies printed in the Atlanta University *Publications,* which Du Bois edited, were his major research projects during these years. Du Bois expressed pride in the wide use that was made of his studies. He said that every study of the race problem made between 1896 and 1920 drew on them. His publications showed him to be a brilliant scholar and a pioneer in developing the new field of sociology.

DU BOIS BECAME A VOICE OF DISCONTENT

The United States of the 1890's and the 1900's was not an ideal environment for solving the race problem by scientific investigation. America was indeed scientific and industrial in its outlook, but this outlook did not apply to the question of race. Racism was at high tide. It was the philosophy of Booker T. Washington that found support throughout the nation. In fact, the road to success for ambitious black Americans ran through Tuskegee. It was almost impossible to get ahead without the backing of Washington. Under these conditions, it was hard for Du Bois to maintain the good will and hope he had gained in Europe.

In Georgia, Du Bois began to see in a new light the problems black people faced in the South. His work took him into the black belt of Georgia. There he met sharecroppers, renters, and those who had nothing. He no longer saw things through his youthful eyes as a Fisk student. Now he viewed conditions as a sensitive, mature scholar. And what he saw disturbed him. "It took but a few years of Atlanta," he wrote, "to bring me to hot and indignant defense." He continued: "I saw the race hatred of the whites as I had never dreamed of it before—naked and unashamed!" It became harder and harder for him to keep from speaking out. And, from time to time, he raised his voice in protest.

DU BOIS CRITICIZED BOOKER T. WASHINGTON

The Souls of Black Folk, published in 1903, contained a mild, well-written criticism of Booker T. Washington. Du Bois praised Washington's leadership and his efforts against injustice. But Du Bois pointed

W. E. B. Du Bois led the fight for equality among Afro-Americans. Du Bois challenged the ideas of Booker T. Washington by demanding full rights of citizenship, as well as jobs and education for blacks.

out the "half truth" upon which Washington's ideas rested. Du Bois called upon blacks to support Washington's teachings of "thrift, patience, and industrial training for the masses." But Du Bois called on them to oppose him in his silence on injustices, his giving up of black political rights, and his opposition to higher education. Up to this time, there had been little basic difference between the views of Du Bois and Washington. This criticism by Du Bois, however, drew an attack from Washington's followers. And from this time on, the two men moved further and further apart.

DU BOIS FAVORED COLLEGE-TRAINED LEADERS

The "talented tenth" was Du Bois' solution to the problem of intelligent leadership for black Americans. He said that "the Negro race, like all other races, is going to be saved by its exceptional men." For this reason, Du Bois became concerned about Washington's strong emphasis on industrial education. Du Bois called for educating that 10 percent of the race with leadership ability to help lift up the rest.

Du Bois did not oppose industrial education. But he believed that in order to advance, black people needed a system of education that would achieve several things for them. They needed education that would strengthen character, that would increase knowledge, and that would prepare them to earn a living. Du Bois did not think that one kind of education could do all these things. Du Bois felt that the regular public schools were dealing with character and knowledge, and the industrial schools provided training in job skills.

Teachers were needed to run all of these schools. Du Bois saw these teachers as a part of the "talented tenth" who needed higher education. He pointed out that teachers educated at Fisk, Howard, Atlanta, and other black colleges were operating the schools of the South, including Tuskegee Institute. Such teachers and the other leaders needed by the race did not receive adequate training in industrial schools. This was work for the black colleges. "The Talented Tenth of the Negro race," Du Bois said, "must be made leaders of thought and missionaries of culture among their people. No others can do this work, and Negro colleges must train men for it."

A UNITY MEETING WAS HELD

By 1903, there was concern among blacks and some whites about the growing division among black leaders. Booker T. Washington took the lead in calling for a meeting to promote black unity. Washington also provided funds to finance the conference. After a year of planning, the conference was held at Carnegie Hall in New York City in January, 1904.

About fifty people were present, including most of the leading black supporters and opponents of Booker T. Washington. One leading opponent of Washington, William Monroe Trotter of Boston, did not attend. A number of whites were present. They included Andrew Carnegie, William H. Baldwin, Jr., Oswald Garrison Villard, William Hayes Ward, George F. Peabody, and Carl Schurz. Du Bois felt that most of them came to urge the conference to accept Washington's point of view.

The meeting ended with statements from Washington and Du Bois. Although what happened at the meeting was kept secret, news leaked out to black newspapers. It was reported that the questioning of Washington about his views became heated at times. At the end, Washington expressed his support for higher education and agreed to support "peaceful and rational" methods to abolish segregation. Washington promised to speak out publicly on these issues. The conference appointed a Committee of Twelve to continue to work for united action.

But the conference did little to bring the black factions together. Washington did not speak out against segregation as he promised to do. He also kept control of the Committee of Twelve. The money to run the committee came through Washington, and the committee organized and adopted a plan of operation while Du Bois was absent. Before long, Du Bois resigned from the Committee of Twelve. In the end, the conference probably did more to push the black factions apart than to bring them together.

DU BOIS CALLED MILITANT BLACKS TOGETHER

The Niagara Movement began in June, 1905, when Du Bois sent out a call to "a few selected persons" to meet near Buffalo, New York. Only twenty-nine of those who had been invited came to the meeting. It was reported that some who wanted to attend had been pressured not to do so by white friends of Booker T. Washington. In any case, those who attended moved across the Canadian border to Fort Erie and held their meeting there.

The meeting was aimed against the accommodation ideas of Washington, and it set forth a philosophy of protest. The statement of principles drawn up at the meeting denied that black Americans were willing to accept an inferior status and submit to oppression. Black women and men accepted their status as second-class citizens only because they were helpless to do otherwise. Now they must speak out against oppression. Those attending the meeting declared that "the voice of ten million Americans must never cease to assail the ears of their fellows, so long as America is unjust." The declaration went on to condemn discrimination based on race or color. According to the statement, the purpose of the movement was "to protest against disfranchisement and Jim Crow laws and to demand equal rights of education, equal civil rights, equal economic opportunities, and justice in the courts." Further, it was proclaimed, "persistent manly agitation is the way to liberty, and toward this goal the Niagara Movement has started." The delegates elected Du Bois as general secretary.

Those who gathered at Fort Erie went home to begin local branches of the Niagara Movement. Within a short time, the Baltimore branch was working to defeat a move to disfranchise blacks. But generally the movement grew slowly. By the end of 1905, there were still only 150 members spread out in local branches in seventeen states. Du Bois claimed that the movement remained small because it was so selective in taking in new members.

WASHINGTON FOUGHT THE NIAGARA MOVEMENT
Washington tried to keep the Niagara Movement from growing and becoming effective. At first, he tried to keep blacks from learning about the organization by keeping the black press from mentioning it. But Washington's followers helped to publicize the movement by attacking it in the newspapers friendly to Washington.

Washington's supporters also tried to start an organization to compete with the Du Bois group. Bishop Alexander Walters reestablished the Afro-American Council. The Council was first organized in the late 1800's. It was taken over by Washington's supporters, then remained inactive between 1902 and 1905. Controlled by Washington from behind the scenes, the Council was started up again and pushed as a more effective protest organization than the Niagara Movement. Washington also sent spies to the meetings of the Niagara Movement.

A MEETING WAS HELD AT HARPERS FERRY
The second conference of the Niagara Movement was held at Harpers Ferry. Du Bois arrived early and tried to get support from local blacks.

He was largely unsuccessful. The local people were afraid to follow Du Bois because they feared trouble. Also, Du Bois was not the type of man to stir the masses and win their loyalty. He was too much of the intellectual for this role. Nevertheless, a hundred delegates who supported Du Bois' ideas of militant protest gathered at Storer College in August, 1906. On the last day of the meeting, August 18, 1906, the delegates walked barefooted to the heights above Harpers Ferry. There they sang the "Battle Hymn of the Republic" and spent time in reverent silence to honor the memory of John Brown.

Du Bois wrote the resolutions, or demands, of this second meeting. These resolutions expressed black demands for the right to vote, for the end of segregation in transportation, for the freedom to choose one's friends, for equality under the law, and for opportunities for higher education. The delegates condemned the Republican Party for betraying blacks. Du Bois and his supporters hoped to make the Niagara Movement the basis of a nationwide protest movement to fight against discrimination in every state.

Branches in several states did begin work to carry out the aims of the movement. The Illinois branch opposed efforts to segregate schools in Chicago. This same branch also fought against showing an anti-black play, *The Clansman,* in Chicago. The Massachusetts branch worked against segregation on railroads and opposed discrimination at the Jamestown Exposition then being planned by the state of Virginia.

THE NIAGARA MOVEMENT WAS SIGNIFICANT

By the time of the third annual meeting at Boston in 1907, the Niagara Movement was weakening. The membership was still small, and financial support was falling off. The delegates adopted a strong statement of protest, but there was no longer much excitement about the movement. In 1908, the Niagara group met at Oberlin, Ohio, the great abolitionist center of the pre-Civil War years. The following year, they met at Sea Isle City, New Jersey. By this time, it was clear that the Niagara Movement could not continue. After the NAACP was formed in 1909, Du Bois urged those who had supported the Niagara Movement to join that organization.

The Niagara Movement failed as an organization, but it had a lasting effect on black thought. Other voices of protest were already being raised here and there. William Monroe Trotter and George Forbes founded the Boston *Guardian* in 1901. They used this newspaper to make strong attacks on Washington. Such organizations as the

New England Suffrage League and the Equal Rights League of Georgia took stands similar to that of the Niagara Movement. But the Niagara Movement was the first organized black protest movement. It was Du Bois' Niagara group that made protest a matter of public interest. After Niagara, the philosophy of accommodation no longer went unchallenged in the United States.

Chapter 6

The National Urban League

Although the years between 1896 and World War I were marked by efforts to push black Americans into an inferior status, some tried to better their condition. Progress here was greatest in the Northern cities. Northern social scientists, social workers, and journalists helped to bring about a change in attitudes on the race question. They and others they influenced formed interracial organizations to work for black advancement. One of the first of these organizations was the National Urban League, which was formed in 1911 out of three other organizations.

A GROUP WAS FORMED TO PROTECT BLACK WOMEN

The National League for the Protection of Colored Women was one of the groups that helped to form the National Urban League. This group to protect black women resulted from a study of employment agencies made by Frances A. Kellor. Frances Kellor found that young women looking for jobs often had to seek help from labor agents.

Many of these agents did not deal fairly with women who were new to the city.

Although this was not the first time the problem had been studied, Frances Kellor wrote a book describing the experiences of black women seeking jobs. As early as 1898, the problems faced by Southern black girls who went to Northern cities were discussed at the Hampton Negro Conference. But no thorough investigation was made until the Kellor study in 1902.

In March, 1905, Frances Kellor called for public support of an organization to work among black women. She wrote an article telling about the immoral, dishonest, and unfair practices these women suffered at the hands of labor agents. The Travelers' Aid Society and immigrant aid groups helped many white women to avoid the labor agents. But black women received no such help. Miss Kellor wanted to start an organization that would protect black newcomers to the city.

Such an organization, the National League for the Protection of Colored Women, was started in the summer of 1905. Branches of the League were formed in Philadelphia and New York City, and both were run by interracial boards of directors. The League furnished workers to meet travelers arriving from the South and to protect them from dishonest labor agents. The League kept a list of reputable lodging houses where young women could stay. Later the organization began to help the newcomers find suitable jobs. The League also sent workers to Southern cities from which the migrants came to help arrange transportation for those planning to move to the North. Such travel agents worked in Norfolk, Baltimore, and Memphis.

A COMMITTEE STUDIED INDUSTRIAL CONDITIONS
At about the same time that the League for the Protection of Colored Women was formed, another group was being organized. The Committee for Improving Industrial Conditions of the Negro in New York City was organized around 1905. Several of the white members of the committee were supporters of Southern black schools, especially Hampton and Tuskegee Institutes. The purpose of the committee was to investigate industrial conditions among blacks in New York City and to educate public opinion in favor of giving blacks better jobs.

A COMMITTEE HELPED NEW YORK WORKERS
In 1910, the third group that was to form a part of the National Urban

58

League was organized. A young black man, George E. Haynes, saw the need for a different type of organization working among blacks. Haynes was studying for his doctorate at Columbia University. As a part of research, he made a study of economic conditions among blacks in New York City. He came to feel that a major need of blacks was help in adjusting to urban life. "My research suggested," he said, "that in a period of less than 30 years one-half the Negro population of the nation would be living in the urban sectors." Therefore, Haynes strongly believed that black "educational institutions should begin training social workers and other leaders to serve city newcomers and that general welfare agencies should be encouraged to place and utilize these trained workers to help the newcomers to learn to live in town."

Haynes discussed these ideas with Frances Kellor and Ruth Standish Baldwin. Ruth Baldwin was the widow of William H. Baldwin, Jr., who had been a strong supporter of Tuskegee Institute. Out of these discussions came the suggestion that the Committee for Improving Industrial Conditions be urged to add the training of social workers to its program. But the Committee for Improving Industrial Conditions refused to broaden its program, and instead a new organization was formed.

In 1910, Ruth Baldwin called a group together at the New York School of Philanthropy. Haynes presented a report of his findings. His conclusions were that the situation called for more than jobs and the protection of black women. There was a real need, he felt, for "broader, basic social action." Enough of those present agreed with him to form a new organization, the Committee on Urban Conditions Among Negroes in New York.

The new committee had broader purposes than the two older organizations. It planned to study social and economic conditions in cities and to work with "all agencies seeking to better urban conditions among Negroes." Where there were no agencies working in behalf of blacks, the committee intended to create some. It also proposed to train black social workers.

Haynes completed his work at Columbia University in 1910 and went to Fisk University in Nashville, Tennessee, to teach sociology. He remained the director of the Committee on Urban Conditions Among Negroes, and he returned to New York City from time to time to keep the work going. Emanuel W. Houstoun, a graduate of Atlanta University, was employed part time to carry on while Haynes was in Nashville.

THE NATIONAL URBAN LEAGUE WAS ORGANIZED

It soon became clear that one organization would be better than three. Many of the same people were involved in all three groups, and the three organizations were concerned about many of the same problems. In October, 1911, the three organizations combined. The Committee for Improving Industrial Conditions of the Negro in New York, the National League for the Protection of Colored Women, and the Committee on Urban Conditions Among Negroes in New York became the National League on Urban Conditions Among Negroes. Before long, this name was shortened to the National Urban League.

In 1911, Eugene Kinckle Jones became associate director of the combined organization. Later, he was given the title of director. Jones was a graduate of Virginia Union and Cornell Universities. He was teaching in a high school in Louisville when he was invited to come to New York City and help start the Urban League's operation. Now, Haynes gave full time to his teaching at Fisk and to the League's work in the South.

Until World War I, the National Urban League remained primarily a New York City organization. Nevertheless, the founders intended it to become a national movement. They set out to develop a program and an organizational structure suited to cities all over the country. In a few years, program activities and methods which had been tested in New York City were being used in branches in other cities.

THE URBAN LEAGUE IMPROVED JOB OPPORTUNITIES

The work of the League's Industrial Department became very important to the growth of the organization. This department tried to help blacks become better workers by opening ways for them to increase their skills and to learn new skills. The League also organized associations of workers and tried to persuade employers who had never used black workers before to employ them. The League did not set up workers' associations for the purpose of putting pressure on employers but to serve as means for improving the workers. For example, a Colored Public Porters' Association was organized to "guard the traveling public against unscrupulous porters" and to raise "the reliability and efficiency of its members." Training classes were held for elevator operators and other workers in apartment houses. These workers were organized into an association to try to screen men entering these jobs and to improve living conditions of the workers. The

The National Urban League soon became a leading group working to help black Americans. Some of the first members of the Washington, D.C., branch are shown here.

League also worked with chauffeurs, longshoremen, musicians, carpenters, and other craftsmen.

Placing workers in jobs was a natural outgrowth of the League's efforts to open new jobs to black workers. By 1913, a Vocational Exchange had been opened. This office was not supposed to send workers directly to jobs. It was to be a "clearing house" from which people looking for work would be sent to employment agencies. But soon the League was dealing directly with employers and sending workers to jobs. The Urban League helped to bring black students from the South to work in the tobacco fields of Connecticut. It helped place other workers in pump works in Massachusetts and in industrial plants in New York. When it was first organized, the League followed the lead of Booker T. Washington in urging blacks to remain in the South. But, before long, it was encouraging Southern blacks to move North by finding jobs for them.

THE LEAGUE WORKED TO IMPROVE HOUSING

The League's work in housing was carried on along social work lines. The organization did not attack the problems of prejudice and discrimination that kept blacks living in Harlem and other separate communities. The League's program was aimed at making living conditions better within the existing system. A policy of selection was called for within the black communities. "Reputable and disreputable persons" would be segregated in different tenement houses and neighborhoods. A list of houses that the League found to be "physically clean and wholesome" was drawn up. The League sent people who wanted such surroundings to these houses to seek lodging. Blacks were urged to insist on good management of the houses they rented. To help tenants do their share, a program of education was started to teach sanitation, proper upkeep, and knowledge of city services and regulations. The League also tried to get real estate men to build houses that blacks could afford to buy.

TRAVELERS' AID HELPED BLACKS

Probably more was being done in travelers' aid than in any other area when the Urban League was organized. The National League for the Protection of Colored Women sent workers to several cities to assist the traveling woman. The National Urban League continued this service and extended it to include men. It ended this work in 1915 when the

Travelers' Aid Society began serving black travelers in New York.

THE LEAGUE BEGAN WELFARE PROGRAMS

A large number of welfare activities were undertaken for blacks in New York City. Juvenile and adult delinquents received special attention. The League's greatest emphasis was on prevention and correction of delinquent behavior among children and youth. Big brother and big sister programs were an early feature of this effort. The big brothers and sisters gave friendly adult supervision to boys and girls who had gotten in trouble with the law.

Efforts to improve recreation were important in the program to prevent juvenile delinquency. As early as 1911, the League urged that more play areas be established in Harlem. The organization even operated a playground to show the good effects play areas could have. When the city opened two playgrounds in Harlem in 1915, the League felt that its work was bringing some results. Boys' and girls' clubs also provided opportunities for recreation. In addition to regular social clubs, boys in Harlem were organized into a Juvenile Park Protective League to report violations of city ordinances. It was hoped that such activity would ease gang tensions between black and white youth.

Fresh air programs were another feature of the League's work with young people. Each summer, about 150 boys 12 to 16 years of age were given a two-week outing at a camp in Verona, New Jersey. The League operated the camp because other camps would not accept black children throughout the summer. Some camps had one or two special weeks for black children. This situation changed after World War I, and the League stopped operating summer camps.

Health improvement became a part of the Urban League's program around 1915. In March of that year, the League began cooperating with the National Negro Business League in sponsoring National Negro Health Week. Urban League workers handed out literature, held mass meetings, and delivered health addresses in churches and Sunday schools. In July, 1915, the League opened a convalescent home. At first, the home cared for women only; then it was enlarged and began accepting men.

THE LEAGUE TRAINED SOCIAL WORKERS

Compared to what the League was doing in New York City, the national program during this period seemed rather limited. But as far as the future was concerned the national work was just as important. The League concentrated on two important national efforts—training social workers, and organizing branches in other cities.

Three methods were used in training social workers. The League cooperated with Fisk University in providing training through the Fisk department of social science. Scholarships were offered to undergraduates at selected black colleges. And fellowships were awarded for graduate study in New York City.

The training course at Fisk started on a small scale. In 1912–13, this program consisted of "courses in Economics, Sociology, Negro History and Social Investigation and . . . lectures by experts in Social Work from various cities." The Urban League paid for the "experts in Social Work" who took part in the program.

The following year, 1913–14, plans were made for a special course in social service training. Seniors in sociology were given field work through Bethlehem House, a settlement house in Nashville operated by a church group and the University. By 1915, the training course had been separated from the regular social science courses and was designed specifically to train social and religious workers. Students were prepared to work as probation officers, settlement workers, kindergarten directors, executive secretaries of civic betterment organizations, institutional church workers, church and charity visitors, and home and foreign missionaries.

The League also worked through other black colleges to train social workers in the South. Students in these institutions were encouraged to study sociology and economics and to consider social work as a career. In 1914, the League held a scholarship contest open to students at Howard and Virginia Union Universities, as well as at Talladega, Morehouse, and Paine Colleges. Examinations were given to those who applied in either economics or sociology. Students at only three of the schools took the examinations. This lack of interest led the League to discontinue the program. The money was used to sponsor lectures at black colleges.

Fellowships offered for study in New York City, however, produced immediate results training black social workers. Starting in 1911, living expenses were provided for two students a year to study at the New York School of Philanthropy. Those who received these awards had to promise to become social workers. After completing their training, many of the Urban League fellows took positions in the national office or with branches as they were organized. The League was able to list six fellows in 1915 who had completed their year of study in New

York. One of the six was still in school, and five had accepted jobs, generally as teachers. They all had some connection with social work, either in part-time jobs or as volunteers. William N. Colson, a teacher at Virginia Union University, was director of the Urban League branch in Richmond, Virginia. James H. Hubert, who received the first fellowship, later became executive secretary of the New York Urban League.

THE URBAN LEAGUE GREW SLOWLY

In spite of its progress in developing programs, the League did not grow rapidly before World War I. In 1913, it had branches in only four cities besides New York City. None of the branches had programs nearly so well developed as those in New York. The Philadelphia branch was the League for the Protection of Colored Women. It limited its work to travelers' aid and help for women in trouble. In St. Louis, the Committee for Social Service Among Colored People had a rather varied program. But the committee had no formal organization and it did not employ a professional social worker. Richmond, Virginia, formed a new organization in 1913, and the work in Norfolk consisted of two travelers' aid workers. Of these branches, only St. Louis and Philadelphia were still operating at the end of World War I.

The failure rate remained high among branches organized during the prewar years. The League had branches in twelve cities in 1916, but only six of these were still in existence in 1919. A number of reasons explain the slow rate of expansion. The League placed the blame on lack of money and of trained people to run the branches. But a major part of the problem was the League's difficulty in setting up interracial organizations in the South.

THE LEAGUE TRIED TO ORGANIZE IN THE SOUTH

At the time the League was organized, few people thought that the northward movement of blacks would increase very much. The census of 1910 showed that 84 percent of the black population still lived in the South. True, there was a growing movement toward cities, but it appeared that blacks might make their home in Southern cities. Of the forty-three cities having 10,000 or more blacks in 1910, thirty-three were in the South. Three Northern cities were the homes of the great majority of those who had left the South. These cities were Philadelphia, New York City, and Chicago.

So it is not surprising that the National Urban League looked to the South as a possible area of expansion. Many of the early branches were in the South, including Savannah, Augusta, and Atlanta in Georgia. Other local branches were set up in Birmingham, Alabama, and in Memphis, Nashville, and Chattanooga, Tennessee. Large numbers of blacks lived in these and other Southern cities, and blacks made up a high percentage of the total populations of these cities.

RACISM BLOCKED THE LEAGUE IN THE SOUTH

Even the Urban League's "conservative" social work program was out of step with the growing racist feelings in the South. The principle of interracial cooperation was very important within the Urban League. But in most Southern cities, it was almost impossible to set up boards of blacks and whites. Nor were these cities ready to meet even the mild social service demands made by League branches. As a result, Southern branches were very limited in their choice of program areas. They found it hard to find people to serve on their boards, as well as very hard to raise money in the South to support their work.

Nine of the fourteen branches listed by the League in 1916 were in Southern or border cities. Many of these branches had very hectic and checkered histories between 1916 and 1950. Most of them went out of existence long before 1950. The border cities of St. Louis and Louisville maintained continuous League connections. St. Louis, in particular, developed a very active and progressive branch.

The situation was different in states of the Deep South. Only Atlanta and Memphis were listed as League cities in both 1916 and 1950. Memphis had a hard time trying to survive, and the so-called "Atlanta Plan" helped the League in that city to avoid the fate of other Southern branches. The Atlanta League was run by two boards, one black and the other white. These groups met separately three weeks each month and held one joint monthly meeting. Branches in Nashville, Savannah, Augusta, Richmond, and Huntsville suffered periods of inactivity or went out of existence altogether. By way of contrast, only one of the five Northern branches listed in 1916 stopped operating. That was the branch in Indianapolis, Indiana.

THE URBAN LEAGUE LOOKED NORTHWARD

Conditions during World War I caused the South to promise to ease its racial policies somewhat. The great increase in the number of blacks moving North after 1915 caused concern in the South about the loss of workers. This continuing flight of Southern blacks to Northern cities thus brought promises that changes would be made in the conditions of black life.

The great demand for labor that came with the period of mobilization and war assured blacks jobs in Northern industry. This situation also opened greater opportunities for service by the Urban League in Northern cities. Now the League had a choice between trying to handle racial matters in the South and taking advantage of the more promising opportunities for service in the North. The Urban League turned its attention to the cities of the North.

Chapter 7

Founding the NAACP

Another major interracial organization was founded during the years just before World War I. This was the National Association for the Advancement of Colored People, better known as the NAACP. The NAACP developed different programs from those of the National Urban League. Emerging as one of the responses to widespread racial violence, the NAACP became the voice of black militance.

A TERRIBLE RIOT TOOK PLACE IN SPRINGFIELD

A court case and the resulting riot that broke out in Springfield, Illinois, in 1908 started the chain of events which led to the founding of the NAACP. Mabel Hallam, the wife of a streetcar conductor, claimed that she had been criminally assaulted. She identified George Richardson, a black man, as the guilty person. Richardson was arrested and jailed. When called before a special grand jury, Mabel Hallam admitted that she had lied. She had been beaten by her white lover, whom she refused to identify. She confessed that she made up the story about being attacked by Richardson in order to explain the beating and to protect her lover. She told the grand jury that Richardson had nothing to do with the matter.

News of Richardson's arrest kindled the kinds of feelings which cause mob action. The local authorities realized this, and to protect Richardson they took him by train to Bloomington, Illinois, a city just north of Springfield. When the members of the mob learned that Richardson had been moved to safety, they turned their fury on others. When they learned that a local businessman's car had been used to take Richardson to the train, this man's restaurant was wrecked. The mob broke into stores and took axes, guns, and other weapons.

These weapons were then used against the black community in Springfield. An effort was made to disperse the mob, but it failed. For nearly two days, blacks were the objects of violent attacks. Their homes were looted and burned, and those unfortunate enough to fall in the hands of the mob were beaten and driven out of town.

Two black men lost their lives during the riot. The first of these was a barber named Burton. When the mob failed to find Richardson, it set fire to Burton's barber shop. The barber was killed, and his body was mutilated and burned. On the second night of the riot, an 84-year-old black man, William Donegan, was lynched. The mob killed Donegan less than a block from the state capitol building.

Order was finally restored on the second night. The state militia was called in, and it finally stopped the violence. It required over 5,000 militiamen to break up the mob. At the end, two black men and four white men were dead, and over seventy people had been injured. Many arrests were made, but the mob leaders were not punished.

Before order was restored, the city's black community had been thoroughly terrorized. An estimated 1,000 blacks fled the city to make their homes elsewhere. Among them were some of the leading black citizens of Springfield. The city and state governments also helped to force blacks to leave by dismissing them from city and state jobs. News of this racial violence in the city of Abraham Lincoln, only a few blocks from his home, shocked blacks and liberal whites throughout the country.

THE SPRINGFIELD RIOT SHOCKED SOME AMERICANS

Writer and journalist William English Walling and his wife Anna Strunsky were in Chicago when the Springfield riot broke out. They rushed to Springfield to investigate. The Wallings were very sensitive to such violence. They had just returned from Russia, where they had witnessed violence against Jews. Mrs. Walling had been imprisoned for a time by the Russian government as a suspected revolutionary.

Conditions in Springfield alarmed the Wallings. They had seen nothing in Russia to compare with the hatred and lawlessness they found in Springfield. The people were not ashamed that their city had been the scene of such terror. Some were even proud of taking part in the violence.

Walling wrote a stirring article, "Race War in the North," which appeared in *The Independent* on September 3, 1908. He appealed to white Americans to take up the cause of Afro-Americans. "Who realizes the seriousness of the situation," he asked, "and what large and powerful body of citizens is ready to come to their aid?"

Although no "large and powerful body" responded, a small group did act. Mary White Ovington, a wealthy white social worker, wrote Walling a letter as soon as she read his article. Mary Ovington had been studying conditions among blacks for several years. She said that she was impressed by Walling's call for blacks and whites to unite in the "spirit of the abolitionist" in order to work for better conditions. She expressed her willingness to cooperate and asked Walling to arrange a meeting to be attended by the two of them and by Charles Edward Russell.

A meeting was held at Walling's home. Russell was unable to attend, but Henry Moskovitz, a social worker, joined Walling and Mary Ovington. They agreed to ask Oswald Garrison Villard, the grandson of William Lloyd Garrison and president of the New York *Evening Post* Company, to write a call to a meeting.

A CONFERENCE WAS CALLED

Villard wrote the call. In it, he told of the wrongs being suffered by black Americans, and he urged those receiving the call to come to a National Conference. The purpose of the meeting was "the discussion of present evils, the voicing of protests and the renewal of the struggle for civil and political liberty."

Other black and white leaders were asked to sign the call. Of those asked, fifty-three signed. Six blacks were among the signers. They were William L. Bulkley, a New York school principal; Ida B. Wells Barnett of Chicago; W. E. B. Du Bois; the Reverend Francis J. Grimké of Washington; Bishop Alexander Walters of the African Methodist

Episcopal Zion Church; and J. Milton Waldron of Washington. The white signers included Jane Addams, John Dewey, William Dean Howells, Rabbi Stephen S. Wise, and the Reverend John Haynes Holmes. The call was issued on February 12, 1909, the one-hundredth anniversary of Abraham Lincoln's birth.

THE NATIONAL CONFERENCE MET IN 1909

According to Du Bois, "two or three hundred persons" of all shades of opinion responded to the call. They gathered at the United Charities Building in New York City on May 31, 1909. The conference denounced violence against blacks and condemned segregation. It demanded academic and professional education for gifted black students, and the right of black Americans to vote and enjoy all other civil rights.

The conference made progress, despite some difficulties. Often the discussion became heated. Many of the militant blacks did not trust the whites present. Du Bois told how at one point a woman participant "leapt to her feet and cried in passionate, almost tearful earnestness— an earnestness born of bitter experience—'They are betraying us again —these white friends of ours.'"

But the conference was the beginning of a permanent organization. A committee of forty was set up to plan a permanent organization. A nominating committee selected people to serve on the permanent committee. Some choices were obvious. Among the whites, Boston liberals Moorfield Storey and Albert E. Pillsbury were early choices.

The selecting of black members created some disagreement. Bishop Alexander Walters and Dr. Charles E. Bentley, the Chicago dentist, were included without question. But some were troubled that the organization might fail if Booker T. Washington was not included on the committee. They were afraid that if Washington were excluded, the new organization would not be able to raise money.

Finally, as a compromise, Washington was not included, but two of his most bitter critics were also excluded, Ida B. Wells Barnett and William Monroe Trotter. Mrs. Barnett made an angry protest, however, and she was added to the permanent committee.

THE NAACP WAS FORMED IN 1910

The permanent committee held a second National Conference in May, 1910. This meeting, like the 1909 conference, was held in New York

City. During this meeting, the permanent committee became a permanent organization—the National Association for the Advancement of Colored People (NAACP).

The new organization represented a forward step in the struggle for the rights of black Americans. It brought together black militants from the Niagara Movement and white Progressives. The interracial character of the NAACP was probably fundamental to its success, because it won a wider audience for the efforts to secure black rights. And in addition, it won greater financial support for these efforts.

In addition to Villard, Storey, Walling, and Ovington, a number of other white Progressives came forward as leaders. These included industrialist John Milholland; prominent social workers Lillian Wald of New York and Jane Addams of Chicago; John Haynes Holmes, the well-known clergyman; Franz Boas, an anthropologist; and Clarence Darrow, the famous lawyer. Moorfield Storey served as President of the NAACP, and William E. Walling was chairman of the executive committee.

DU BOIS JOINED THE NAACP STAFF

W. E. B. Du Bois was invited to join the staff of the NAACP soon after the organization was formed. He left his teaching position at Atlanta University to become Director of Publicity and Research for the NAACP. Du Bois was risking a great deal in changing jobs at this time. He was not certain he would receive a salary from the NAACP. Villard, who served as treasurer, told Du Bois when he arrived in New York City that there was no money on hand to pay him. In spite of this uncertainty, Du Bois set to work. Between 1910 and 1917, he was the only black officer of the NAACP. His major achievement during these years was the founding of *The Crisis* magazine.

The Crisis was the official magazine of the NAACP, and Du Bois set the tone of the magazine. Under his control, it became a journal of militant protest. The name of the magazine showed how concerned the editor and his assistants were about the dangers that racial discrimination posed to the future of the country. They believed, Du Bois said, that the magazine was founded during a "critical time in the history of the advancement of men."

Du Bois, at that time, believed that one way to fight prejudice was with truth. He believed that America would change if the facts were made known, and if blacks waged a strong fight for their rights. Thus, *The Crisis* had to awaken the nation to the truth concerning black people. Du Bois considered this a vital task, because he believed white magazines and newspapers assumed that blacks were an "undesirable race destined to eventual extinction of some kind." He thought that it was his job to combat the influence of the white press by giving fair treatment to news about black people.

The range of the magazine was quite broad. Du Bois made it both a literary magazine and a news journal. It published news about black people throughout the United States. In addition, poets, writers of fiction, and scholars were able to have their works printed in the pages of *The Crisis*.

During the early years, *The Crisis* grew faster than the NAACP itself. Before the end of 1910, the magazine was selling 12,000 copies a month. When the NAACP held its first annual meeting on January 4, 1912, it did not yet have 1,000 members; *The Crisis* already had a circulation of 16,000 copies. The total income of the NAACP to that time was only $9,771. Of this amount, $5,208 had come from the sale of *The Crisis*.

DU BOIS WAS IMPORTANT TO THE NAACP

Both Du Bois and the NAACP gained when Du Bois joined its staff. The success of *The Crisis* was due, in large measure, to the fact that it had the backing of a growing organization. Du Bois did not have such backing for two earlier magazines, the *Moon* and the *Horizon*, and they both had failed. On the other hand, the NAACP needed Du Bois' experience as a protest leader and his great prestige among black intellectuals. The Niagara Movement had made him an important leader of black intellectual protest against racial discrimination.

Du Bois held a unique position in the NAACP. Although he did not take an active role in policy decisions during board meetings, he exercised great influence over policy. He is credited with setting the militant tone of the NAACP from the very beginning. Du Bois used *The Crisis* to influence NAACP policy. He announced policies in the magazine in the name of the organization.

This practice caused conflict between Du Bois and some members of the board. When Oswald Garrison Villard became chairman of the board, his relations with Du Bois grew very strained. Villard wanted Du Bois to accept the wishes of the board and to stop publishing his own views. Du Bois refused to give up his freedom of action, and, in 1913, Villard resigned as chairman of the board in protest. This did not end the conflict between Du Bois' personal policy and the policy of the Association. And it was probably fortunate that it did not. In spite of these conflicts, *The Crisis,* through its editor, continued to shape the image of the NAACP as a militant organization.

THE NAACP USED PROTESTS AND LEGAL ACTION

The program of the NAACP followed the course set by the National Negro Conference of 1909. To end the evils resulting from racial discrimination, the conference declared, "... We demand of Congress and the Executive:

(1) That the Constitution be strictly enforced and the civil rights guaranteed under the Fourteenth Amendment be secured impartially to all.

(2) That there be equal educational opportunities for all and in all the States, and that public school expenditure be the same for the Negro and white child.

(3) That in accordance with the Fifteenth Amendment the right of the Negro to the ballot on the same terms as other citizens be recognized in every part of the country."

The NAACP used publicity, protest, and legal action to work toward its goal of equal rights for all. Publicity and protest were used in efforts to get Congress to pass a law to stop lynching. The NAACP gathered information about every reported lynching. Protest meetings were held, and anti-lynching publicity was published in newspapers. Another early campaign was carried on by the group against the film *Birth of a Nation,* which the NAACP denounced as degrading to blacks. The group used publicity, picketing, and protest efforts to try to influence city officials to ban the film.

THE NAACP WON A MAJOR COURT VICTORY

The Association became best known, however, for its fights in the courts. Several well-known lawyers were among the leaders of the NAACP. Arthur Spingarn led the team of white and black lawyers who handled NAACP cases.

The first legal battle won by the NAACP dealt with voting rights. Oklahoma followed the example of several other Southern states and added a "grandfather clause" to its state constitution. The "grandfather clauses" were designed to allow whites to register to vote without being able to read and write. At the same time, blacks were denied the right to register and vote. The Oklahoma constitution said that all

WE HOLD THESE TRUTHS TO BE SELF
EVIDENT THAT ALL MEN ARE CREATED
EQUAL THAT THEY ARE ENDOWED BY THEIR
CREATOR WITH CERTAIN UNALIENABLE
RIGHTS THAT AMONG THESE ARE LIFE
LIBERTY AND THE PURSUIT OF HAPPINESS.

IF OF AFRICAN DESCENT TEAR OFF THIS CORNER

The NAACP organized peaceful marches in Northern cities to protest lynchings and racial violence. This march was held to condemn a race riot in St. Louis.

persons descended from persons who had the right to vote on January 1, 1866, could vote without passing a literacy test. This included all whites and excluded almost all blacks. The question was whether or not the state's action was lawful under the Fifteenth Amendment to the Constitution.

An NAACP-backed case questioning the Oklahoma "grandfather clause" reached the United States Supreme Court in 1915. The Court ruled in *Guinn v. United States* that the clause violated the Fifteenth Amendment. Oklahoma, the Court said, was attempting to restore and continue "the very conditions the Amendment was intended to destroy." This was the first of many legal battles the NAACP was to win in its long and continuing struggle for first-class citizenship for black Americans.

BOOKER T. WASHINGTON OPPOSED THE NAACP

Booker T. Washington was no more friendly toward the NAACP than he had been toward the Niagara Movement. Washington was opposed to the methods of agitation and protest used by the NAACP. Some leaders of the NAACP probably hoped that Washington could be ignored. They believed that if the NAACP did not criticize him, he would not bother the Association.

But Du Bois knew that this was not possible. In later years, Du Bois summed up the situation when he said that "to discuss the Negro question in 1910 was to discuss Booker T. Washington." Although those members who opposed Washington succeeded in keeping Washington's influence out of the NAACP, the organization did not weaken his leadership position. The NAACP was considered a radical organization in the period before World War I. Most whites who supported efforts to improve the lives of black Americans favored Washington's methods.

But changes began to take place during World War I. When Washington died in November, 1915, the NAACP became the leading spokesman for blacks. Blacks became more militant and gave greater support to the NAACP program. More college-educated blacks became members of the Association. By 1914, the NAACP had 6,000 members in the fifty branches it had established throughout the United States.

UNIT THREE

BLACK AMERICANS AND PROGRESSIVISM

Chapter 8

The Republican Years

The results of the loss of voting rights by black Americans began to become clear in the years after 1900. The political parties ignored the problems facing blacks, and violence directed against blacks increased. Some black Americans still hoped that a President might be elected who would lead the nation toward justice and understanding. Many of them thought such a man had been found when Theodore Roosevelt became President. But both Roosevelt and the next Republican President, William Howard Taft, proved to be disappointments. Some black leaders urged their people to turn away from the party of Lincoln and to support the Democrats or a third political party. Many followed this advice.

POLITICAL PARTY PLATFORMS IGNORED BLACKS

During the election of 1896 the Republican, Democratic, and Socialist Labor Parties gave weak support to the rights of black citizens to vote. The Republicans also stated their opposition to lynching. This was the last time during the years before World War I that the Democrats and third parties had planks favorable to black Americans in their platforms. In the elections of 1900, 1904, and 1908, all of the parties except the Republicans remained silent on the right to vote and on ending violence against blacks.

The Republican Party continued to make token gestures to keep black support. During the 1900 election campaign, the party expressed regret that the Fifteenth Amendment was being violated. But it made no promise to do anything to prevent such violations. The 1904 Republican platform called for reducing the number of Congressmen and the number of Electoral College votes in any state which kept its citizens from voting because of race. A stronger statement was made in the 1908 Republican Party platform demanding equal justice for all people. The Republicans said that they opposed all methods of denying black Americans the vote. And they demanded enforcement of the Thirteenth, Fourteenth, and Fifteenth Amendments to the Constitution.

The Democrats broke their silence regarding blacks only one time during these years. In 1904, the Democrats accused the Republicans of trying to stir up racial and sectional problems. The Democrats said that the nation had healed its wounds, and all would be well if the Republicans would drop the race question.

BLACK STRENGTH DECREASED
IN THE REPUBLICAN PARTY

Even after blacks lost the vote in the South, the Republican Party organizations in Southern states remained in black hands. This meant that black leaders participated in the Republican National Conventions and helped to name the candidates. It also meant that jobs were given to blacks during Republican administrations.

Black leaders had to fight many attempts to weaken black influence in the party. This was a losing struggle because as black voting power decreased it was certain that black influence would also decrease. But black delegates gave loyal support only to candidates they believed would work in the interest of blacks and other oppressed people. The presence of blacks also made it impossible for the Republicans to completely avoid the question of civil rights during their national conventions.

Beginning in the 1880's, some Republican leaders tried to reduce Southern representation in the Republican National Convention. They favored basing representation on the number of Republican voters in a state rather than on the size of its total population. John R. Lynch of Mississippi led the fight against reduction of delegates for many years. Moreover, he called upon the party to urge a decrease in representation in Congress of any state that violated the Fifteenth Amendment. Henry Lincoln Johnson of Georgia took up the fight against reducing Southern representation in 1908. The matter came up again in the election campaign in 1912. Finally, in the 1916 election, the selection of delegates was based on the number of Republican voters. As a result of this change, the Southern states lost seventy-eight delegates.

RACIAL VIOLENCE GRADUALLY INCREASED IN THE SOUTH

As black citizens lost political power, violence against them increased. In fact, terror became a method by which the white South forced blacks into second-class citizenship. Blacks had been able to join together against organized white violence during the years of Reconstruction. But during the 1880's, such efforts by black Southerners were seldom tried. Individuals were left to the mercy of white mobs. Lynching became the means of enforcing "white supremacy" and for keeping "the Negro in his place."

In only one year between 1885 and 1915 were fewer than fifty black Americans lynched. The number of blacks who lost their lives at the hands of white mobs increased greatly up to 1892. Mobs lynched 1,400 blacks from 1882 to 1892. The number killed each year began to decrease in 1892, but lynching remained a major problem during the pre-World War I period. A total of 1,100 blacks were lynched between 1900 and 1915.

Each year, stories of brutal murders came out of the South. In 1900, white mobs roamed the streets of New Orleans for three days. Blacks were beaten, and their homes and businesses were looted. An argument on a streetcar in Augusta, Georgia, led to the death of a white man and the lynching of the black man who killed him. The black man was tortured and mutilated before he was hanged by the mob.

Similar incidents took place each year after 1900. Throughout the South, blacks met death by being hanged, burned at the stake, or shot. Those who died quickly were fortunate. These mob actions usually included such torture as cutting off fingers and ears, and other forms of mutilation.

THE ATLANTA RIOT CLIMAXED THE VIOLENCE

The question of disfranchising blacks was a major issue in the Georgia election of 1906. Hoke Smith, who was running for governor, made racial hatred a main part of his campaign. Tensions were increased by reports of crimes committed against white women by black men. The *Atlanta News* played up the crimes, and fear and anger grew in the city. The newspapers reported four attacks on white women on Saturday, September 22. Whites from outside the city caused trouble on Saturday night, but Sunday was rather quiet.

On Monday, white mobs began attacking black citizens living in Brownsville, a suburb of Atlanta. Many blacks fled to local black colleges, seeking safety. They gathered at Gammon Theological Seminary and other schools. Some blacks decided to get weapons and resist. In the meantime, white mobs were attacking every black person they could find. Police and soldiers began shooting and arresting blacks for having weapons. Several blacks were killed, and many more were injured. The president of Gammon was beaten by the police when he demanded protection.

W. E. B. Du Bois, who was teaching at Atlanta University then, was out of the city when the riot broke out. He took the first train back to Atlanta to be with his family. On the way back, he wrote the poem "A Litany at Atlanta." Du Bois set down the deep feelings and frustrations of blacks in the face of white violence. In one stanza he wrote:

> "Bewildered we are, and passion-tost, mad with the madness of a / mobbed and mocked and murdered people; straining at the armposts / of Thy Throne, we raise our shackled hands and charge Thee, God, / by the bones of our stolen fathers, by the tears of our dead mothers, by / the very blood of Thy crucified Christ: *What meaneth this?* Tell us the / Plan; give us the Sign!"

ROOSEVELT CAUSED SOME BLACKS TO HOPE

When Theodore Roosevelt became President in 1901, some blacks hoped that they now had a friend in the White House. But they were not certain, because Roosevelt had a mixed record. For example, he first praised the black soldiers who fought in Cuba during the Spanish-American War, but later he said they were lacking in courage.

Several of President Roosevelt's early actions gave blacks hope. Soon after he became President, Roosevelt invited Booker T. Washing-

President Theodore Roosevelt consulted Booker T. Washington about appointing blacks to government posts. But Roosevelt's policies did little to improve the lives of most black Americans.

ton to the White House for an interview. Washington remained and had dinner with the President. The white South and some white conservatives were very upset by this event, but black Americans were pleased.

Roosevelt also followed a policy of equal rights in making his first appointments. He insisted that color should not bar a qualified Republican from a job. He held to this belief when the whites of Indianola, Mississippi, forced Minnie Cox to resign as postmistress in 1903. Mrs. Cox was first appointed by President Benjamin Harrison and was reappointed by President McKinley in 1897. Mrs. Cox was a respected property owner in Indianola, and she had performed her job as postmistress well.

Finally, when threats were made to harm her, Mrs. Cox resigned. The town officials said that they were unable to protect her unless she resigned. Roosevelt closed the post office when Mrs. Cox refused to serve. Indianola remained without mail service for several months. Although the post office later reopened with a white postmaster, blacks were cheered by Roosevelt's stand.

At about the same time, Roosevelt named Dr. William D. Crum as Collector of the Port in Charleston, South Carolina. There was much opposition in the Senate to appointing a black person to such a position in the South. But Roosevelt insisted, and he finally obtained Senate approval.

BLACK HOPES DIMMED AFTER BROWNSVILLE

The more militant blacks began to change their minds about President Theodore Roosevelt after his actions during the Brownsville, Texas, incident. In August, 1906, a group of armed men shot up the town of Brownsville, Texas. The trouble started when the First Battalion of the 25th Infantry, a black unit, was sent to Fort Brown. The people of Brownsville showed their displeasure at the soldiers' presence in every way possible. One incident after another took place until this led to the final shooting up of the town. The black soldiers were blamed for this shooting.

The evidence connecting the soldiers with the incident was very weak. Because of the trouble the black troops had to face from the time they arrived, they had been ordered to stay at the fort. And they were at the fort not long after the incident happened. In addition, an inspection of their rifles showed that none had been fired recently. Still, several white citizens swore that the black soldiers were guilty.

In spite of the weak evidence, Roosevelt issued an order on November 9, 1906, dismissing all 167 men of B Company from the service "without honor." The men were denied the right to be appointed to civil service jobs or to receive pensions. Black opinion was strongly opposed to Roosevelt's actions. Even those black newspapers that received money from Booker T. Washington to assure their loyalty denounced the President. Sixty-six years later, in October, 1972, the Secretary of the Army finally reversed Roosevelt's order and made the discharge "honorable." This action cleared the men of all guilt on army records.

BLACK MILITANTS OPPOSED TAFT

When President Roosevelt supported William Howard Taft for the Presidency in 1908, some militant black leaders supported the Democrats. Some of Du Bois' associates in the Niagara Movement were major critics of Roosevelt. The Reverend Reverdy C. Ransom had been urging blacks to break their attachment to the Republican Party. William Monroe Trotter, Alexander Walters, J. Milton Waldron, and other militants organized the National Negro American Political League in 1908. The League took a strong anti-Republican stand.

The militants called for the election of William Jennings Bryan as President in 1908. This was largely a protest against Roosevelt's changing policy toward blacks. It was also a protest against Taft. In the minds of blacks, Taft, as Secretary of War under Roosevelt, shared the blame for the Brownsville affair. Taft also had spoken in favor of the South's disfranchisement policy. These militant blacks also opposed Roosevelt and Taft because of the political influence they gave to Booker T. Washington, who served as political adviser to both men.

It was argued that a vote for the Democrats in 1908 would be in the best interests of the blacks. The election of a Northern Democrat with the help of black votes would end the Northern Democrats' dependence on the "solid South." This would free the Progressive group in the Democratic Party to carry out a program in the best interest of blacks and other oppressed groups. At the same time, the Republicans would be punished for mistreating loyal blacks.

REPUBLICANS APPOINTED BLACKS TO JOBS

Supporting the Democrats was a gamble, but the jobs provided by the Republicans were real. For years blacks had played an important part in every Presidential campaign. Booker T. Washington had general control of the main campaign effort, but several politicians usually served on the advisory committee. Cyrus Field Adams, a Chicago newspaper editor, and Ernest Lyons of Baltimore managed the Republican campaign among blacks in 1900. Henry Lincoln Johnson of Georgia joined Adams to direct the campaign among blacks in 1904 and 1908.

Blacks received a number of minor job appointments from the Republican Party in the South. Republican Presidents down through the Taft administration made such appointments. In 1900, the Republicans boasted that the 15,868 blacks in the federal service were earning $5,538,612. Nearly all of these 15,050 employees were in the army, however. Only 818 blacks were employed in nonmilitary federal jobs.

But in 1900, there were a few important positions held by black Americans. Eleven were members of the foreign service. These included officials serving in Russia, Brazil, Paraguay, Santo Domingo, and France. And in the United States, some blacks served as collectors of internal revenue, collectors of ports, collectors of customs, and postmasters in small cities and towns. The highest positions held by black appointees were Recorder of Deeds of the District of Columbia, Register of the Treasury, and Minister to Haiti.

Roosevelt added more black office holders. Soon after he took office, Roosevelt began calling upon Booker T. Washington to seek his advice on new black appointees and in some instances Southern white appointees as well.

CONDITIONS BEGAN TO WORSEN UNDER TAFT

Booker T. Washington also served as adviser to President Taft, but Taft did not rely on him as much as Roosevelt had. Taft began to listen more to white Southern ideas on black appointments. He did not reappoint blacks to jobs when whites objected. Soon a number of federal jobs as postmasters and port collectors were lost by blacks in the South. Taft defended his policy by pointing out that he had appointed many blacks to office. Several of these, he said, were "offices of essential dignity at Washington." But, he added, "What I have not done is to force them upon unwilling communities in the South itself."

The significant black appointments under Taft came because of strong urgings from Washington and other black leaders. Washington had already succeeded in having Roosevelt and Taft appoint several blacks to important jobs. These included the appointment of Robert H. Terrell as judge of the municipal court in Washington, D.C., and

Charles W. Anderson as collector of internal revenue in New York City. As black opinion began to turn against Taft, Washington insisted that Taft must make some gesture to hold the black vote. Finally, Taft appointed William H. Lewis as Assistant Attorney General of the United States. This was the highest position a black person had held in the federal government up to that time.

BLACKS ORGANIZED INDEPENDENT GROUPS

While the majority of blacks remained loyal to the Republican Party, many tried to find other ways to obtain political power. But they had few real choices. In the South, disfranchisement decreased the power of the black vote, and the laws segregating blacks in the South forced them into second-class citizenship. The Republican Party took the black vote for granted because the Democrats made no efforts at the national level to attract black support. Still, militant blacks felt that some protest against Republican policies had to be made. Some dreamed of uniting black voters into a movement that might win recognition from both parties. Others favored supporting the Democrats to show that party the value of the black vote. After the Brownsville affair and the election of Taft, most militant blacks were strongly anti-Republican.

The National Liberty Party was an early attempt at black political independence. This party was organized at St. Louis in July, 1904, largely under the leadership of Stanley P. Mitchell of Memphis, Tennessee. Mitchell tried to use the Civil and Personal Liberty Leagues in the South as the basis for the new political movement.

The National Liberty Party set out to form organizations in every state. The organizers hoped that white Progressives would join with blacks in reforming the old parties. If this united group could be formed, the leaders believed that it would shake "the very foundations of the two dominant political parties." They hoped that Republican and Democratic leaders would be "brought to a realization of the danger which threatens their organizations." However, this movement had little impact as a political force.

DEMOCRATS GAINED SOME BLACK SUPPORT

Blacks in some places found it profitable to split their support between Democrats and Republicans. Northern blacks often found that they were able to obtain more from local Democratic organizations than from Republicans. In cities like St. Paul, Chicago, and Boston, the Democrats attracted a sizable black vote. Frederick L. McGhee of St. Paul was an example of a black leader who favored the Democrats locally but wanted Roosevelt elected President in 1904.

The Democrats had great success among black voters in 1910. Those blacks who had supported William Jennings Bryan in 1908 continued their organization after the election. The National Independent Political League, as the black Democrats called their organization, met at Atlantic City in 1910. Bishop Alexander Walters of the African Methodist Episcopal Zion Church was elected president of the League.

From its New York City headquarters, the League took an active part in the 1910 election campaign. Du Bois joined this group in urging blacks to vote for the Democratic Party. Considerable attention was centered on the state of New York. The campaign publicity promised black policemen and firemen in New York City and a black regiment in the New York State Guard. When the Democrats won, Du Bois hailed their victory as significant to blacks. It did show political independence among blacks, as well as their dissatisfaction with the Republicans.

But the New York Democrats did not fulfill their promises to their black supporters. Some of Du Bois' enthusiasm cooled when the New York legislature took no action to organize a black regiment. Consequently, blacks were not unhappy when the Democrats lost control of the legislature in 1911. Even so, at the national level some blacks still considered it best for blacks to divide their votes. A National Negro Democratic Convention was held at Indianapolis in May, 1911. This group argued that it was not good for blacks always to follow one party. Those at the meeting pledged their allegiance to the Democratic Party. They urged other blacks to support the Democrats in the Presidential election of 1912.

Chapter 9

Woodrow Wilson and Jim Crow

In the Presidential election of 1912, blacks split their vote among William Howard Taft, Theodore Roosevelt, and Woodrow Wilson. And the Democrats tried to win black voters' support. Many black voters, particularly the more militant blacks, decided to vote for Wilson. But when Wilson won, the Democrats were even more ungrateful to black supporters than the Republicans had been. Under Wilson, blacks lost many of the jobs they had long held in the federal government. Still worse, segregation became firmly established within the federal government.

SOME BLACKS SUPPORTED THE DIVIDED REPUBLICANS
In 1912, both President Taft and former President Roosevelt wanted the Republican nomination. When the Republican Convention picked Taft, Roosevelt and his followers left the convention. They then formed a new party, the Progressive Party (or Bull Moose Party). In the summer of 1912, at their convention in Chicago, the Progressives

named Roosevelt as their candidate for President.

Black politicians now were divided in their loyalty. The regular delegates from the South had been members of the Republican Convention, and most of them remained supporters of Taft. Henry Lincoln Johnson and Charles W. Anderson, Collector of Internal Revenue in New York City and close associate of Booker T. Washington, directed the Taft campaign among blacks.

Theodore Roosevelt, too, sought the support of Northern blacks. James H. Hayes, a Richmond attorney and critic of Booker T. Washington, and Perry Howard, leader of Mississippi Republicans, led the Progressive Party campaign.

Du Bois was impressed with the Progressives at first. He liked their reform views, many of which he felt would benefit blacks. The main thing missing in the party's platform, he believed, was a plank supporting black rights. Du Bois wrote such a plank, therefore, to place the Progressives on record as condemning racial discrimination. It also stated, "The party . . . demands for the American of Negro descent the repeal of unfair discriminatory laws and the right to vote on the same terms on which other citizens vote."

Three of Du Bois' white liberal associates in the NAACP—Joel Spingarn, Henry Moskowitz, and Jane Addams—took his plank to the Chicago convention. They tried to get it accepted by the Progressive Convention, but the Progressives refused to support a statement of any kind dealing with the rights of blacks. To make matters worse, Roosevelt refused to seat black delegates from the South. Roosevelt openly tried to get white support in the South. He only allowed the "lily white" Republican delegates to be seated at the Progressive Convention. Du Bois said of the situation, "To explain the action of his Progressive convention, one must realize Mr. Roosevelt's attitude toward black men. He does not respect them."

DEMOCRATS TRIED TO GAIN BLACK SUPPORT IN 1912
In 1912, for the first time, the Democrats made an organized effort to win black votes. The campaign was directed by Judge Hedspeth of New Jersey. Bishop Alexander Walters and Dr. Joseph D. Johnson, an outstanding Columbus, Ohio, physician, were also active national campaign leaders.

Support for the Democrats was especially strong among militant blacks. When Du Bois left the Progressives, he turned to the Democrats. Actually, he viewed Wilson as the least of three evils. Personally, Du Bois favored Eugene V. Debs, the Socialist candidate. Debs was the only candidate who took a courageous stand on "human rights." But after Wilson's nomination, a number of things led Du Bois and other blacks to hope that Wilson might give blacks fair treatment.

The first hopeful sign was a conference on July 16, 1912, between Woodrow Wilson, J. Milton Waldron, and William Monroe Trotter. Waldron and Trotter were old colleagues of Du Bois from the Niagara Movement. After the meeting, Waldron wrote a report about Wilson which was very favorable. But Waldron's report was published before Wilson was told about it. A month later, Oswald Garrison Villard talked to Wilson about his views on the racial question. Villard left satisfied that Wilson deserved black support. But when Wilson later read Waldron's statement, he denied it agreed with his views. Wilson then asked Villard to write a statement for him that promised blacks only that they need not fear "unfair discrimination."

DU BOIS WROTE A STATEMENT

Villard asked Du Bois to write the statement for Wilson. The statement that Du Bois wrote asked blacks to support the Democrats. It pledged Wilson to become, if elected, "President of the whole nation and treat every citizen according to the spirit of our institutions."

The Du Bois statement also was too strong for Wilson. In the end, Wilson's only promise to blacks was that he would guarantee them "justice executed with liberality and cordial good feeling." In spite of Wilson's failure to take a strong stand, many black leaders continued to support him. This can be explained in part by the strong feelings that men like Du Bois had against Roosevelt, Taft, and Washington.

BLACKS STRONGLY OPPOSED TAFT

President Taft had done a number of things which angered blacks. They considered him weak. Roosevelt, on the other hand, while not dependable, had stood firm at important times. But Taft seemed to be lacking in principles. He had come out in favor of the South's refusal to allow its black citizens to vote. In addition, he had refused to help in the campaign against lynching. In June, 1911, the NAACP and other groups called upon Taft to ask Congress to pass an anti-lynching law. Taft told them that lynching was a matter for state legislatures to handle.

President Taft's statements drew a strong reaction from black militants. Du Bois, in his *Crisis* editorials, expressed the views of this group. After the elections of 1911, Du Bois said that Taft would need "every black vote in the North" to be reelected. But Du Bois did not believe Taft would get these votes with "his silence on lynching and his treatment of colored officials." "Any colored man who votes for Mr. Taft," Du Bois said, "will do so on the assumption that zero is better than minus one."

BLACKS HOPED TO GAIN
BY SUPPORTING THE DEMOCRATS

Many black leaders still believed that blacks had some political power. They assured black citizens that their case was not hopeless. Black people still were "a half million votes this side of disfranchisement." And every election since the Civil War had been "settled by a margin of less than a half million votes." The leaders reasoned further that the distribution of this vote was also important. In a close election, black voters in the Middle Western states, New York, and New Jersey probably would be the deciding voice.

Bishop Walters, Lester A. Walton, and William M. Trotter were important black Democratic leaders. They hoped that by working to defeat the Republican administration blacks would earn the appreciation of the Democrats. If the new Democratic administration treated black Americans fairly, black voters would have a real choice.

When the election returns were in, however, it was clear that the black vote had not been important in Wilson's victory. The split in the Republican Party had caused Wilson to win an overwhelming majority in the Electoral College. Still, black leaders pointed to the fact that Wilson had received 100,000 blacks votes. Some were worried, but most looked forward to the Wilson administration with hope of justice for blacks.

WILSON FAILED TO APPOINT BLACK OFFICIALS
TO GOVERNMENT JOBS

It was clear from the organization of Wilson's Cabinet that the South was in power in Washington. The South also had control of Congress. What this meant to black Americans became clear when the Democrats began to fill the federal government's offices. Few black job holders remained after this Democratic change in office holders.

There were a number of important black officials when Wilson took office. Assistant attorney general William H. Lewis was the top black official. Register of the Treasury, J. C. Napier, Recorder of Deeds, Henry Lincoln Johnson, and Ralph W. Tyler, an auditor for the Navy Department, held jobs the Republicans usually assigned to blacks. Lewis had an annual salary of $5,000, and the other officials earned $4,000 to $4,500. Blacks holding lower-level jobs in Washington paying $2,000 to $2,500 included C. F. Adams, Assistant Register of the Treasury, and James A. Cobb, special assistant district attorney in Washington, D.C. Such salaries were much higher than most Americans earned in those years.

Other blacks held office as collectors of internal revenue, collectors of ports, and were in the foreign service. The collectors of internal revenue earned salaries as high as the top black officials in Washington. The collectors of internal revenue were Charles W. Anderson in New York City; Joseph E. Lee in Jacksonville, Florida; and Charles A. Cottrell in Honolulu. Collectors of ports and receivers of public moneys earned between $1,500 and $2,500. Several black men held these positions. J. E. Bush was receiver of public moneys in Little Rock, Arkansas. T. V. McAllister held this position in Jackson, Mississippi. Former Congressman Robert Smalls served as collector of the port at Beaufort, South Carolina, and N. W. Alexander was register of the land office in Montgomery, Alabama.

The highest-paying position held by a black official was in the foreign service. Henry W. Furniss had a salary of $10,000 as envoy extraordinary and minister plenipotentiary to Haiti. George H. Jackson was consul at Cognac, France, and James W. Johnson served at Corinto, Nicaragua.

President Wilson replaced blacks in all of these offices with white Democrats. He left only two offices in the hands of blacks. He appointed Dr. George W. Buckner of Indiana as Minister to Liberia. When Dr. Buckner later resigned, Wilson appointed James L. Curtis, a New York lawyer, to replace him. The other official who remained in office was Robert H. Terrell, whom Wilson reappointed as a municipal judge in the District of Columbia.

When President Taft had left office, 22,440 blacks were in government service and had total earnings of $12,456,760. Wilson made little change in the lower positions. But he changed the top office holders and downgraded others. By 1915, the total number of black employees had been reduced to 22,387, and the income received by black workers in governmental service had been reduced by more than a million dollars.

WILSON ORDERED A JIM CROW POLICY

Black Americans were shocked by the official policy of segregation begun by the Wilson administration. As soon as Congress met, a flood of measures discriminating against blacks were offered. Among the laws asked for were laws to segregate public transportation in Washington, to keep blacks out of military service, and to segregate federal offices.

When Congress failed to pass most of the segregation bills, the President himself acted. Wilson's Postmaster General, Albert Burleson of Texas, called for the segregation and downgrading of black civil service employees during a Cabinet meeting on April 11, 1913. Wilson then issued an executive order putting this policy into effect. Some unofficial segregation had taken place under Taft, but now it became official policy.

Protests were made by both black and white organizations. Trotter's pro-Democratic National Independent Political League sent an appeal to Wilson. The League accused the Democrats of betraying black voters. Trotter's group tried to get signatures on a petition to present to the President. The National Council of Congregational Churches also sent in an appeal.

DU BOIS TRIED TO EXPLAIN
THE REASONS FOR WILSON'S ACTION

Du Bois blamed the South for Wilson's policies. He said that the "Bourbon South" was struggling "to control Mr. Wilson's Negro policy." For this reason, Wilson did not dare to give blacks offices. Du Bois called upon Northern Democrats to counter this pressure from the South. He also called upon black Americans to unite and act in their own behalf.

In early 1914, Du Bois wrote another mild defense of Wilson. He pointed to the problem Wilson faced in getting his progressive reform program approved and in working for justice for blacks at the same time. Du Bois said that Wilson was powerless to do anything for blacks, because Wilson had to maintain good relations with Congress in order to get his reform program passed into law. The problem was, according to Du Bois, the "abnormal advantage over the Northern votes" that the Southern voters enjoyed. He believed that the way to end this advantage was a reduction in the representation of the South, "in order to release the West and North from its intolerable political dictatorship."

ANTI-BLACK BILLS WERE PROPOSED IN 1914

Another group of anti-black laws were proposed in 1914. Bills were offered to make segregation permanent in federal jobs. In a bill providing money for agricultural education, the usual guarantees that blacks would get a fair share of the funds were left out. In addition, James K. Vardaman of Mississippi started a drive to repeal the Fifteenth Amendment.

Some of the blacks who had supported Wilson in 1912 decided to protest directly to him. A delegation led by William Monroe Trotter went to the White House on November 12, 1914. The group demanded equal treatment for black civil servants. Wilson defended segregation on the grounds that it protected black workers from friction with whites. But Trotter denied that there had been any friction among federal job holders before segregation started. The delegation reminded Wilson that they were Democrats and had supported him in 1912. Wilson insisted that segregation was not a political question.

Wilson became very upset over the way Trotter presented the group's protest. The President told the group that if they came to see him again they must have another spokesman. Both Wilson and Trotter lost their tempers. A rather heated argument followed. Finally, Wilson ordered Trotter out of his office. The President said that he had been insulted by Trotter's language. This incident received wide coverage in the newspapers. Only the Southern press coverage was completely favorable to Wilson.

REPUBLICANS GAINED BLACK SUPPORT IN 1916

The Republicans tried to reunite their party before the 1916 Presidential election. A large campaign group was organized with members from all factions. Charles W. Anderson served as chairman, and Perry Howard was secretary of the group. Many prominent black Republicans took part in the campaign to elect Charles Evans Hughes as President. The campaign advisory committee included as members Fred H. Moore of New York, W. Justin Carter, Sr., of Pennsylvania, William P. Dabney of Ohio, William H. Lewis and W. C. Mathews of Massachusetts, R. R. Church and J. C. Napier of Tennessee, Benjamin Davis and Dr. Ernest Lyons of Georgia, and James A. Cobb of Washington, D.C.

Henry Lincoln Johnson also took an active part in the Republican campaign. Johnson emphasized the bad appointment record of the Democrats. He defended the record of past Republican presidents by pointing to the large number of blacks they had appointed to government jobs. He also told black voters that there was a secret group, the so-called Fair Play Association, in the federal civil service that worked to limit the appointment of blacks to the lowest level jobs.

BLACKS WERE NOT CERTAIN ABOUT HUGHES

Although many efforts were made to attract black votes, the Republicans did not include a strong equal rights statement in their platform. And Hughes did not state his own view on the issue. His only statement during the campaign was to a gathering of 2,000 blacks at Nashville, Tennessee, where Hughes declared, "I stand for the maintenance of the rights of all American citizens, regardless of race or color."

In September, 1916, Du Bois and three other NAACP officers asked Hughes to state his views on lynching and other problems facing blacks. But the NAACP officials never received a reply from Hughes. Du Bois was unwilling to support Hughes on faith, as he had done Wilson. Thus, in *The Crisis,* Du Bois advised the black voter not to vote for Hughes, "unless Mr. Hughes satisfies him by some statement more *specific* than the Nashville speech."

FEW BLACKS CAMPAIGNED FOR WILSON

President Wilson did not receive much support from black leaders during the 1916 election. Judge Hedspeth and Dr. Joseph D. Johnson still led campaign efforts aimed at black voters. But militants like Bishop Walters and Trotter no longer supported Wilson. They had received no recognition from Wilson after their efforts in 1912, and their followers deserted them. And in any case, as militants they were unable to support Wilson's policies. In the past, they had opposed Booker T. Washington for ignoring Republican policies which had not been as bad as those under Wilson. As a result, the black Democratic organization, the National Independent Political League, ceased to exist.

In the 1916 election campaign, Wilson simply restated his views of 1912. Wilson also realized that he had not lived up to the vague promise of equality during that campaign. Du Bois and other militants did not let blacks forget this.

THE MILITANTS WERE DISILLUSIONED

As the election of 1916 approached, Du Bois and other militants could find little to encourage them. The only encouraging thing to Du Bois was the appointment of a liberal Jewish Justice, Louis D. Brandeis, to the Supreme Court. Du Bois said that the black man's only hope in politics was in a "move of segregation." Blacks, he said, had to vote as a unit. He called for an all-black party that would support candidates on individual records, rather than support parties. It was too late for such a group to form for the election of 1916.

When Wilson was reelected, Du Bois said that the campaign had been "distracting and unsatisfactory." "Few men," he said, "could vote according to their consciences, because neither candidate represented their conscience." Wilson had a good record on economic matters, Du Bois stated, but he was controlled by the black-hating leaders of the South. On the other hand, Hughes had written several of the best rulings in favor of blacks by the Supreme Court. But "on specific Negro problems he was curiously dumb," Du Bois concluded.

As the victorious Democrats took office in 1917, Du Bois described what seemed to him to be the sad state of things for blacks. He wrote, "We see an impotent government: a President reassuming office to which he has been elected by fraud and disfranchisement in the Rotten Boroughs of the South; . . . a valiant nation too cowardly to stop lynching . . . And yet, with all, our country and the land of our dream. . . ." And Du Bois seemed here to summarize the despair of black Americans on the eve of the nation's entry into World War I.

Chapter 10

Saving Democracy for Whom?

World War I marked a turning point in race relations in the United States. Blacks found themselves fighting abroad and working at home to "save democracy." Yet many black Americans who went to fight in Europe found more freedom there than they had known at home. And those who remained on the home front were still denied many rights enjoyed by white Americans. Even so, almost 400,000 black men served in the armed forces. On the home front, black workers found jobs in fields never before open to them. At the same time, these wartime changes sharpened the conflicts between black and white Americans.

BLACKS ANSWERED THE CALL TO ARMS

At first, the regular army, volunteers, and the National Guard were expected to provide the manpower needed to fight World War I. Four regiments of black soldiers, containing about 10,000 men, were in the regular army when war was declared. These black regiments were the

9th and 10th Cavalry and the 24th and 25th Infantry. The soldiers of the 9th and 10th Cavalry had won fame during the Spanish-American War by their actions in rescuing Theodore Roosevelt and the Rough Riders at San Juan Hill. The two infantry units also had fought in the war with Spain, serving in the Philippines.

In addition, the National Guard of several states had black units. Among these National Guard units were the 8th Illinois, the 15th New York, the 9th Ohio Battalion, and the 1st Separate Battalion of the District of Columbia. In addition, Massachusetts, Connecticut, Maryland, and Tennessee had separate black National Guard companies. Altogether, about 10,000 black soldiers served in these units.

Black Americans were especially proud when the 1st Separate Battalion of the District of Columbia National Guard was called to active duty on March 25, 1917. This black unit was assigned the duty of protecting the nation's capital. This was considered a great honor, and the officers and men carried out their duty with special care. But the record of the Wilson administration with respect to black Americans caused some blacks to wonder why black soldiers were called upon for this duty. One view was that President Wilson and his advisers did not want to force white workers to leave their jobs. Another theory was that black soldiers were called because there was no doubt as to their loyalty to the country.

BLACKS WERE URGED TO FIGHT FOR DEMOCRACY

When World War I broke out, blacks hoped that some improvements would take place in their condition. They had reasons for this new hope. White Americans began to place great emphasis on making the world "safe for democracy." And some talked about the need for more democracy at home. Little was said about the specific grievances of black people, however. From long experience, blacks did not assume that speeches about democracy and "the American way of life" necessarily included them. At the same time, black Americans became more aware of the difference between America's professed ideals and the real conditions of their own lives. They became more sensitive to the peculiar situation of America's trying to "save democracy" abroad, while Afro-Americans at home were denied the ballot, segregated, and lynched.

In spite of this, Afro-Americans were proud of their record of loyalty to their country. Black leaders called upon their followers to maintain that record during World War I. W. E. B. Du Bois called for unity in 1918 in his "Close the Ranks" editorial in *The Crisis*. Du Bois said that black people had a special interest in the outcome of the war. A victory by Germany, he felt, would spell "death to the aspirations of Negroes and all dark races for equality, freedom, and democracy." Consequently, he advised: "Let us not hesitate. Let us, while the war lasts, forget our special grievances and close ranks shoulder to shoulder with our white fellow citizens and the allied nations that are fighting for democracy. We make no ordinary sacrifice, but we make it gladly and willingly with our eyes lifted to the hills."

Earlier, Roscoe Conkling Simmons had urged a similar view. Simmons, who lived in Chicago, was an active Republican politician and one of the best-known black orators of his day. Speaking at Louisville, Kentucky, in March, 1917, Simmons called upon his audience to disregard German efforts to encourage disloyalty among Southern blacks. Woodrow Wilson was his leader, Simmons declared, and he urged blacks to answer the call to serve.

Yet Simmons knew the many grievances black people had against their government. He called for loyalty in spite of this. "Injustice to me there is," Simmons said, "bad laws there are upon the statute books, but in this hour of peril I forget—and you must forget—all thoughts of self or race or creed or politics or color. That is loyalty."

BLACKS WERE NOT WELCOMED IN THE ARMY

When volunteers were called for, large numbers of young black men offered their service. Only enough of these men were accepted to bring the black units up to full strength. Then the War Department ordered recruiters to stop accepting black volunteers.

This was a great blow to the morale of black Americans. Pressure came from black leaders and from the black press to have the War Department accept blacks as soldiers. Du Bois, at this point, expressed doubts about his country. He said that black youth might now ask themselves, "Why should we want to fight for America or America's friends; and how sure could we be that America's enemies were our enemies too?"

Another blow to black morale came in June, 1917, when the War Department retired Colonel Charles Young. Young, who was a graduate of the United States Military Academy, was the highest-ranking black officer in the regular army. He was commissioned a second lieutenant in 1889, led a regiment during the Spanish-American War as a major, and was promoted to lieutenant-colonel in 1916. Blacks followed his activities with great interest, and they expected he would receive an appropriate assignment during World War I. The reason given for his retirement was that he was not physically fit for service. To demonstrate his good physical condition, Young rode on horseback from Ohio to Washington. Nevertheless, the decision to retire him was not changed.

Continued protests from blacks finally resulted in Colonel Young's being recalled from retirement late in 1918. He then served briefly at several military posts in the United States before World War I ended.

BLACKS WERE DRAFTED BUT SEGREGATED

The United States government soon realized that not enough military manpower could be obtained through the volunteer system. It also realized that black men were needed. Congress passed a Selective Service, or draft, law on May 18, 1917. Between June 5, 1917, and September 12, 1918, a total of 2,290,527 black men registered for service. Of these, 458,838 were called for physical examinations.

A large percentage of the blacks examined were accepted by the army. A total of 367,710 blacks entered the service. Southern draft boards seemed especially unwilling to reject black draftees because of family hardship or other reasons.

Yet black soldiers faced segregation from the moment they were drafted. The draft law required that blacks and whites be called into service separately and trained separately. In several Southern states, white politicians objected to black soldiers being trained at camps located in the South. They were especially opposed to Northern blacks being sent into Southern states.

At first, the War Department tried to satisfy Southern demands. It tried to send drafted Southern blacks to camps located in the states where they lived. But all regiments of each state's National Guard were trained at the same camp. However, the National Guard from many Northern states with black regiments and companies did receive training in the South. This meant that while Northern black draftees and black draftees from neighboring Southern states were kept out of a particular Southern state, blacks in National Guard units from Northern states were not. So much confusion resulted from the policy of keeping black draftees in their home states that the policy had to be changed. Before the war ended, black soldiers from all over the country were being trained in most Southern camps.

A BLACK ADVISER WAS NAMED
FOR THE WAR DEPARTMENT

The tense racial situation resulting from wartime conditions caused several black and white leaders to ask for a black adviser in the War Department. Dr. Robert R. Moton, who replaced Booker T. Washington at Tuskegee Institute, asked the Secretary of War to appoint such an adviser. Julius Rosenwald, the Chicago philanthropist, also supported the idea.

On October 5, 1917, Secretary of War Newton D. Baker named Emmett J. Scott as Special Assistant in the War Department. Scott had earlier been confidential secretary to Booker T. Washington and was serving as secretary of Tuskegee Institute when appointed to his new post. Scott's duty was to serve as "confidential adviser in matters affecting the interests of the 10,000,000 Negroes of the United States, and the part they are to play in connection with the present war."

BLACK OFFICERS WERE TRAINED

Black citizens were greatly concerned about the need to have blacks commissioned as army officers. A number of the National Guard regiments and companies had black officers, but the army units of black draftees were largely staffed by white officers. Blacks began to demand some black officers for these draftees. The 92nd Division, for example, was an all-black division with few, if any, black officers. But the opposition to black officers was strong. The War Department resisted the demand for black officers, claiming that few trained black officers were available. No camp for training black officers existed, and the Selective Service law made it illegal to train blacks and whites together.

Individual blacks and whites and organizations such as the NAACP began agitating for an officer-training camp. This was a difficult problem for some. Leaders of the NAACP were working to end segregation. But, on this problem, they had to choose between having a segregated camp in order to train black officers or having no camp and no black officers. The NAACP and most blacks supported the demand for a separate camp in order to have some black officers.

The pressure on the War Department to establish a camp became great. Students at several black colleges, including Fisk and Howard Universities, joined the campaign. Finally, the War Department gave in and opened Camp Dodge at Des Moines, Iowa, to train black officers. The training program began during the summer of 1917. The men were supposed to finish in three months, but an extra month was added. This caused some unrest among the trainees and among blacks generally. But in October, 639 black officers were commissioned, including 106 captains, 329 first lieutenants, and 204 second lieutenants. The new officers were sent to the seven different camps where units of the 92nd Division were being trained. Before the war ended, a total of about 1,400 black soldiers received commissions.

BLACK CIVILIANS AIDED THE WAR EFFORT

Black civilians gave generously to support the war activities. When the government called for financial support in Liberty Loan campaigns, blacks helped more than was expected. They bought Liberty Bonds and War Savings Stamps to the limit of their means. The black citizens of the District of Columbia bought $2,200,000 worth of bonds in four Liberty Loan campaigns. In 1918, South Carolina blacks bought $1,294,540 worth of War Savings Stamps. It was estimated that blacks contributed a total of over $225 million in these money-raising campaigns.

Blacks also gave the Red Cross support. Contributions were asked for through churches, schools, and other black organizations. The Negro Auxiliary of the Fort Worth, Texas, Red Cross raised $4,484 in one week. Generous sums came from other areas. The black community of Birmingham, Alabama, gave about $80,000 to the Red Cross.

Black civilians also helped the armed forces. Black nurses worked in hospitals at six army camps. Black women worked in army canteens in the United States and in France. And about 350 Young Men's Christian Association secretaries worked among the soldiers.

RACIAL TENSIONS CAUSED CONFLICT

Given the attitude of whites toward black soldiers, it was not surprising that violent incidents took place. Problems arose between blacks and whites in army camps and in the towns near camps.

Black soldiers had many reasons to complain about their treatment by the military. Northern blacks did not like the segregated training in Southern camps. The white officers assigned to black units often were openly prejudiced. Sometimes black soldiers were beaten as punishment for breaking rules.

Black soldiers disliked the open discrimination they faced in the army. Blacks were placed in labor battalions no matter what kind of training or skills they had before entering the service. It became clear that ability meant little as far as the treatment of black soldiers was concerned. White officers picked unqualified blacks as noncommissioned officers and passed over more able black soldiers. Many white soldiers refused to salute black officers. Black soldiers were not allowed to use recreation facilities in the camps. And the military police enforced Southern racial customs and Jim Crow policies of racial segregation, which caused frequent trouble between black soldiers and the military police.

White civilians showed their dislike of black soldiers. It was especially difficult for white Southerners to accept the fact that blacks were being trained as soldiers. They realized that this new experience would change the attitude of black people toward life in the South. And they were not wrong. Black soldiers showed on a number of occasions that they would not accept insults and mistreatment without striking back.

AN INCIDENT TOOK PLACE THAT LED TO A RIOT IN HOUSTON

Feelings of fear and bitterness grew between the men of the A Battalion of the 24th Infantry Regiment and the white citizens of Houston, Texas. The citizens objected to the black soldiers being there and openly showed their hostility. Soldiers were insulted and beaten while in Houston. This situation broke into open violence in August, 1917, when a soldier was arrested for protesting the brutal treatment of a black woman by a Houston policeman.

When his fellow soldiers at Camp Logan learned of the arrest, they armed themselves and went into Houston. In the fighting which followed, seventeen people were killed. When order was restored, the battalion was moved to a camp in New Mexico. Charges of murder were brought against thirty-four of the men, and thirteen of them were hanged. Others were charged with various crimes, and forty-one were sentenced to life in prison.

None of the whites involved were punished. The "Houston riot" caused great excitement throughout the country. Blacks began to wonder if this was the kind of "democracy" they were asked to defend. It seemed to many that Afro-Americans were being asked to give all and receive nothing. The NAACP began a campaign to have the men in prison freed, and it finally did obtain their release. But reports of insults and attacks on black soldiers continued to come from camps all over the country.

A RIOT WAS AVOIDED IN SPARTANBURG

Another blow to black morale came from Spartanburg, South Carolina. The units of the New York National Guard were trained at Camp Wadsworth near this South Carolina town. The black 15th New York Regiment, which became the 369th Infantry, was among the units at the camp. At first, the regiment was under the command of a black officer, Colonel Benjamin O. Davis. Then Colonel Davis was replaced by a white officer, Colonel William Hayward. But this change did not end the complaints of the white citizens of Spartanburg nor their attempts to teach the black men from New York to "know their place."

One Sunday evening in 1917, Noble Sissle, a musician and soldier in the 15th Regiment, went to a white hotel to buy a newspaper. The owner walked up to Sissle, cursed him, and knocked the soldier's hat from his head. When Sissle reached for his hat, the hotel owner struck him and then kicked him as he moved toward the door to leave.

A group of white and black soldiers of the 15th Regiment went to the hotel when they heard of the attack on Sissle. Lieutenant James R. Europe, a black officer who was bandmaster of the 15th, stopped them before they could storm the hotel.

The following night, a group of the men decided to go to Spartanburg and "shoot up" the town. Colonel Hayward learned of their plan and overtook them before they reached the town. He brought the men back to camp and prevented a riot. But this did not ease the tension, and violence still seemed possible.

The War Department sent special assistant Emmett J. Scott to Spartanburg to try to calm things down. Scott tried to convince the black soldiers that in spite of the insults and attacks they should not fight back. Scott's appeal to the men to have patience succeeded. He later praised their action as serving the "Great Cause, even in the face of studied insult and maltreatment."

The War Department's reaction to the problem at Spartanburg was to send the black regiment overseas. The men of the 369th Infantry, 92nd Division, fought with valor in France. When they returned, their commander could boast, "They never lost a trench or a foot of ground."

COMPLAINTS CAME FROM OTHER CAMPS

Reports of mistreatment of black soldiers came from camps in both the South and the North. Camp Lee in Virginia had a very bad record. Unfair treatment by military police was common, and black soldiers com-

104

plained that they were not given passes as freely as white soldiers. Reports of discrimination in working conditions, promotions, and the use of camp facilities also came from Chicago and St. Louis.

An incident that received wide publicity occurred at Camp Funston in Kansas. The manager of a theater in Manhattan, Kansas, refused to admit a sergeant from the 92nd Division. The manager gave as his reason that white customers might object to the presence of the black soldier.

On March 28, 1918, General C. C. Ballou issued a "bulletin" to the black officers and men under his command. In it he said that black soldiers should not insist on their right to go places where whites might object. This was necessary, the general felt, in order to prevent racial friction. Black people throughout the country protested the general's action, and the black press strongly criticized him. General Ballou said that his order had been misrepresented. He pointed out that he had taken action against the theater manager, and that his "bulletin" had nothing to do with any policy of segregation. Rather, he said, "its purpose was to prevent race friction, with the attendant prejudice to good order and military discipline."

BLACK SOLDIERS SERVED WELL IN EUROPE

In spite of problems at home, black soldiers served with great bravery overseas. About 200,000 men were sent to France during the war. Most of them were assigned to labor battalions to do the heavy work needed to support combat troops. Black stevedore battalions unloaded most of the goods shipped to French ports. Working long hours, often in rain and mud, these black battalions helped to keep the Allied armies fighting.

Black American units placed under French command fought at the war front. About 42,000 of the 200,000 black soldiers sent to France became combat troops. Most of these were in units of the 92nd Division. Plans were drawn up for a 93rd Division of black soldiers, but only four regiments were organized. These regiments—the 369th, 370th, 371st, and 372nd—fought as part of French units.

The 92nd Division was formed on November 29, 1917. About four-fifths of the commissioned officers were black. The Division was never brought to one main camp for training. Instead, units of the Division were trained at seven different camps. In May, 1918, the Division was ordered overseas to join the American Expeditionary Force. After eight weeks of training in France, the 92nd was ordered to the front line.

Many black soldiers fought in France during World War I. These troops took part in the fighting in the Argonne Region.

From August 25 to September 20, 1918, the 92nd Division held the St. Die sector of the line near the Rhine River. The Germans attacked the sector the very first day the 92nd arrived. But the only major fighting took place on August 31, when the enemy tried to retake the village of Frapelle. Most of the time, the men participated in patrols and raiding parties.

The 92nd fought in two other sectors before the war ended. In late September, 1918, the Division moved to the Argonne Region. The 368th Infantry Regiment of the 92nd Division took part in the battle for Binarville. The Regiment captured the town but at a heavy price. It lost 450 men, and another 14 were wounded. On October 5, 1918, the Division joined the advance toward Metz. The 92nd was ordered to attack Metz on November 10, but it was ordered to stop fighting the next day because of the Armistice.

THE 92ND DIVISION WAS CITED FOR BRAVERY

One of the most outstanding units of the 92nd Division was the 367th Infantry Regiment. The unit, nicknamed the Buffaloes, was trained at Camp Upton in New York. The entire First Battalion of the 367th was awarded one of France's highest military honors, the *Croix de Guerre*, for bravery during the advance on Metz. The 365th Regiment also received the *Croix de Guerre*.

Individual soldiers of the 92nd Division also were cited for bravery. They carried messages through enemy lines, rescued wounded comrades, and defended positions under enemy attack. A total of fourteen officers and forty-three enlisted men received the Distinguished Service Cross for bravery in action.

OTHER BLACK REGIMENTS SAW ACTION

The four regiments of the proposed 93rd Division saw action as parts of French divisions. The 369th Infantry Regiment was one of these units. It was formed from the 15th Regiment of the New York National Guard. After the incident at Spartanburg, South Carolina, the regiment shipped out for France. Their arrival was delayed by bad weather, a ship collision, and measles; and they did not reach France until December 27, 1917. When they arrived at Brest, the men were put to work building roads and unloading supplies.

Then in February, 1918, they were placed under French command. Almost immediately, the 369th was moved to the front. The

French trained the men for combat and sent them to a sector in the Champagne region. Although they lost many men in the fighting at Boise d'Hauze, they were sent to Minancourt to stop the German advance there. In October, 1918, the 369th became the first Allied unit to reach the Rhine.

The "Hell Fighters," as the 369th was called by the French and the Germans, had an outstanding combat record. The regiment was cited eleven times for bravery in action, and the French awarded the 369th the *Croix de Guerre* for the advance to the Rhine.

Two soldiers of the 369th were the first men of the American Expeditionary Forces to receive the *Croix de Guerre*. They were Henry Johnson of Albany, New York, and Needham Roberts of Trenton, New Jersey. Early on the morning of May 14, 1918, a German raiding party of twenty men attacked their post. Both men were wounded by German grenades, but they fought off the attack. Roberts was seriously wounded, but he threw hand grenades at the enemy. Johnson fired all the cartridges in his rifle, then used his rifle as a club, and finally fought using a knife. Johnson killed four of the attackers and wounded several others.

Black Americans were especially interested in the activities of the 370th Infantry Regiment. This unit had been the 8th Illinois National Guard Regiment, under the command of Colonel Franklin A. Denison. It was commanded entirely by black officers and noncommissioned officers. Because the regiment was under black officers, the War Department seemed to move slowly to send it overseas. The 370th reached France in June, 1918, and was sent to defend a part of the St. Mihiel sector. In July, the regiment was moved to the Argonne Forest. The 370th and French units drove the Germans across the border into Belgium. The 370th captured Gue d'Hossus in Belgium only a short time before the signing of the Armistice.

Their heroic deeds earned decoration for many men of the 370th. Sergeant Matthew Jenkins received both the Distinguished Service Cross and the *Croix de Guerre* for capturing an enemy position and holding it alone for thirty-six hours. Corporal Isaac Valley was awarded the Distinguished Service Cross for covering a grenade with his foot to protect the other soldiers in his trench. In all, twenty-one men received the Distinguished Service Cross, sixty-eight received the *Croix de Guerre*, and one was awarded the Distinguished Service Medal.

The 371st Infantry Regiment reached France in April, 1918. This regiment was organized at Camp Jackson, South Carolina, in August, 1917. In France, it became a part of the 157th French Division and fought in the Champagne sector. The 371st lost 1,065 men in this battle. It also received many awards for its part in the fighting in the Champagne. The regiment's colors were decorated by the French government, one soldier received the Legion of Honor, twenty-two men the Distinguished Service Cross, and 123 men the *Croix de Guerre*.

The 372nd Infantry Regiment was made up of National Guard units from several states as well as draftees. As a part of the French "Red Hand" Division, the 372nd took part in heavy fighting in the Argonne region. The regiment received the *Croix de Guerre* for its part in the Champagne offensive. Twenty-one of its men earned the Distinguished Service Cross, sixty-eight the *Croix de Guerre*, and one the Distinguished Service Medal.

BLACK UNITS BROUGHT JAZZ TO FRANCE

Several black regiments had very good regimental bands. Two of the most famous were the bands of the 369th Infantry Regiment and the 350th Field Artillery. Lieutenant James Reese Europe led the 369th band, and Lieutenant J. Tim Brymm led that of the 350th.

An article in *The World Magazine* reported how the 369th band "jazzed its way through France." The band introduced jazz to France even before it left the port of Brest. Lieutenant Europe and his men spent two months playing for soldiers at a rest center there. People came from miles around to listen.

PREJUDICE FOLLOWED BLACKS TO FRANCE

Black soldiers in the American Expeditionary Force found that white Americans brought discrimination with them to France. Black officers were special objects of this prejudice. Black officers were segregated at meals and given living accommodations inferior to those furnished white officers. Some white commanders believed black soldiers should be used only in labor battalions, and many soldiers who had been trained for combat were assigned to these labor units.

Conditions in the labor battalions were very difficult. The men worked long hours under terrible conditions. They were housed in makeshift tents and barracks that often lacked heat and toilet facilities. Their food was not adequate, and sickness was widespread among the men.

Many white American soldiers urged the French to follow their example in handling black soldiers. The commander of the 92nd Division ordered black soldiers not to talk to French women and had the military police arrest anyone who disobeyed the order. French officers were urged not to mix socially with black officers and not to praise blacks for their military accomplishments when white Americans were present.

On August 7, 1918, Americans had the French military mission with the American army issue secret instructions to French commanders. The order said that the French needed to understand the position occupied by blacks in the United States. It said that blacks were dangerous because they attacked women. The French were asked not to treat the blacks as equals because Americans feared that this might give them "undesirable aspirations." However, the French did not understand this racist attitude and did not fully adopt it. When the French Ministry of War learned of the secret instructions, it ordered all copies burned.

News of discrimination abroad soon became known and increased tensions in the United States. Black Americans were angered by reports of unjust punishment of men overseas and by stories about attacks on black soldiers by mobs of white soldiers. Black Americans had good reason to wonder for whom democracy was being saved.

Chapter 11

The Great Migration

One of the most significant events of the World War I period was the movement of black people from Southern farms to Northern cities. The Great Migration, as this movement was called, brought as many as a half million black Americans to the North in less than three years. The outbreak of war in Europe stopped the flow of cheap immigrant labor from Europe. As a result, Northern industry was short of labor at the very time that factories and steel mills needed more workers to produce weapons and war materials, as well as other products needed by the nation. Employers in the North now became interested in using the labor supply available in the South. And, for many reasons, the black worker was ready to take advantage of the opportunity to leave the South. By doing so, black workers improved their condition; yet they did not find the North to be the "Promised Land" they had hoped for.

FORCES "PULLED" AND "PUSHED" SOUTHERN BLACKS

All that was needed to make many blacks leave their Southern homes was the promise of better conditions in the North. Many had already lost hope that conditions would improve in the South. In other words, to use ideas from the history of immigration, a "pull" and a "push" were operating. The "pull" of the North was better political, social, and economic conditions. The Southern "push" was violence, great poverty, and unfair treatment.

Why did black people not move out of the South in greater numbers before 1915? A number of explanations have been offered. Blacks did not go West in large numbers because they did not have the money and the skills to move and start new lives there. In addition, whites in the West strongly opposed black settlement. Blacks also faced competition for jobs from Mexicans in the Southwest. And in the North, they had to compete for jobs with European immigrants.

Nevertheless, Southern blacks came to regard the North and West as places which promised better conditions. Although both these sections accepted the doctrine of racial superiority, political and social conditions in the North and West were different from conditions in the South. The differences were great enough that the North, in particular, remained through the years the Southern blacks' beacon of hope.

Even before the Great Migration, relatively large numbers of blacks were moving into the North and into Northern and Southern cities. This movement continued in spite of the objections of some black leaders, such as Frederick Douglass and later of Booker T. Washington. Although the number of those who moved was not great, several Northern states had sizable increases in black population during the pre-World War I years. The total increase in the black population between 1870 and 1910 was 200 percent. But the increase averaged 250 percent in New York, Pennsylvania, Illinois, Ohio, Indiana, New Jersey, and Massachusetts. But unlike the Great Migration, this early migration was not a mass movement of people.

TENANT FARMING WAS A "PUSH"

The typical Southern black in 1915 was a tenant farmer. Conditions varied from state to state and from one section of a state to another section. But generally, the black tenant farmer worked on farmland owned by white landlords. He planted his own crop, and cultivated and harvested the crop. He also supplied his own farm animals. For his work, he usually received half of everything he grew, except the cotton seed. If the tenant farmer did not have his own farm animals, his share of the crop was only a third.

The Southern system of land holding kept black farmers in debt. The landlord did not settle the farm accounts each year until the next crop had been planted in late spring. By this time, it was too late for a tenant farmer or sharecropper to move to another farm, and he had to accept the terms his landlord offered. In addition, by Southern custom, the black farmer dared not ask to see the landlord's account books. The landlords regarded it as an insult to be required by anyone, even by the courts, to show their records. They usually declared that it was not necessary to settle an account as long as the tenant was in debt. And from one year to the next, the tenant or sharecropper only went deeper in debt, according to the landlord's bookkeeping. The black farmer who was able to make money each year and was able to get out of debt was considered a troublemaker. Such tenants often were forced to leave by their landlords.

The lending practices connected with sharecropping helped to keep the tenant in debt. To get through each year, tenants had to get "advances," or loans, from their landlord and local merchants. They had to pay very high prices for the loans or goods bought on credit. In addition, the tenant had to contract for his money in January. He did not receive it until March, yet he had to pay interest on the loan for the whole year.

Even the black farmer who had the money to rent land was often at the mercy of the landlord. In Mississippi, the renter could not sell his crop. Under Mississippi law, only the landlord was able to give a clear title to the cotton being sold.

THE BOLL WEEVIL CAUSED HARDSHIPS

The boll weevil, too, helped to "push" black farmers out of the South. The boll weevil came from Mexico into Texas in 1892. Within three decades, this insect destroyer of cotton had spread throughout the entire cotton-growing region of the South. By 1904, the weevil had moved into Louisiana, and within five years it had crossed the Mississippi River into Mississippi. From there, the boll weevil spread north into Oklahoma and Arkansas and eastward into Alabama, Georgia, Florida, and South Carolina.

The boll weevil brought financial ruin to many plantation owners, but the greatest sufferers were the black farmers. Because the planters could not grow cotton, banks refused to lend them money. As a result, the landlords were not able to give their tenants credit. The situation became critical for many blacks. Many areas such as Lowndes County,

Alabama, and neighboring cotton-growing counties suffered great hardships. During the winter of 1916–17, there were many blacks without food, clothing, and adequate housing. As temporary help, some money was given by the federal government. But, by mid-winter, the money was gone. Conditions became so bad that the Red Cross sent food to the area. Weekly food rations were given the needy during the remaining winter months.

Still, the boll weevil's part in causing black migration should not be overemphasized. Actually, the black migration and the boll weevil's spread were in opposite directions within the South. While the boll weevil was advancing through Texas, blacks were beginning to move out of Florida and the Southeast. Black migration moved across the South from east to west, while "the march of the boll weevil" was from west to east. Blacks began leaving South Carolina in large numbers, for example, before the boll weevil arrived in that state.

OTHER CAUSES LED TO BLACK DISCONTENT

Great stress has been placed on the economic causes of migration. But black writers criticized this overemphasis on economic forces. They pointed to the desire for education and the right to vote and to discontent over segregation and mob violence as equally important causes. W. E. B. Du Bois said that those who blamed black unrest on anything other than "natural resentment against wrong" were clouding the issue. "Such persons," Du Bois said, "are making such absurd statements either through ignorance of the facts or because they know the facts and are attempting to shift the responsibility for the half-century of lynching, disfranchisement, peonage, 'Jim-Crowism' and injustice of every sort practiced on the Negro."

Many migrants at this time said that they moved North because of better schools. Black parents realized the disadvantages they suffered because of their lack of education. They wanted their children to receive a good education. Yet many counties in the South had no high schools for black children.

Afro-Americans also strongly objected to the terror and violence they suffered in the South. Lynching had become largely a Southern evil, and the victims of mob violence were usually black. The Division of Records and Research of Tuskegee Institute reported the lynching record each year. Black victims of mob violence numbered fifty-four in 1915, fifty in 1916, thirty-six in 1917, and sixty in 1918. In 1917, lynchings and terrorism drove 2,500 black residents out of Dawson and

Forsyth counties in Georgia. Other victims in 1917 included Jesse Washington, who was burned alive in the public square at Waco, Texas, and two women and three men who were lynched near Gainesville, Florida.

THE *CHICAGO DEFENDER* URGED MIGRATION

Black newspapers in the North helped blacks to make up their minds to leave the South. Chief among these was the *Chicago Defender.* Robert S. Abbott, the militant editor of the *Defender,* used the Illinois Central Railroad to get his paper into the South. The porters on the trains left bundles of the newspaper at train stops all through the South, from Kentucky to New Orleans. Abbott published the details of Southern terrorism and urged his readers to leave the South. He invited them to come North, where jobs and freedom were waiting for them.

Abbott's glowing reports on conditions in Chicago helped strengthen the ideas many blacks had about that city. Many of them had heard stories of the city of great white buildings where the Columbian Exposition of 1893 had been held. Many Southern blacks began to think of Chicago and the North generally as the "Promised Land."

INDUSTRY CALLED LABOR FROM THE SOUTH

Labor agents representing Northern industry brought Southern blacks "visions of a promised land just a few hundred miles away." One of the first organized efforts to bring black workers North was carried on by the National Urban League. In the spring and summer of 1916, the Continental Tobacco Corporation and other companies in the tobacco-growing district of the Connecticut Valley used large numbers of black students to harvest tobacco. These students were brought from black colleges in the South by the National Urban League. The tobacco growers were very pleased with the student workers.

The publicity given these tobacco workers helped to call the attention of other Northern industries to the labor supply in the South. The Erie and Pennsylvania Railroads sent trains to Southern cities to bring back laborers to work for them. The response to this effort was astonishing. Stories were told of blacks who dropped whatever they were doing and boarded the trains. Some left teams of horses standing in the streets. The entire black population of one town in North Carolina reportedly left for the North. Other reports told of entire church congregations, led by their ministers, leaving Southern towns. Between July 1, 1916 and July 1, 1917, the Pennsylvania Railroad brought 13,-223 black workers North to work as railroad laborers. Many of these men soon found even better jobs and better living conditions in Philadelphia and other large cities.

The Illinois Central Railroad also sent South for black workers. The company sent extra cars South, put them on sidings at major stations, and used agents to spread the word that free transportation and jobs were available. The stockyards in Chicago also had great need of workers. Agents for the meat packers spread the word in Mississippi and Louisiana that 50,000 men were needed. Blacks were told that the Chicago packers would furnish them housing and would care for them until they were well established in their new home. To Southern blacks, who earned only a few cents a day or a few dollars a week, the promise of from $3.00 to $4.00 a day made Chicago sound like the land of plenty.

SOUTHERN WHITES OPPOSED THE MIGRATION

As the Great Migration continued, it became increasingly difficult for blacks to get out of the South. Southern newspapers demanded that labor agents from the North be "run out of town." Florida required them to buy a license costing $1,000 or face 60 days in jail and a $600 fine. Macon, Georgia, required a license fee of $25,000 plus recommendations from 45 citizens. To operate legally in Birmingham, a labor agent had to pay annual fees of $1,250.

Many blacks now found it as difficult to leave certain parts of the South as it had been during the days of the Underground Railroad. When a black person tried to buy a ticket for Chicago or some other Northern city, he was not sold the ticket. Therefore, blacks often had to travel northward short distances at a time. Then when they reached Tennessee or Kentucky, they usually were able to buy a ticket to the Northern city where they planned to settle.

BLACK WORKERS FOUND JOBS IN INDUSTRY

The Great Migration and America's entry into World War I gave blacks an opportunity to enter industrial jobs in large numbers. Black workers found jobs in most of the industries in the North. Many found work in the iron and steel industries. The number working in the stock-

Black workers made important contributions to the war effort. Shipbuilding provided many jobs for laborers like those shown here.

yards also increased greatly. For example, in 1910 only 33 of the 4,414 semi-skilled workers and 34 of 8,426 laborers in the Chicago stockyards were blacks. In 1920, these figures had changed dramatically. Now there were 1,558 blacks among the 6,931 semi-skilled workers and 1,397 blacks among the 7,032 laborers. Jobs in the automobile industry also opened up for black workers. During the war, shipbuilding was under the control of the United States Shipping Board. Some 26,648 black workers performed 46 of the 55 different jobs connected with shipbuilding. When the war ended, 39,000 blacks were working in plants under the Shipping Board.

The federal government recognized the importance of black workers to the war effort. In June, 1918, the Division of Negro Economics was set up in the Department of Labor. Dr. George E. Haynes, a founder of the National Urban League and professor of social science at Fisk University, was appointed director of the Division. Haynes set to work trying to improve white attitudes toward black labor. Conferences were held in Southern and Northern cities for this purpose.

In spite of the work of the Division of Negro Economics, discrimination was still widespread. But the labor shortage was so great that employers had little choice as to whom they would hire, and blacks proved that they could handle the new jobs. Charles Knight, who worked in the shipyard at Sparrow's Point, Maryland, set a world's record for driving rivets in building steel ships. A black pile-driving crew set the world's record at Hog Island near Philadelphia.

In spite of such achievements, the number of blacks employed in war industries remained rather small. The excellent work done by blacks at Sparrow's Point and Hog Island did not bring an increase in the number of blacks working at these places. And even in industries operated by the government, when the numbers of blacks increased, black workers were not promoted to higher-level jobs.

BLACK WOMEN MADE IMPORTANT GAINS

The greatest job gains in industry during the war were made by black women. In some states, including Maryland and Florida, they were given training as mechanics and as drivers so that they could take the place of those who were drafted into the army or who found better jobs. Black women were also welcomed into such dangerous jobs as making weapons and munitions. Women were victims of special discrimination. They were paid less than all men doing the same work and less than white women in the same jobs.

118

Still, black women found a greater variety of jobs open to them than ever before. In Chicago, they replaced men in such jobs as washing and polishing taxicabs. In addition, they were employed in tobacco factories, in garment, button, and box factories, as ushers in theaters, as stock girls in department stores, and as elevator operators. In 1918, Sears, Roebuck and Company hired 600 black women during the Christmas season "rush" to do clerical work. This company also opened what it called a "special division" in which it employed 1,400 young black women.

CITY HOUSING CONDITIONS WERE POOR

Housing was a serious problem for the migrants. Discrimination forced the black newcomers to live in the worst housing in the cities. Because housing was scarce, landlords charged high rents and refused to repair their buildings. The limited supply of housing and the high rents caused overcrowding. To find better homes, some blacks moved into white neighborhoods. This led to violence and increased racial tensions.

The situation in Chicago was typical. In the summer of 1917, the Chicago Urban League talked to real estate dealers who supplied houses for blacks. The League found that on a single day 664 people wanted houses but only 50 houses were available. When new areas were open, the black tenants had to pay 5 to 30 percent higher rents than whites paid.

Even so, the experiences of black migrants were not all bad. A study made of Southern migrants in Philadelphia found that most of them had improved their standards of living. The majority of the families studied had adequate diets, and only a few families were underfed. Housing conditions also varied. Many families lived in crowded, rundown houses. Others enjoyed larger, more comfortable houses. In any case, most families had better housing than they had had in Mississippi, Alabama, Georgia, and the other Southern states from which they came.

UNIONS DISCRIMINATED AGAINST BLACK WORKERS

Black workers faced racial prejudice when they tried to join labor unions. Many unions refused to accept black workers as members. And they attacked blacks who were forced to accept jobs as strikebreakers in order to work. The American Federation of Labor (AFL) showed organized labor's attitude toward black workers at its 1917 convention.

The convention was asked to pass a resolution against discrimination. The resolution called for an end to disfranchising black voters and condemned segregation in transportation, housing, schools, hotels, theaters, and other public places. It also favored fair representation for blacks in local and state government, and called for an end to lynching. The committee on resolutions presented the resolution to the convention without recommending its approval. In fact, the committee disclaimed responsibility for all statements in the resolution. Several delegates spoke against the resolution, and an amendment to the committee's report was passed which rejected everything in the resolution. The result of the convention's action was to put the AFL on record as favoring discrimination and inequality.

During the war, a committee of nationally known black leaders met with the AFL's Executive Council. The group criticized labor's policy of racial discrimination and asked the union to organize black workers. Samuel Gompers, president of the AFL, defended the union's policy of having segregated unions for black workers. He claimed that this was the only way it had been possible for unions to be organized in the South. Gompers also told the group that the AFL was powerless to end discrimination.

Six months later, the committee sent Eugene Kinckle Jones of the National Urban League back to see Gompers. Jones made several recommendations on behalf of the committee. He asked the AFL to issue a statement making clear its racial policies. The union was urged to employ a black labor organizer and was asked to consult the committee from time to time. However, the AFL Executive Council turned down all of these recommendations. The council said that it found no fault with the actions of the AFL.

VIOLENCE BROKE OUT IN EAST ST. LOUIS

White laborers, both union workers and unorganized workers, were opposed to blacks working in Northern industries. Most white workers did not want to compete with blacks for jobs. They claimed that blacks would lower the standards of labor. The same whites also were against blacks moving into white communities. Such views caused strong opposition to black workers in East St. Louis, Illinois.

The Central Trade and Labor Union of East St. Louis appealed to the city government for action to stop the "growing menace" of black labor. The union asked the city "to devise a way to get rid of certain portions of those who are already here." This appeal was made in the late spring of 1917. By this time, over 10,000 black workers had moved to East St. Louis to work in industries there. Some of these blacks had been brought in to help break a strike at the Aluminum Ore Company. Labor problems and racial prejudice combined to cause one of the worse race riots the United States ever had known.

The city government cooperated with the white workers in trying to keep blacks out of the city. Blacks became the target for police actions. Innocent blacks were arrested and charged with vagrancy or loitering. Minor racial incidents became numerous. In one such incident, William Engram was arrested by patrolman Thomas Gebhardt and charged with spitting on the sidewalk. Gebhardt took his prisoner to a bar run by Thomas Boston while he called for help to take Engram to police headquarters. Several blacks, angered by the discriminatory action in arresting Engram, followed Gebhardt to the bar. Boston ordered the crowd of blacks to leave. When the crowd failed to leave immediately, Boston shot and wounded one of them.

Violence broke out again on May 28, 1917, when a crowd of whites leaving city hall heard that a white man had been shot during a robbery. Wild rumors began to spread. It was reported that a white woman had been insulted. Another rumor was that two white girls had been shot. The crowd became a mob and began demanding a lynching. The mob went downtown and began beating every black they saw. Restaurants and shops were broken into and damaged.

The East St. Louis police did not act, and the mayor was unable to contact anyone who could order out the National Guard. Finally, the violence ended on May 29, when the members of the mob became tired and went home. But during weeks that followed, attacks on blacks by white gangs continued.

Blacks finally struck back on July 1. That night a car driven by whites drove through the black community, shooting into homes. When the car came back, blacks returned the fire. Police rushed to the area to investigate reports that blacks had weapons. Blacks fired on the police car, killing one policeman and seriously wounding another. For the next two days, East St. Louis was ruled by a mob. The mob burned and looted, and killed any blacks it found. Members of the National Guard sent in to stop the violence stood by and watched. Some soldiers helped the rioters. Newspapers reported that the mob's actions were unbelievably cruel and brutal. White women and children also took part in some of these actions. The commander of the National Guard shut himself up in the city hall. Finally, the rioting ended on July 4.

By this time, many people had been killed and a great deal of property destroyed. Estimates of property damage were as high as $400,000. No reliable figures of the number of dead and wounded were ever given. The number killed may have been as high as 100, with another 750 wounded. Some claimed that many blacks were burned alive in their homes and their deaths not reported. Another report stated that 100 blacks were burned in empty theaters where they went to hide from the mob. During the rioting, over 6,000 blacks fled from East St. Louis across the Mississippi River into Missouri.

THE GREAT MIGRATION WAS IMPORTANT

Blacks gained from both the Great Migration and World War I. In spite of the problems involved, the great movement of people out of the South represented a turning point in the black American experience. As to the war, those who served in the army gained new skills and were changed by the experiences they had in the army camps at home and on the battlefields of Europe. The war and the migration opened many economic opportunities and caused important changes in black life.

The Great Migration created large black communities in Northern cities. Although these black communities soon had to face the problems of the black ghetto, they opened the way for future changes. Soon these Northern black communities also formed the basis for black economic development, for political power, and for cultural development.

UNIT FOUR

THE UNCERTAIN YEARS OF THE 1920's

Chapter 12

The "Red Summer" of 1919

The war did not bring a lessening of discrimination toward black Americans. In fact, racial tensions increased as a result of the Great Migration and the new industrial opportunities opened to blacks. When the war ended, the competition between black and white workers for jobs increased. The struggle for housing in the cities also remained bitter. At the same time, blacks had come to expect more and were not willing to go back to the way things were before the war. This condition led to a great increase in violence.

WHITES FEARED NEW BLACK ATTITUDES

During the war, white Americans became aware of the changes taking place in the social and economic condition of blacks. The white reaction was an increase in prejudice and discrimination. Mob violence greatly increased in the South, and racial incidents became widespread in Northern cities. Fear of the returning black soldiers was especially strong in the South. Rumors spread about unruly soldiers who were unwilling to act as they had before the war. Many black soldiers were lynched on their way home from the army while still in uniform. Lynchings increased generally. The number of lynchings had decreased from 50 in 1916 to 36 in 1917. But in 1918, there were 60 lynchings, and in 1919, 76 blacks were killed by mobs.

The fear and distrust among whites led to a new Ku Klux Klan. The new Klan was organized in 1915 by a small group headed by William Joseph Simmons. This group met near Atlanta, Georgia, to start what they called a fraternal and social organization. The Klan remained small until 1919. In that year, Edward Y. Clarke and Elizabeth Tyler joined Simmons as leaders. Membership drives were held, and the Klan began to grow. It spread to all parts of the country, including the Middle West, and by the end of 1919, the Klan had about 100,000 members. As the Klan grew, violence increased. Its members took part in floggings and tar-and-feather parties, and often attempted to terrorize blacks by sending them warnings to leave town.

THE BLACK ATTITUDE HAD CHANGED

Thousands of black men enjoyed the greater freedom they found in Europe while in the army. They recognized the great difference between that life and life at home. They talked of changing conditions at home. The Reverend Francis J. Grimke voiced the new attitude when he declared that black troops in France had sniffed that country's "free, invigorating liberty-loving air." When they returned from France, Grimke said, "There has got to be a change. . . . They know now what it is to be a man, and to be treated as a man." W. E. B. Du Bois wrote about this new spirit in *The Crisis*. "We return from fighting," Du Bois wrote. "We return fighting. Make way for Democracy! We have saved France and by the Great Jehovah, we will save it in the U.S.A. or know the reason why."

The War Department became concerned about reports that black soldiers in France, waiting to be brought home, were out of control. Officials in Washington were afraid that serious trouble would occur when these soldiers returned to their home communities. The War Department asked Dr. Robert R. Moton, who replaced Booker T. Washington at Tuskegee, to go to Europe and look into the situation.

Moton was supposed to help prepare the men for their return to civilian life. He found that most of the wild rumors about disorderly behavior were not true. But he warned the men that they could not expect to enjoy the same freedom at home that they had enjoyed in France. Many of the men did not like this advice from Moton.

MANY INCIDENTS TOOK PLACE IN 1918

Lynchings and other acts of racial violence increased greatly in 1918. News of heroic deeds from France was sometimes overshadowed by news at home. Pennsylvania was the scene of two riots in 1918. The tensions resulting from the migration of blacks to Chester, Pennsylvania, led to a riot there from July 25 to 28. Rioting broke out in Philadelphia on July 26 and lasted until July 29. It started when a black woman bought a home on a formerly all-white block. The rioting resulted in the deaths of three whites and one black, as well as injuries to many others.

Many reports of mob violence came from the South. A white employer was shot in Brooks County, Georgia, in May, 1918. The employer was shot after he had beaten a black worker. A few days after the shooting, mobs lynched eleven blacks. One of those killed was a woman. Hundreds of blacks fled from the county. In December, two men and two women were taken from the Shubuta, Mississippi, jail and lynched. In Tennessee, three persons were burned at the stake.

BLACKS BEGAN TO FIGHT BACK ✓

Out of the violence and frustrations of the war years came a "New Negro." In 1918, and particularly in 1919, blacks fought back. They seemed determined to protect themselves at any cost. This was the "New Negro" about whom the black poet Claude McKay wrote:

Like men we'll face the murderous, cowardly pack,
Pressed to the wall, dying but fighting back.

This new attitude helped in bringing on the "Red Summer" of 1919, so called because of the bloody violence during those months. As blacks tried to better their condition in the South, riots broke out in several places. The struggle for jobs and housing caused riots to flare up in many Northern cities, too. About twenty-five racial riots took place during the "Red Summer."

VIOLENCE BROKE OUT IN CHARLESTON

One of the first major riots took place in Charleston, South Carolina. Fighting began there on May 10, 1919, between local blacks and white sailors from the naval training base. The first incident was a fight that Saturday evening between a black man and two sailors. The black was killed, and this led to fights between blacks and white sailors. Hundreds of white sailors decided to march into the black community. The sailors looted to get weapons, which they used to beat and shoot blacks along the way.

The city officials asked the navy to help restore order. Marines were sent in to patrol the city and control the mob. The marines used bayonets to break up the sailors' march and send the sailors back to the base. When blacks started shooting at the sailors, all black citizens were ordered off the streets. Before morning, the violence had ended. But by this time, two blacks had been killed and seventeen wounded. Among the whites, seven sailors and one policeman had been wounded.

Firm action on the part of the authorities kept violence from breaking out again. The sailors were not permitted to return to the city the next day, and after that only a few minor incidents took place. The mayor of Charleston and the NAACP asked the navy to pay for all black property destroyed by the sailors. This was not done. However, at the urging of the NAACP, the Navy Department did investigate the riot, and several sailors were tried and convicted for their part in the violence.

A RIOT TOOK PLACE IN EAST TEXAS

The next major riot was at Longview, Texas. Longview, located in eastern Texas, had a population of about 5,000. About 30 percent of the population was black. This part of Texas was a part of the South's cotton-growing area. And blacks in Longview were trying to improve their economic condition as the war ended.

One of the leaders of this movement for economic progress was Dr. C. P. Davis. Davis organized a Negro Business Men's League in Longview. The League was successful in helping black farmers to get higher prices for their cotton by sending it to Galveston. This angered local white merchants, who usually bought their cotton from local black farmers cheaply and sold it at a large profit. Davis and the members of the League also opened cooperative stores. These stores sold products and goods to blacks at great savings. This meant that white merchants lost customers and profits. Longview whites were ready for an opportunity to put the blacks "in their place."

Their opportunity came in early July. The July 4 issue of the *Chicago Defender* carried a story which greatly angered Longview whites. The story was about a lynching that had taken place near Longview a few months earlier. The black man who was lynched had been accused of attacking a white woman. The *Defender* said that the woman had been in love with the man and that she was very sad over his death.

Longview whites believed that Samuel L. Jones, a black school-teacher, had written the *Defender* article. They did not like Jones because he was involved with Davis in the Business League. A white mob attacked Jones on July 11 and ordered him to leave town. Later that day, a large mob of whites went into the black community looking for Jones. Blacks opened fire on the mob and wounded four members. The whites left to get help, and the blacks fled while they were gone. The angry white mob returned and burned down homes, shops, and offices.

The police finally took action. They arrested six blacks and charged them with rioting. The mayor asked the governor for help, and the National Guard was sent to restore order. By the afternoon of July 12, the militia had things well in hand. Joined by Texas Rangers, the soldiers arrested twenty-three white men and charged them with arson. Some were charged with the attacks on blacks. Twenty blacks also were arrested, but most of them were not charged with anything. The whites were released on bail. The blacks were taken to Austin and put in jail. Through the efforts of the NAACP, the blacks were finally released.

BLOOD WAS SHED IN WASHINGTON, D.C.

The riot in Washington, D.C., was the first to receive attention throughout the country. Conditions in Washington had been building toward an explosive point for some time. The anti-black policies of the Wilson administration caused racial tensions to increase in the city. Then, during the war, blacks migrated to Washington, D.C., seeking a better life. For some, economic conditions improved, but segregation and discrimination also increased. Blacks grew increasingly angry over the situation. In addition, large numbers of Southern whites migrated to Washington. And they tried to make racial conditions there as much like those in the South as possible.

The local newspapers helped to increase tensions to the point of violence. The *Washington Post* was having a running battle with local officials over the law against drinking. Washington police were strict in enforcing the law, and the editor of the *Post* opposed this policy.

To get back at the police, the *Post* claimed that Washington was in the midst of a "crime wave." The editor criticized the police for not stopping robberies and attacks on local citizens. The paper claimed that there were many attacks on white women by black men.

On Saturday, July 19, the *Post* had a story headlined, *"Negroes Attack Girl . . . White Men Vainly Pursue."* The so-called attack turned out to be a minor incident. The story told how two blacks had bumped into a secretary and tried to take her umbrella. When she resisted, they ran. But that night a group of sailors and marines set out to find the blacks. The secretary's husband worked in the Naval Aviation Department, and about 500 of his comrades set out to uphold his honor. This mob marched into southwest Washington. They stopped every black person they saw, beating those they caught. Other whites joined the mob and helped to chase blacks through the streets.

Finally, Washington police and military police broke up the mob. But in making arrests the police discriminated against black citizens. They arrested eight blacks and only two white men. It was not until the arrests started that blacks committed any violent acts. When three blacks were stopped after the first arrests, one of them fired at the police. One policeman was wounded.

The fighting continued on Sunday night. The police arrested a young black man on Pennsylvania Avenue and charged him with a minor offense. A white crowd gathered, took the prisoner from the police, and began beating him. The police took the man back, but they did not arrest any of those who had beaten him. For several hours until midnight, mobs roamed up and down Pennsylvania Avenue. Blacks on their way home from work were chased and beaten. Streetcars were stopped, and black passengers were dragged off. The police did nothing.

The *Washington Post* further inflamed the situation on Monday. It ran a story on the rioting. The story said that there would be more action. According to the *Post,* all servicemen were going to assemble at nine o'clock on Pennsylvania Avenue. Their "purpose is," the story said, "a 'clean-up' that will cause the events of the last two evenings to pale into insignificance."

Black leaders and Washington officials protested this story. Efforts were made to try to keep order on Monday night. The NAACP demanded that the white mob members responsible for the earlier incidents be punished. It also called for better police protection for black citizens and their property. But, by this time, blacks felt that they would have to protect themselves. Guns were brought in from

Member of the Associated Press

The Associated Press is exclusively entitled to the use for republication of all news dispatches credited to it or not otherwise credited in this paper and also the local news published herein. The Washington Post is a member of the Associated Press, receiving the complete services of the world's greatest news-gathering organization.

The Washington Post.

Weath... ery tod... cloudy; temperat... Tempe... imum, ...

NO. 15,743. DAILY AND SUNDAY ENTERED AS SECOND-CLASS MATTER POSTOFFICE, WASHINGTON, D. C. WASHINGTON: TUESDAY, JULY 22, 1919.—SIXTEEN PAGES. COPYRIGHT, 1919, BY WASHINGTON POST

OLICE OFFICER AND TWO NEGROES KILLED, OTHERS FAT HURT, AS RACES BATTLE IN THE STREETS OF WASHIN DEFYING TROOP OF U. S. CAVALRY, INFANTRY AND

ATION'S CAPITAL HELD AT MERCY OF THE MOB; STERN ACTION TONIGHT

ighting Spreads to Many Sections After Troops Form a Cordon Around Center of City.

etective Sergeant Harry Wilson Shot Dead by Negro Woman and Marine Killed When Streets of City Are Turned Into Battlefields—Detective Sergeant Thompson Probably Fatally Wounded—Other Officers Badly Injured—Scores Treated at Hospitals. Blazing Race Hatred Defies Police and Military Authority—Hospitals Crowded.

Blazing race hatred turned the streets of Washington into ttlefields last night. Surging mobs of blacks and whites prov- themselves stronger than the law in the nation's Capital.

All authority, represented by the city's police force and the tion's cavalry, infantry and marines, was set at nought.

As the night of terror struggled toward morning one police cer had been killed outright and four wounded, one of them rtally. Two negroes were killed and of the many wounded, probably will die. One marine was killed.

Wounded Crowd Hospitals.

The hospitals of the city were thronged throughout the long ht of turmoil with wounded whites and negroes.

By early this morning the police system of reports had prac- ally broken down under the continued strain, and only frag- ntary and incidental reports of developments in the outlying tions of the city were available.

Negro Rioters in Autos.

ntil almost daylight groups of belligerent negroes, armed to the teeth, e touring the streets of the city in automobiles, evading or defying the y police and military parole, particularly in the outlying sections.

he downtown section, where a riotous mob of more than 1,000 had ged earlier in the night, had by that time been practically deserted.

t was plain as the tumultuous night crept toward dawn that the of- als in charge of the police and the military forces in the city were rehensive concerning what may happen tonight.

May Declare Martial Law.

Whether a practical condition of martial law will be declared will be ermined today.

The temper of the opposing elements indicated beyond any doubt that ess the sternest measures are adopted there will be further and more ous outbreaks.

Surge Against the Cordon.

The whole strength of the Washington police force with the aid of 400 more United States troops struggled with the race rioters.

n the downtown district their efforts succeeded in keeping the mobs ving, but it was an endless task.

A cordon of cavalry had been thrown around the downtown section m Seventh street to Fifteenth street, and from the mall south of the nue to above H street northwest.

Times afer times the mobs surged with more or less good nature inst the lines south of the avenue. But no serious effort was made break through to the objective of the rioters, which was the negro tion in the southwest.

Cavalry Charges Mob of 1,000

North of H street the mob made several efforts to break through the rdon.

Nearly 1,000 white men, who had thronged up Ninth street after a re- se in the Mall, moved over to Seventh street and had moved north as as H street bound for the negro section at Seventh and U streets rthwest.

Just above H street the mob was confronted with a detachment of valry. A single charge which swept street and sidewalks drove the wd back in confusion, with no more damage than a few slight injuries. After this attempt the mob turned its attention to the downtown district d during the remainder of the night it ranged along F street, and G eet from Seventh to Fifteenth street, and the cordon held.

Murder of Sergt. Wilson.

Negroes in the downtown section ed badly. They were torn from eet cars and manhandled. They re pummeled into unconsciousness d left lying in the street.

Here the crowds and the police xed indiscriminately, and it was parent that the police looked with athy upon the task of taking any ident measures to break up the mob.

northwestern part of the city were swamped with demands for help long before midnight.

Here a small group of whites would meet small group of negroes. A few words, a knife or firearms, and the throng would scatter.

The hastily summoned police would find only the embers of the blaze of murderous feeling, and the wreck of one or more of the victims lying in the street.

THE DEAD AND WOUNDED.

THE DEAD.

Detective Sergeant Harry Wilson, Headquarters.
N. W. Randall, colored, 22 years old, 1458 N Street N.W.
Thomas Armstrong, colored.

FATALLY SHOT.

Private Albert Luck, U. S. M. C.
Detective Sergeant Bernard W. Thompson, Headquarters.

SERIOUSLY WOUNDED.

Policeman Herman Glassman, No. 8 Precinct.
Policeman J. C. Bunn, No. 8 Precinct.
Policeman Michael Mahany, No. 8 Precinct;
James Richards, white, 68 years old, 344 M Street S.W.
Mrs. Hannah Singer, white, 30 years old, 1109 Ninth Street N.W.
Robert Broadus, colored, 47 years old, 910 E Street S.W.
L. J. Hill, colored, 21 years old, 1623 Sixteenth Street N.W.
William Tolliver, colored, 28 years old, 4907 Sheriff Road, Deanwood.

supplied with ammunition. And they did not hesitate to use their arms the casualty list shows.

One negro, on a street car near Seventh and G streets, confronted by a mob of hooting white men, drew his revolver and emptied it into the mob. He wounded two men with his bullets and two were cut with glass from the window throug which he fired.

Shot Five Times by Policeman.

A few minutes later the negro, with five bullets from a policeman's revolver in his body, walked into police headquarters dripping with blood.

Throughout the northwest sections guns flashed throughout the night, and bullets whizzed through street car windows and about passing automobiles.

The panic of fear among the negroes had become a panic of indiscriminate destruction, and they fired indiscriminately at passersby, policemen, soldiers and even among crowds of their own race.

The whole U street section was ablaze. Throngs of negroes swept the streets, and as rapidly as they could be dispersed they gathered again.

The police found it utterly impossible to keep the streets clear. The temper of the negroes was well illustrated by the demeanor of one negro, who was taken into the Eighth precinct station out of the crowd.

In the station house he struggled away from the officers holding him and, drawing a gun, attempted to shoot. He was quickly overpowered.

Negroes Sweep Section Clear.

While the white mob ranged downtown, the negroes swept their own section in the northwest clear. They began early, and before dark half a dozen white men had been badly beaten on U and T streets between Seventh and Fourteenth streets.

The panic gathered force as the night of terror wore on, and the shooting became epidemic. After one policeman was shot early in the evening, shooting followed without surcease.

Toward midnight the negroes had organized regular bands of raiders. Eight or ten high-powered automobiles had been commandeered, and each, with a load of well-armed negroes, scoured the northwest.

Three Carloads Captured.

Three of these cars and their crews were captured by the police, but the others were pursuing their career of death at an early hour this morning.

Wherever the negro sections abutted on trolley lines there was indiscriminate firing into street cars and passing autos. As the morning drew near, the negroes cleared gradually from the streets, the mobs weakened in strength, and the race struggle became a house-to-house battle.

Here and there the police and soldiers found houses barricaded, windows and doors strengthened and loop holes arranged through which negroes fired indiscriminately on passersby.

Repulse Raid by Police.

One of these at Seventh and O repulsed a police raid. Another at Seventh and M streets was apparently prepared for a formidable resistance. A force of soldiers and policemen

Where Serious Rioting Took Place Last Night

Second and G streets northwest, where Detective Sergeant Harry Wilson was shot to death by a negress as he forced his way in a house.

Fourth and N streets northwest, where Randall Neale, negro, was killed.

Seventh and G streets northwest, George Dent, negro, was shot and probably fatally wounded after he had shot and seriously wounded two white men.

Eighth and T streets northwest, where Policeman Herman Glassman was shot in the leg by negroes in an automobile.

In Ball's court, where Policeman A. C. Thompson was shot and seriously wounded by a negro.

At Fifteenth street and New York avenue, where Private Edward Licek, marine corps, was shot in the back of the neck by a negro watchman at the Treasury. Condition serious.

At Seventh street and Pennsylvania avenue, where William H. Thomas was shot in the hip by a negro firing from a street car.

At Fourth and G streets northwest, where Benjamin Scott, negro, was shot in the leg by a man in an alley. Scott also was cut in the stomach and hit over the head.

At Fifth street and Massachusetts avenue, where an unidentified soldier was shot from his horse.

Seventh and T streets, where Policeman Michael J. Mahaney was cut on the leg by a stone thrown by a negro.

Twenty-second and N streets, where Phelon Eatman was attacked by four negroes and cut on the arm and shoulder.

Seventh and M streets, where Sergt. Murphy, marine provost guard, was shot in the neck by a negro.

Fourth and G streets, where John Washington, negro, was shot in the side. Condition serious.

At Seventh and M streets, where Thomas Armstrong, negro, was shot dead.

individuals or small groups of whites and blacks, and they pale into insignificance beside the pitched battles that raged in the northwest.

Toward morning what was left of the downtown crowd had concentrated at the Treasury. After a brief struggle with the police there they forced their way through, and a mob of nearly 2,000 surged past the White House and out Pennsylvania avenue toward

CROWDS FILL JAILS

Cells Packed With Men Taken in Streets by Police.

BEDLAM INSIDE AND OUT

Hospital Cases So Many No Count Is Taken of Injured.

Force of 400 Soldiers and Police Utterly Inadequate to Protect City From Mobs' Fury Despite Yeoman Service Done—3 Times as Many Men Needed to Restore Order in Nation's Capital.

Three persons dead, two dying, three probably fatally injured and two score treated at hospitals are the major casualties, as reported early today, of Washington's night of terror.

At 8 o'clock last evening came the first clash between a crowd of white men and negroes which was the prelude to a swift succession of lurid and bloody scenes—the surgings of mobs through uptown streets, the rattle of shots, the dashings to and fro of automobiles laden with police and soldiers the clang of ambulance gongs and the thousand alarming sights and sounds of the most serious race riot in the Capital's history.

Killed Arresting Negress.

The dead are Detective Sergt. Harry Wilson, of headquarters, who fell with a bullet through his heart while attempting to arrest a negro woman in a house, and Randall Neale, a negro, who was shot and killed while rioting at Fourth and N streets northwest.

Private Herman Glassman, of the Ninth precinct, is dying at Casualty Hospital from a bullet wound in the abdomen, and Private A. C. Thompson, Sixth precinct, is at Emergency with a bullet lodged against his spinal column, and his life is despaired of. Albert Luck, a private in the marine corps, is the other man believed fatally wounded.

A force of 400 soldiers, sailors and marines forming a hastily organized provost guard in combination with Washington's 700 available policemen, was the only bulwark against mob fury—and it was inadequate. With more square miles of city streets to patrol and guard, the men no sooner dispersed one mob of battling whites and negroes than strife began in another locality.

Great Work by Armed Forces.

Yeoman service was done by both the civil and military police as their sacrifice in comrades dead and wounded and their many bruises and cuts at the hands of enraged negroes testify, but there was needed at least three times their number to stamp out with an iron heel the rampant lawlessness. Last night's need, no man could forsee until too late to provide adequate forces to combat the mobs. Today in all probability will witness Washington under military law for the first time in half a century. It is felt that only the introduction of substantial forces of soldiery will check rase rioting and return the city to its normal condition of peace and order.

Sergt. Wilson's death was directly in the line of duty and in accord with the best traditions of the police department. Charging up a flight of pitch-black steps in the house at 220 G street from a second-story window from which a volley of shots had been fired, he was met with a bullet, said to have been fired by Carrie Minor, Johnson, a negress aged 17, as she lay under a bed.

An army captain coming behind him in turn shot the girl in the groin as Wilson fell to the floor. He was rushed to Emergency Hospital in a

CONTINUED ON FIFTH PAGE.

500 GUNS BOUGHT IN D. C., POLICE SAY

No Parley With Element Of Disorder Now, Says Chief of Police Pullman

Maj. Pullman, superintendent of police, after receiving reports from the various precincts and after conferences with the army and navy officers in charge of the troops on duty in Washington at an early hour this morning, said:

"It is difficult to discuss this situation in the face of the casualties which the police department has suffered.

"The combined authorities charged with the duty of preserving order in Washington are determined that following the night's events, there will be no parleying with the elements of disorder.

"All the power of the Federal government is behind the police department and these combined forces will see to it that order is restored.

"Every law-abiding citizen will keep cool and go quietly about his business, avoiding curious crowds and all possible sources of disturbance."

Commissioner Brownlow last night declined to make any comment.

in downtown shops is certain, said the police.

"I have not the slightest control over the sale of firearms in the District," said Commissioner Brownlow last night. "I have no doubt that a large number of weapons were purchased in the District. The situation is deplorable, but one over which I have no control."

Maj. Pullman added that the police department was without authority to regulate the sale of guns and knives. He said that more than 500 revolvers were sold to both whites and negroes yesterday.

Although many dealers sold firearms to all comers yesterday, some of the large dealers refused to sell unless they were positive that the gun was not to be used in the impending trouble.

PRESIDENT WILSON ILL

Confined to His Bed, but Condition Is Not Serious.

CANCELS HIS ENGAGEMENT

Did Not See Visitors Yesterday and May Not Be Able to Meet Republican Senators Today—Trouble May Prevent His Journey to Pacific Coast.

President Wilson was in a weakened but nowise serious condition last night after having spent the day in bed with acute dysentery. Rear Admiral Cary T. Grayson, his personal physican, said the President had been in considerable pain during the day and had been very "uncomfortable." Admiral Grayson said he would insist that Mr Wilson remain in bed until he had completely recovered.

The President's appointments for today with Republican senators had not been postponed last night, but at the White House it was considered extremely doubtful whether Mr. Wilson would be able to keep them.

First Complained Friday.

While none of those close to the President would say whether his illness would result in postponement of his trip through the West, there seemed to be an opinion that should the illness be prolonged it could have no other effect. Rear Admiral Grayson was uncertain when the President might be able to resume his dutues.

The President first complained of feeling ill Friday when he went to the Capitol to confer with Senator Hitchcock, of Nebraska, ranking Democratic member of the foreign relations committee.

Caught Cold on Trip.

He told Secretary Tumulty then he was slightly indisposed and expressed his intention of going down the

Index to Today's Iss

TOLD HUN SECR

Two "Prisoners" at New Germans of High Ra

GAVE HELP TO PER

Were Close to Von Hind in Last Big Offensive

Enabled American Comman Strike at Proper Time and Finally Suspected by C Associates, They Are Brou America Under Guard t Lives—Clerk Reveals Na

A story of the betrayal of t man high command through forts of the American militar service and of the orga among German officers of a v aimed at the lives of the trait brought to light with the ar New York yesterday of "two prisoners of war consigned to rector of military intelligence ington, D. C.

According to information mysterious prisoners who from the Agamemnon unde guard formerly were German of high rank, occupying pos great responsibility under V denburg.

Before the inauguration American offensive in 1918 tives of the American mili telligence corps prevailed up through inducements which been divulged to deliver plan German general staff cove proposed movements on the front, probable lines of retrea at which stands would be m other detailed information o mable value.

Helped Pershing to W

With these plans before h Pershing was able to lay campaign with great freedom is believed that a result wa the cost of the American practically in half.

The German officers inter dered themselves to the A forces. Certain of their for ciates had become suspicio ever, and are believed to hav together to mete out stern Utmost precautions were tak within the allied lines to pr informers, but as officials that as long as they were France their lives would be ger, orders were given fo transfer to this country.

Disclosed by a Clerk

Preparations for the movi prisoners were kept a close se it was only through the car of some clerk that they were in the roster of the Agamem she left France.

The plan was to send the to some isolated army post w might be given military prote a time. Eventually, it is they would have been per "escape" to some other coun to begin their lives anew. Of

Newspaper reports of the rioting in Washington, D.C., helped to increase racial violence during the riot in the nation's capital.

Baltimore, and black veterans brought out weapons they had obtained in the service.

Blacks began to fight back and even formed mobs. On Monday, blacks stopped streetcars to attack whites. One group marched toward the Navy Yard, but police stopped them before they could get there. During the fighting on Monday night, four men were killed and eleven badly wounded. Those killed or seriously wounded included six white policemen, one white marine, three white civilians, and five black civilians. Hundreds of persons were arrested. Most of them were blacks charged with carrying concealed weapons.

By Tuesday, the local newspapers were calling for an end to the violence. Alarmed government officials brought in enough soldiers, sailors, and marines to patrol the city. By Thursday, the situation was under control.

BLACKS LEARNED LESSONS FROM THE WASHINGTON RIOT

The Washington riot taught black people several important lessons about their relations with the press and with the police. It was clear that the white newspapers discriminated against blacks in news coverage. Crimes committed by blacks were given so much coverage that it often appeared that only blacks had committed crimes. Black leaders warned that such reporting was a cause of racial violence.

Police did nothing, in the beginning, to stop white mobs from attacking blacks. They arrested blacks who fought back, and disarmed blacks and left them at the mercy of white mobs. Blacks became angry and suspicious of the police. They learned that they could expect no protection from the police. They learned that they often needed to defend themselves against those who were supposed to protect them.

A significant lesson of the riot was that it stopped when blacks began to fight back. The fact that blacks fought back sent a sense of determination through black America. Black leaders thought that this was a step forward for black people. In the riots that occurred after the Washington riot during 1919, Northern blacks followed the example of black people in Washington, D.C.

THE CHICAGO RIOT STARTED AT A BEACH

One of the bloodiest racial riots of the "Red Summer" of 1919 took place in Chicago. The causes of the violence in Chicago were similar to those which caused riots in other cities. Large numbers of blacks had come to Chicago during the war seeking better social and economic conditions. But they had to compete with white workers for jobs. Housing was hard to find, and when blacks tried to move into white neighborhoods, white residents resisted. Struggles also took place over blacks using parks, playgrounds, beaches, and other places of amusement. All of this built up an explosive racial situation that needed only a spark to set it off.

The spark came on July 27. On that hot Sunday afternoon, Eugene Williams and three other black youths decided to go swimming in Lake Michigan. It was a good day for a swim. The temperature in Chicago was above 90 degrees, and it had been that hot for several days. Williams and his friends did not have much choice about where to go to take their swim. The beach at 29th Street was nearer their home, but it was used by whites. Blacks usually went to the beach at 25th Street. But blacks had not given up their right to use the 29th Street beach. In fact, on July 27 a group of blacks were at 29th Street facing a group of hostile whites.

Williams and his friends had their own special spot between the two beaches. There they kept a crude raft to use in their water games. As the boys played, their raft drifted toward 29th Street, where a rock-throwing fight was underway. A white man spotted the boys and began throwing rocks at them. Williams was struck and lost his hold on the raft. His friends were unable to save him, and Williams drowned.

Blacks demanded that the white policeman on duty at 29th Street arrest the guilty person. But instead of arresting the white man, the policeman arrested a black man against whom a white man made a complaint. Then rioting began on the beach when the black crowd attacked several whites. Rumors spread throughout the city, many of them enlarged the incident into a general racial war in Chicago.

Gangs of white youths went into action that Sunday night. Many of these gangs, called "athletic clubs," operated in neighborhoods near the black community. These gangs took revenge by beating, stabbing, or shooting thirty-eight blacks they found in white areas. On the first day of the riot, two people were killed and fifty were injured.

The South Side black community was calm on Monday morning. Blacks went to their jobs as usual. Many Chicagoans viewed the violence on Sunday as just another of the many minor incidents that had been going on all year. The newspapers did not give the violence special attention. Nevertheless, disorder broke out again late Monday afternoon. White gangs attacked black workers returning home from the stockyards. Mobs pulled blacks from streetcars. Black mobs, in turn, gathered and attacked whites who worked in black areas. Later Monday night, whites drove through black neighborhoods in automobiles, firing shots into homes.

Violence continued until Tuesday and spread to new areas of the city. Two blacks were killed by a mob in the downtown business district. The following day mob action slowed down. On Wednesday evening, the state militia was called out, and the soldiers did their job well. They kept mobs from forming and stopped cars from raiding black neighborhoods. Rains at the end of the week also helped to cool things off.

The riot caused great suffering and sorrow. The dead numbered 23 blacks and 15 whites; 520 persons were injured, including 342 blacks and 178 whites. But the arrest record told a different story. Of the 229 persons arrested, 154 were blacks and only 75 were whites.

The Chicago riot was the worst of the summer of 1919, and lasted the longest before troops were brought in. But, as in Washington, blacks showed that they were going to fight back. They also showed a deep distrust of the police. The police record proved their distrust was justified. Arrests were not handled fairly. And, in many instances, the police joined in the rioting.

RACIAL VIOLENCE CONTINUED INTO THE FALL

Lynchings, rioting, and the burning of property went on in different parts of the United States into the fall of 1919. In early September, black schools and churches were burned in Georgia. A riot took place in Knoxville, Tennessee, on August 30, when a white mob stormed a jail looking for a black prisoner. They tore up the jail and released some white prisoners. The National Guard was sent in to restore order. Disorder spread from the jail into the black community. When whites tried to march into the black area the next day, they were met by gunfire. The soldiers marched into the black area, but the blacks fired on them, too. Several people were killed before the trouble ended on September 1.

Trouble broke out in Omaha, Nebraska, at the end of September. In Omaha, the press had inflamed feelings with wild stories of black crimes. On September 28, a mob formed to drag a black prisoner from jail and lynch him. The mob attacked the jail when officials would not hand over the prisoner. Blacks on the streets were beaten. After setting fire to the jail, the mob obtained the black prisoner, hanged him, burned his body, and hung the body downtown.

Soldiers from a United States Army unit stationed nearby finally arrived to restore order. They kept close watch until tensions eased. In a few days, blacks returned to work under army protection.

ARKANSAS HAD A RIOT ✓

The violence in the town of Elaine, Arkansas, in Phillips County, arose over farm problems. Black tenants there, as in the rest of the South, were forced to borrow from their landlords and to buy their supplies from them. They also had to accept the landlord's word concerning the value of their share of the crop. Black farmers in Arkansas felt that they were being cheated by this system. In 1919, a group of black farmers decided to hire a lawyer to get fair treatment for them. A white lawyer from Little Rock agreed to take their case. Some of the blacks also decided to charge certain white planters with peonage, or forcing tenants to remain as workers against their will. The black farmers held meetings and collected money to pay the lawyer. All of this was done in secret.

The same problems caused black cotton pickers to form an organization. The cotton pickers formed a union to force planters to raise their wages. They decided that they would refuse to work until they received higher wages. The white planters learned what the blacks were doing. They decided to stop this effort, and to put the blacks "in their place." The planters also found out that the blacks were buying weapons to defend themselves.

Trouble began after an incident at a church at Hoop Spur. A group of blacks met on September 30 to decide on hiring a lawyer to represent them. A deputy sheriff, another white man, and a black trustee passed the church in an automobile. The whites claimed that the blacks in the church shot at the deputy without cause. The blacks said that the deputy tried to enter the church. When he was not allowed to do so, he fired into the building. The blacks returned the shots. The deputy was wounded, and the other white man was killed.

News then went out that there was a "Negro uprising." Armed bands of whites roamed the county, killing blacks and herding black men and women into a stockade. Federal troops were called in to help put down the "uprising." The soldiers arrested over a thousand blacks. A "committee of seven" was formed to investigate those arrested. No black person was allowed to go back to work until a white person spoke for him. Blacks were forced to return to work on the planters' terms before they were released.

134

Many blacks lost their lives in the Elaine riot. The NAACP said that between twenty-five and fifty blacks were killed, along with five whites. Others said as many as 200 blacks were killed. Of the 1,000 blacks arrested, 122 were charged with crimes. Many were tortured to force them to confess. In trials that lasted only a few minutes, black defendants were sentenced to death or long prison terms. The NAACP worked for several years to free these men. Some received new trials and were set free. Others had their death sentences changed to prison terms.

Chapter 13

The Search for Better Times

Neither riots nor the hard times that followed World War I lessened the attraction of the North for Southern blacks. Southern migrants continued to find jobs in industry, even though discrimination by the labor unions remained a serious problem. As large black communities formed in Northern cities, important economic and political changes began to take place. Movements toward a "separate economy" and toward more independence in political activities developed.

THE BLACK MIGRATION CONTINUED

Immediately after World War I, industries and business began to slow down. Factories began to cut down the number of workers they employed. This started a new wave of movement among blacks. The unskilled black worker who had been the last to be hired when industries expanded was the first to be fired when hard times came. But these unemployed black workers did not return South. Instead, they left the smaller manufacturing towns, the mill towns, and the mining industries, and they streamed into the large Northern cities to look for jobs there.

No jobs were available, but the migrants came anyway, hoping against great odds to find jobs or at least some means of survival. The Pittsburgh Urban League reported that in one week 1,027 persons applied to it for jobs. The League was able to find jobs for only eight of them. Institutions in the black community gave what help they could. The churches led the way in providing food and shelter for the hungry and the homeless.

When business and economic conditions improved by 1921, a new wave of migration from the South began. An estimated 500,000 Southern blacks went north between 1921 and 1925. The census showed that the number of blacks born in the South and living in the North increased from 737,423 in 1920 to 1,355,789 in 1930.

This mass movement during the 1920's was from the same states blacks had left during the Great Migration. About 80 percent of the migrants in 1923, for example, were from Florida, Georgia, and Mississippi. It was claimed that Georgia alone lost 100,000 blacks each year between 1921 and 1923.

The reasons for this movement were similar to those causing earlier migration. When business conditions improved around 1921, the opportunities for jobs also increased. And Congress passed laws which greatly limited the number of immigrants coming from Europe. Once again, Northern industry looked to the South for labor. Farm conditions in the South were still difficult. The boll weevil severely damaged Southern crops from 1920 to 1923, and black farmers suffered. Blacks also were distressed because of the activities of the Ku Klux Klan and the increased mob violence.

For the first time, Southerners began to fear that the South might have a shortage of cheap labor. Efforts were made to try to stop the black migration. Some claimed that labor agents from the North were causing blacks to leave by making false promises. Blacks were told that they would not be able to stand the cold Northern winters. Violence, too, was used to try to stop the movement to the North.

Some Southerners realized that fair treatment was the key to keeping black workers. Men like Richard W. Edmonds of the *Manufacturers Record* called for higher wages. Edmonds pointed out that the whole South would gain from a higher standard of living among blacks. Others called for an end to lynching, and for fair treatment in the courts.

During the winter of 1923–1924, Southern employers tried to get black workers to return South. Some states and employers actually sent agents to Northern cities. An official of a Southern railroad tried to recruit 500 workers in Chicago and neighboring towns to work for Southern planters. He claimed that 500 blacks said they were interested in returning; however, only 28 actually returned. The agent blamed Northern labor agents for his lack of success. The Southern agent said that the Northern agents talked the workers out of leaving. But, in fact, blacks were not willing to return South to the same conditions they had left.

SOME FOUND JOBS IN THE NORTH

Even though jobs were not as easy to find as they had been during the war, some blacks still found work in industries in the North. In the South, most black workers remained agricultural workers. And black women still worked mainly as domestic and service workers. But many of the Northern industrial jobs that had opened to black workers during the war remained open.

Migrants moved into the industrial centers to take these jobs. Large numbers worked in the stockyards of Chicago, St. Louis, and Kansas City. They remained a part of the labor force in the steel industry and the automobile industry. Jobs were also available to them in glass factories, tobacco factories, and the food industries. Although the textile industry remained closed to blacks in the South, some found work in this field in Northern centers, such as Chicago and New York City.

UNIONS REMAINED CLOSED TO BLACKS

Labor unions continued to discriminate against black workers. This kept blacks out of all but the lower-paying, unskilled jobs. Organized labor controlled the higher-paying jobs, and many of the unions which made up the American Federation of Labor would not accept blacks as members. In 1927, an attempt was made at the AFL convention to order all AFL unions to accept black workers. The convention refused to do this and many of the AFL unions continued to favor separate unions for blacks.

The railway brotherhood unions were completely closed to blacks. This kept black workers out of the better jobs on the railroads. White workers even tried to force blacks out of the jobs they held. This was especially true in the South, where most firemen on steam locomotives were black. When the railroads would not give these jobs to whites, attempts were made to frighten black firemen into leaving their jobs. Some who would not be frightened were killed.

THE FIRST BLACK UNIONS WERE UNSUCCESSFUL

The hostility toward black workers in the 1920's caused blacks to try to organize to protect themselves. Chandler Owen and A. Philip Randolph worked for unity among black workers and unity with all working people. Owen and Randolph were editors of the *Messenger*, which they called a magazine of "scientific radicalism." They stood for unionism and socialism among blacks.

Owen and Randolph made several attempts to organize black workers in labor unions. Back in 1917, they formed the United Brotherhood of Elevator and Switchboard Operators. But the union was slow to develop, and the organizers turned to other projects. Next, they joined with the organizers of the National Brotherhood Workers of America in 1919. This movement aimed at bringing every black worker into a union. The National Brotherhood did not get much support, and it ended operations in 1921.

The *Messenger* editors started several other unsuccessful projects in the 1920's. They organized the Friends of Negro Freedom in May, 1920. They hoped to make this a national organization with branches all over the country. The organization aimed to bring black migrants into unions, to protect black tenants, and to teach the masses the advantages of unionism. It planned to use boycotts as the means to fight discrimination. Within three years, the Friends ceased to exist. The National Association for the Promotion of Labor Unionism Among Negroes and The United Negro Trades were two other unsuccessful attempts to promote unionism among blacks.

THE PULLMAN PORTERS ORGANIZED

An important step toward union organization among blacks was taken when the Brotherhood of Sleeping Car Porters and Maids was formed. A. Philip Randolph led in the organization of the Brotherhood in 1925. The Pullman Company refused to recognize the union. The company said that Randolph was a troublemaker and that the Brotherhood was a dangerous organization. White and black groups sided with the Pullman Company. But three important groups gave their support to the

Brotherhood. These were the AFL, the NAACP, and the National Urban League.

It was extremely difficult to convince the Pullman Company to recognize the union. The company favored what was called a company union, or an organization of workers set up by the company itself to handle labor problems. The Pullman Company said that this group served the needs of the workers. Randolph brought a complaint against the company, and a Railroad Mediation Board was set up to hear the dispute. Finally, the company gave partial recognition to the Brotherhood in wage matters. But it took until 1937 for the Brotherhood to gain full recognition.

THE BLACK MIDDLE CLASS DEVELOPED BUSINESSES

Among the black middle class, separate development was centered around business activities. The myth of a separate black economy had strong supporters in the 1920's. A number of forces strengthened this myth. Many still believed in Booker T. Washington's view that black business ownership was one road to complete participation in American life. The National Negro Business League, founded by Washington in 1900, continued to spread this view after his death. Then, too, blacks were forced by segregation to provide many services for themselves. This led to the establishment of drug stores, restaurants, insurance companies, and other businesses.

All of this contributed to the idea that blacks could have a separate economy within the general American economy. It would provide employment for owners and workers. The dollar in the hand of the black man would do "double duty." It would support the black economy and would buy the goods and services black families needed.

BLACK BUSINESSES WERE MAINLY SMALL BUSINESSES

Black businessmen faced many problems. They lacked the experience and the know-how to organize businesses that could compete against large white firms. The competition from white businesses was great. Blacks were unable to obtain the credit they needed from banks and lending agencies. Often they had trouble finding suitable locations for their businesses.

As a result, black businesses remained small. In 1929, blacks operated 25,701 retail stores. These were mainly grocery stores, gas stations, restaurants, cigar stores, and drug stores. Sales totaled

$101,146,043, but only a small part of this total went to the owners and their workers. In a store selling about $12,000 worth of goods a year, the owner received about $1,750. Out of his share, the owner had to pay his workers. Moreover, these small busineses did not provide many jobs. The census showed that 28,243 black owners and members of their families worked in retail stores in 1929. These stores employed 12,561 other persons.

Other black businesses also were small. The number of black banks increased greatly during the 1920's, but they had limited resources. The weaknesses of other black businesses helped keep the banks weak. Insurance companies were small, too. Yet they were the largest black businesses, and many were well run. But all of them together did not have the assets of any one of the large insurance firms. And white companies continued to insure the great majority of black families.

BLACK BUSINESSES WERE IMPORTANT ✓

Although black businesses did not lead to separate economic development, they played an important role. They were symbols of the race pride that resulted from the period of World War I. They represented black racial consciousness and recognition of economic power. This business activity helped to build a black middle class with business experience. Many among this "black elite" became local and national leaders. Finally, it was important that blacks become a part of the business activity of the country. In the 1920's separate businesses were the only means open to them to achieve this.

A number of different types of black businesses existed during this period. Some retail businesses were flourishing operations. Large cleaning and pressing shops were in operation in Winston-Salem, North Carolina, in Atlanta, Georgia, and in Columbia, South Carolina. Charles W. Bryant owned a chain of gas stations in Columbus, Ohio. Blacks also entered a number of new business fields. They opened furniture stores, automobile agencies, and investment firms in several cities. Black also owned many small retail establishments.

Small manufacturing plants also appeared. Plants to make sausages were established in St. Louis and Kansas City. A soap factory was located in Kansas City, and casket factories were opened in several places. In addition, new cosmetic manufacturers joined the businesses established earlier by Mrs. C. J. Walker, Anthony Overton, and others.

A study during the 1920's showed that thirty-two black insurance companies were licensed to do business. The majority were in the South, but new companies were appearing in the North. The oldest of these companies had existed since the nineteenth century. They grew out of fraternal self-help organizations that paid sickness and death benefits to their members. The United Order of True Reformers was one such group that led to a number of insurance companies, banks, and other businesses. The North Carolina Mutual Life Insurance Company began as a fraternal organization in 1898. Under the leadership of John Merrick and Dr. A. M. Moore, it also developed into an insurance company by 1908. Other major companies included the Atlanta Life Insurance Company, Liberty Life Insurance Company of Illinois, National Benefit Life Insurance Company of Washington, D.C., Victory Life Insurance Company of Illinois, and Gibraltar Health and Accident Insurance Company of Indiana.

Black businessmen opened banks in several cities. Thirty-five black-owned banks with assets of about $13 million, were in operation in 1926. A number of these had been in business for some years. The Citizens Savings Bank and Trust Company of Nashville was founded in 1904, and the Forsyth Savings and Trust of Winston-Salem, opened in 1907. One of the strongest of the black banks was the Mechanic and Farmers Bank of Durham and Raleigh, North Carolina. Other important banks were located in Atlanta, Washington, D.C., Richmond, and Chicago.

The bankers and their banks represented success stories. Jesse Binga of Chicago was a good example of this group. Binga arrived in Chicago penniless in 1893. He worked as a Pullman porter and became a real estate speculator. He made enough money in real estate to open a bank. Binga was a strong believer in the "double duty" dollar which supported both the black economy and the black family's needs. And he looked forward to black economic control of the black community. In 1928, Binga's bank had resources of almost $2 million. Binga's dream was destroyed, however, when his bank failed during the Great Depression. Even the best-run black banks had trouble surviving the Depression, and many of them failed in the late 1920's.

BLACKS BECAME MORE POLITICALLY AWARE

The relationship between black Americans and the Republican Party began to change in the 1920's. Black pride and the attitude of the Republicans toward blacks caused black voters to become increasingly restless in that party. But the masses refused to support radical parties,

Banks were among the growing number of successful businesses established by black Americans in the years after World War I.

such as the Socialist and Communist Parties. At the same time, they considered the Democrats worse than the Republicans. For a time, blacks seemed to have no place to go if they changed their party loyalty.

The Republican candidates received solid support from blacks in 1920 and 1924. But they did not expect Warren G. Harding's election in 1920 to bring any improvement in race relations. In many ways, Harding was little different from Woodrow Wilson in his racial policies. He favored white leadership in the South, and he appointed few blacks to office. Harding did call for political and economic equality. But he favored separation in "things social and racial." He said that qualified blacks should be allowed to vote and that unqualified whites should not be able to cast ballots. President Coolidge followed Harding's policies, and he appointed a few more black officials.

During each Presidential election from 1920 on, the Republicans came out against lynching. They urged Congress to pass an anti-lynching law. But some black leaders did not believe the Republicans had worked very hard to try to pass such a law. For example, just before the election of 1924, Republicans let the Dyer Anti-lynching Bill die when Democrats filibustered against it.

COMMUNISTS AND SOCIALISTS WANTED BLACK SUPPORT

The Communist Party worked hard to get black support. Efforts were made to organize black workers and to win their support for the party in this way. The American Negro Labor Congress was formed by the Communists in 1925 for this purpose. Blacks also received legal help from the Communists through the International Labor Defense. The Communists also tried to reach blacks by practicing social equality. Members of the party took part in social activities such as dances and outings with blacks. Blacks were given high offices in the party and named as Communist Party candidates for important political offices.

In spite of this, very few blacks joined or supported the Communist Party. Probably no more than 200 blacks were members by 1928. Then, in 1928, the party's "line," or official policies changed, and the Communist Party became even less appealing to blacks. The Communists began to push for a separate black state within the United States. Even though black nationalism was strong, most black Americans did not favor a forty-ninth state as a solution to the race problem.

The Socialist Party had no better luck than the Communist Party. Although A. Philip Randolph and Chandler Owen tried to convince blacks that labor unity was the answer, they received little support. Blacks viewed racism as more than an economic problem. Their experiences with organized labor gave them little reason to hope for a united movement of black and white workers. Socialist candidates received few votes from blacks. In 1924, the Socialists supported the Progressive Party candidate, Robert La Follette. La Follette set up a special bureau to work among blacks, and he strongly attacked the Ku Klux Klan. Nevertheless, he received little black support.

THE DEMOCRATS WORKED FOR BLACK VOTES

The Democrats made a great effort to attract black voters in the Presidential election of 1924. A special division was set up under the leadership of Ferdinand Q. Morton, a black New York lawyer, and Lester A. Walton, a black journalist from New York. John W. Davis, the Democratic candidate, was described as a man who had worked for the best interest of blacks. He had been involved in cases against Southern farm peonage, and he had helped to win the court case against the "grandfather clause."

The Democratic political bosses in Northern cities worked to attract black voters. The city bosses realized that the newcomers' votes could help to win elections. Therefore, the bosses sent party workers to urge the migrants to register and to vote. The Democratic Party machine also did small favors for the new voters. Baskets of food and minor jobs were given to grateful poor black migrants, just as they had once been given to grateful poor European immigrants.

THE ELECTION OF 1928 SHOWED CHANGES

The election of 1928 showed that blacks were moving away from the Republican Party. During the campaign, Republican candidate Herbert Hoover caused Southerners to believe that he would not appoint blacks to office. Several black Republican leaders from the South were treated badly at the party's National Convention. Ben Davis, a Georgia leader, was not given his place on the Republican National Committee. Perry Howard and S. H. Redmond, leaders of the party in Mississippi, were accused of selling jobs. Charges were brought against them in Mississippi, but they were finally found not guilty.

The Democrats, on the other hand, organized an active black division for the election campaign. Lester A. Walton and Ferdinand Q. Morton were again involved. Other leading blacks also were brought into the campaign. These included Bishop Reverdy C. Ransom and J. Finley Wilson, Grand Exalted Ruler of the Elks.

Alfred E. Smith, the Democratic candidate in 1928, did well among urban black voters. The majority of black citizens still voted Republican in 1928, but enough voted Democratic to show that the old party loyalty was breaking down. In Harlem, in New York City, where Tammany Hall, the Democratic machine, had worked hard for black support, Smith ran particularly well.

BLACK CANDIDATES RAN FOR OFFICE

Blacks showed their growing independence by demanding that black communities be represented by black citizens. In many places, blacks were elected to city councils and state legislatures. More blacks also received appointments to minor local and state positions. However, the main goal was to elect a black representative to Congress. Success here would not achieve much real black political power in Congress, perhaps. But it would be a boost to black morale.

Black candidates ran for Congress in the Twenty-first District in New York City in 1924 and in 1928. Republican Charles Roberts was defeated by his Democratic opponent in 1924, and Republican E. A. Johnson was defeated in 1928. The Republicans ran another black candidate, Hubert T. Delaney, in the Twenty-first District in 1929. Two other blacks also ran, Frank R. Crosswaith on the Socialist ticket and Richard B. Moore, on the Workers Party ticket. All were defeated.

In St. Louis, the Democrats ran a black candidate in 1928. Joseph L. McLemore was nominated to run against the Republican L. C. Dyer. Dyer was well known for his sponsorship of the Dyer Anti-lynching Bill, and the majority of blacks in the Twelfth District voted for Dyer. They suspected that McLemore was being used by white politicians to hurt the anti-lynching movement.

Chicago blacks were the first to succeed in their efforts to send a black representative to Congress. When the white Congressman in the First District died in 1928, blacks demanded that a black replace him. The Republicans responded by naming Oscar DePriest as their candidate. DePriest's victory was a symbolic victory for all blacks. He represented the return of the black American to the Congress of the United States after an absence of twenty-eight years. DePriest was reelected in 1930.

146

Chapter 14

Black Protest and Black Nationalism

Black nationalism, the idea that Afro-Americans had to unite and use their own resources for advancement, was a common theme in the 1920's. The idea took many forms. Some groups working for better racial relations used this growing black consciousness by appealing to blacks to fight against discrimination and to support efforts to achieve an integrated society. Other black nationalist groups preached separation from American society and emigration to Africa as the solution to blacks' problems. But the call for racial pride and self-help was basic to all forms of black nationalism.

THE NATIONAL URBAN LEAGUE LOOKED FOR JOBS

The National Urban League continued to emphasize economic advancement for blacks. But the League found it much harder to achieve results as more blacks moved into industrial centers and jobs became fewer. Finding new job opportunities for black workers usually depended upon making friendly contacts with employers. Many employers were using black workers to break strikes and help keep out unions. When the strike ended, the black workers often were fired. The Urban League wanted to maintain good relations with employers. At the same time, League officials realized that black workers must become a part of the labor movement.

The League tried to work with both employers and organized labor. It worked to organize branches in more cities and to educate blacks, labor unions, and employers about the problems of the black worker. In 1921, the National Urban League set up its department of research. Charles S. Johnson, a sociologist and director of research for the Chicago branch, came to New York City to run the new department. Johnson's job was to gather information on job conditions and send it along to the branches. He also informed employers and others about the problems of blacks and showed them the need for organizing League branches.

The research department made careful studies of industrial conditions and the job situation. An important study of black workers and organized labor was also made. The information gathered was sent out regularly in *The Urban League Bulletin*. To reach more readers, in 1933 the League began publishing the magazine *Opportunity: Journal of Negro Life*.

But information was not enough. Something needed to be done to change conditions. For this reason, the National Urban League set up an industrial department. T. Arnold Hill came from Chicago to become industrial secretary in 1925. Hill worked with labor leaders to try to open unions to Afro-American workers. He also began a "Negro in Industry Week." This week was celebrated all over the country as a means of increasing opportunities. Nevertheless, by 1927 unemployment among blacks was growing extremely serious. The Chicago Urban League decided to take more direct action than promoting the "Negro in Industry Week." Therefore, it helped to begin a boycott of businesses in the black community to open more jobs for blacks there. A black newspaper, the *Chicago Whip,* took over the campaign under the slogan "Spend Your Money Where You Can Work." The boycott received support in Chicago and spread to other cities.

RACE RELATIONS GROUPS WERE ORGANIZED

Two other interracial organizations similar to the Urban League were active in the 1920's. The Commission on Interracial Cooperation (CIC) worked to improve conditions in the South. The CIC began in Atlanta in 1919. It worked through state and local branches, composed of leading white and black citizens. Headed by Dr. Will Alexander, a young white minister, the CIC had a black and a white paid worker in each state.

The CIC depended mainly on educational methods to try to bring gradual change. It distributed pamphlets and other publications attacking the Ku Klux Klan and calling for fair treatment of blacks. The CIC joined the fight to end lynching. It formed the Association of Southern Women for the Prevention of Lynching to carry on this fight. The CIC, however, never called for an end to segregation. It attempted to work for fair treatment within the South's Jim Crow system. Even so, the organization had little influence outside cities and college campuses.

The Federal Council of Churches entered the field of race relations in 1922. In that year, it began its Department of Race Relations. Dr. George E. Haynes, a founder of the National Urban League and a Fisk University professor, became head of the department. Haynes helped to establish local councils throughout the country and started the observance of "Race Relations Sunday" in the churches. The council's purpose was to bring about the general improvement of race relations.

THE NAACP HAD A CHANGE IN LEADERSHIP

A change took place in the leadership in the NAACP in 1920. At this time, blacks held most of the staff positions. James Weldon Johnson became executive secretary. Johnson had joined the NAACP staff in 1916 as field secretary. Before that, he had had a remarkable career as teacher, poet, writer, and diplomat. Johnson's appointment was important because he was able to work with leaders of differing points of view. Although he was considered an ally of Booker T. Washington, both the militants and the conservatives respected him. Robert W. Bagnall, another black staff member, directed the NAACP department branches, and Daisy Lampkin and William Pickens were field secretaries. Walter White served as assistant, and W. E. B. Du Bois remained as editor of *The Crisis*.

But the NAACP remained interracial in its leadership. Mary White Ovington, Oswald G. Villard, and Moorfield Storey helped to shape the organization's policies. The president and the chairman of the board were whites, and the NAACP's legal work was in the hands of white lawyers. A white staff member, Herbert Seligman, handled publicity.

149

Many problems demanded the urgent attention of the NAACP. The organization centered its work in the courts and the legislatures. Voting, segregation in housing, and lynching remained major problems. In addition, the NAACP fought discrimination in many forms. Throughout the 1920's, it worked to end discrimination against blacks in governmental jobs. NAACP investigations of complaints from black workers showed that such discrimination was widespread. In 1926, Monroe Trotter, the militant Boston editor, went to see President Coolidge about this problem. And in 1927 and 1928, NAACP representatives tried to get the President to help. However, these investigations and appeals brought little change in conditions.

A LONG FIGHT FOR VOTING RIGHTS BEGAN

Many blacks believed that the vote was the key to advancement. Although barriers against black voting remained the rule in the South, hopes grew that the courts would open the way for black political participation. In 1915, the Supreme Court ruled that Oklahoma's grandfather clause was unconstitutional. This clause was used in many Southern states to make it possible to register whites who did not meet the qualifications to vote, while at the same time making it impossible for all black citizens to vote. Unfortunately, this victory did not make any difference to black Southerners. White voters who were not qualified continued to be found qualified to register, while black citizens were still found to be unqualified.

Black Americans attacked other practices used to discriminate against them. One of these widely used practices was the white primary. The laws setting up white primaries provided that only whites could vote in the Democratic Party primary election, where candidates were selected. The result was that only one candidate ran for each office in the general election. The reason for this was that the Republican Party had almost no white support in the South, and therefore the candidates selected in the white Democratic Party primaries always won the general election. The few blacks who were able to vote in the general election had no choice of candidates.

The fight against the white primary began in 1927. Dr. L. A. Nixon, a Houston dentist, tried to vote in the primary in Texas. He was not permitted to vote because of his color. The Texas law stated that "in no event shall a Negro be eligible to participate in a Democratic primary election." Nixon took the case to federal court on the grounds that the Texas law violated the Fourteenth Amendment. Arthur B.

Springarn, an NAACP lawyer, argued the case before the Supreme Court.

The Supreme Court in the case of *Nixon v. Herndon* declared the Texas law unconstitutional. Justice Holmes, in the majority opinion, said that the law clearly violated the Fourteenth Amendment because it did not give blacks equal protection. But this decision was only the first step toward destroying the white primary.

Texas and other states passed new laws. This time the states did not say who was eligible to vote in the primaries. Political parties were given the power to choose their own members and to limit voting in the primaries to members only. The Democratic Party in the South made rules that only whites could vote in Democratic primaries. Thus, the court victory in *Nixon v. Herndon* only began the long struggle for the right to vote.

THE NAACP FOUGHT SEGREGATED HOUSING

In cities throughout the country, efforts were made to keep blacks segregated in all-black neighborhoods. Louisville, Kentucky, tried to do this by passing local laws which said that black citizens could not move into neighborhoods where the majority of the residents were whites. White citizens were forbidden to move into neighborhoods where most residents were blacks. The NAACP took this matter to court. In 1917, the Supreme Court of the United States ruled that segregated neighborhoods could not be created by laws. The Court ruled, in *Buchanan v. Warley,* that such laws violated the Fourteenth Amendment because they denied persons the right to use their property as they wished.

To get around this ruling, whites began to make private agreements called "restrictive covenants." That is, white property owners made contracts agreeing not to sell their homes or property to blacks. Often the agreements also prevented white property owners from selling to Jews, Catholics, or Asians. These agreements were supposedly legal because they were not governmental actions. And in 1926, the Supreme Court ruled that these contracts did not violate the Fourteenth Amendment.

Still, the NAACP was successful in having laws declared unconstitutional that aimed to accomplish the same thing that restrictive covenants did. The case of *Harmon v. Tyler* involved a city law. This law made it illegal for blacks to move into white communities unless a majority of the residents gave written consent. Ruling on the case in

1927, the Supreme Court declared that this law deprived white property owners of the full right to their property. The Supreme Court also held that zoning laws which kept blacks out of white neighborhoods were unconstitutional. But private restrictive covenants remained legal throughout the 1920's in spite of all NAACP efforts.

The Afro-American family who managed to find someone to sell them a house in a white neighborhood was likely to be greeted by a mob. This happened to Dr. Ossian Sweet, a Detroit surgeon, in 1925. When Sweet and his family moved into a home they bought in a white neighborhood, a mob tried to drive them out. The mob shot at the house, and one of Sweet's brothers returned the fire. A member of the mob was hit by a bullet and killed. The Sweets were arrested and charged with first-degree murder.

The NAACP entered the case to defend the Sweets. It was able to get one of the most famous lawyers of the 1920's, Clarence Darrow, to take the case. Black people all over the country were greatly alarmed by the Sweet case. They were concerned about the right of black people to defend their own property. Contributions were sent in from all over the country. Darrow presented his case in court skillfully, and after two trials the Sweets were freed.

CONGRESS REJECTED AN ANTI-LYNCHING LAW

The Republican platform in 1920 called upon Congress to act against lynching. James Weldon Johnson spent considerable time attempting to persuade Congress to pass an anti-lynching bill. He offered the assistance of the NAACP to Representative L. C. Dyer of Missouri, who was trying to get a bill before Congress. Dyer introduced his bill to make lynching a federal crime on April 11, 1921. Johnson and the association spent the next two years trying to get support for the bill. Johnson visited friendly members of Congress to seek their help.

The NAACP devoted most of its resources to this campaign. The black press, organizations, and individuals joined the fight. Members of Congress were showered with letters urging favorable action. The National Association of Colored Women raised money and helped to organize NAACP branches. Crowds jammed the galleries of the House when the Dyer bill was debated. It was a day for rejoicing when the bill passed the House of Representatives by a vote of 230 to 119.

However, the Senate still had to act. The bill went to a subcommittee of the Senate headed by Senator William E. Borah of Idaho. Borah told James Weldon Johnson that he did not think that the bill was constitutional. Since lynching was murder, Borah argued, the federal government did not have the power to remove just this one kind of murder case from control by state laws. The committee kept the Dyer bill bottled up, and the NAACP had to work hard to get it out of committee for the Senate to debate. The committee finally released the bill after the Senate received a petition signed by a long list of important national leaders. Among the signers were twenty-four governors, thirty-nine mayors, forty-seven judges and lawyers, eighty-eight bishops and churchmen, and many others.

Getting the Dyer bill introduced in the Senate was only the beginning. The NAACP now began its campaign to have the bill considered and passed. Advertisements were bought in leading newspapers. The National Association of Colored Women ran a full-page ad in *The New York Times*. These ads called lynching the "shame of America."

The Dyer bill never came up for vote in the Senate. The Democrats began a filibuster and used other means of keeping the Senate from voting. Republican leaders such as Henry Cabot Lodge did nothing to try to stop the filibuster. James Weldon Johnson said that the Republicans reasoned that they had "done their duty and cleared their own skirts" when they presented the bill, letting the Southern Democrats kill it. In any case, Democrats would get the blame.

The struggle over the Dyer bill did some good, however. The debate in Congress made Americans more aware than ever before of lynching and all of its horrors. More Southerners now determined to end this terrible crime, and the number of lynchings decreased in the following years.

BLACK AMERICANS LOOKED
TO BLACKS IN OTHER LANDS

During and after World War I, black Americans became much more aware of black people in other parts of the world. Special interest centered in Haiti, when that land was occupied by United States Marines in 1915. Black newspapers reported stories of the treatment of the people of Haiti by the marines. Du Bois wrote editorials and carried stories in *The Crisis*. The NAACP sent James Weldon Johnson to Haiti to investigate the situation. Johnson wrote articles about conditions there, and Harding used some of Johnson's findings during the election campaign of 1920. Harding made some changes after he was elected President, but the marines remained in Haiti.

Du Bois made black Americans more conscious of Africa by helping to organize Pan-African Congresses. Du Bois wanted to bring blacks of "different origins and nationality" together. Four congresses were held. The first met in 1919 in London, Brussels, and Paris. Later meetings were held in 1921, 1923, and 1927. The meeting in 1927 was held in New York City. Du Bois was ahead of his time in hoping that worldwide black unity was possible. But these congresses pointed the way of the future and did influence many individuals.

MARCUS GARVEY AWAKENED BLACK NATIONALISM

The man who brought black nationalism to full flower was Marcus Moziah Garvey. He was a leader able to reach the black masses in the cities and draw them into his movement. And the time was right for his efforts. Blacks were frustrated and disillusioned by life in large cities. They were forced to live in shabby, overcrowded housing. Jobs were hard to find, and their dreams of a better life were overshadowed by the hate and violence of the riots.

Garvey brought the black masses a message of reassurance and hope. He stirred in them feelings of racial pride and gave them a sense of identity. He glorified blackness and called upon black people to study and identify with the exciting history and culture of Africa. Garvey kindled dreams of escape to an African homeland, ruled by black people. He talked of the important role that blacks throughout the world would play in shaping the future. The masses responded when he demanded of them: "Up, you mighty race. You can accomplish what you will."

Marcus Garvey was born in Jamaica on August 17, 1887. He left school at the age of 14 and worked at a number of jobs. Early in life, Garvey became concerned about the condition of black people. He tried to help the black masses of Jamaica as a labor leader and through political activity. He traveled and observed conditions in many Latin American countries. For a time, he worked as a timekeeper on a banana plantation in Costa Rica.

In 1912, Garvey went to London. There he hoped to learn about blacks throughout the British Empire. In London, there were black people from all parts of the empire. Garvey came to know them, and he talked to them about their homelands. He also read and studied in the libraries of London. To support himself, he worked on the staff of the magazine *Africa Times and Orient Review*. He learned a great deal from the magazine's editor, Duse Mohammed Ali.

Marcus Garvey, the founder of the Universal Negro Improvement Association, stressed black pride and economic self-help.

Garvey was not encouraged by his study of blacks in the British Empire. He saw that conditions of black people were the same everywhere. All over the world, black people were poor and being oppressed. According to Garvey, he became determined to do something about this situation after reading the autobiography of Booker T. Washington. "I read *Up From Slavery* by Booker T. Washington," he said, "and then my doom—if I may so call it—of being a race leader dawned upon me." Garvey began writing to Washington, who invited him to come to the United States.

But first Garvey returned to Jamaica. There he organized the Universal Negro Improvement Association in 1914. Under the motto "One God! One Aim! One Destiny!" Garvey set out to unite "all the Negro peoples of the world into one great body to establish a country and government absolutely their own."

GARVEY ESTABLISHED THE UNIA

Garvey arrived in New York in March, 1916, shortly after Washington's death. He traveled to thirty-eight states, meeting people and lecturing. In 1917, he organized a branch of the Universal Negro Improvement Association (UNIA) in Harlem. The association was an immediate success. Within two months, over 1,500 people had joined. Branches were organized in other cities, and by 1919, thirty branches were operating in the United States. By 1922, the UNIA claimed several million members in branches throughout the world, including the West Indies, Latin America, and Africa.

To keep his followers informed about his program, Garvey published the *Negro World*. This was a well-edited weekly newspaper, selling between 75,000 and 100,000 copies at the high point of Garvey's movement. The pages of the *Negro World* emphasized the beauty of blackness, told of black heroes, and called for the liberation of Africa.

GARVEY DRAMATIZED HIS MOVEMENT

Part of Garvey's attraction to the masses was his personality. He was a great showman, who gave his followers a feeling of importance and a sense of belonging to a great movement. In 1920, the UNIA convention met at Madison Square Garden in New York City, where 25,000 people from 25 countries attended the meeting. Before the meeting opened, a colorful parade marched through the streets of Harlem. The military arm of the UNIA, the African Legion, was dressed in blue uniforms with red stripes on the trousers. The Black Cross nurses, dressed in white, also marched through the streets.

At the convention, Garvey was proclaimed head of the African Republic that he planned to establish. He unfurled the red, black, and green flag of that republic. And his followers sang the UNIA anthem, "Ethiopia, Thou Land of Our Fathers." Garvey chose a government and gave titles of nobility to many of his followers.

Members of Garvey's movement could belong to a number of different groups. In addition to the African Legion and the Black Cross Nurses, these included the Universal African Motor Corps, the Juvenile, and the Black Flying Eagles. Garvey was also responsible for starting a new black church, the African Orthodox Church, with the Reverend George Alexander McGuire, a former Episcopal clergyman, as its bishop. Black became the symbol of goodness in this church. Angels were black, and the devil was white. Members learned about the "Black Man of Sorrows" and the "Black Virgin Mother."

GARVEY FAVORED ECONOMIC SELF-HELP

Garvey's economic program centered around the Negro Factories Corporation and the Black Star Steamship Line. His economic ideas were similar to those of Booker T. Washington. Garvey believed in economic self-help and racial advancement through the ownership of stores and factories. The Factories Corporation established grocery stores, a restaurant, a laundry, and other businesses. But these businesses failed because the managers lacked training and experience.

The Black Star Line was vital to Garvey's entire program. He planned to use its ships to take black Americans to their African ancestral homeland. These ships also would bring the products of Africa to the Americas. The first problem Garvey faced in starting this shipping line was the need to raise money. He did not want whites and wealthy blacks to provide the funds. Instead, he offered to sell shares of stock to the masses of blacks to raise the money. These small investors eagerly bought the stock, and, in a short time, he obtained over $600,000. But, again, lack of business know-how and experience caused the project to fail. By 1922, the Black Star Line was hopelessly in debt.

GARVEY FACED SERIOUS PROBLEMS

Garvey never got along well with established black leaders. He said most of them were working for their own selfish interests. He also would have nothing to do with many of them because they were light-skinned. Garvey preached that the darker a person's skin, the better he was. He did not recognize those of mixed blood as being black. Black American leaders returned his dislike. W. E. B. Du Bois, A. Philip Randolph, Robert Abbott of the *Chicago Defender,* and other leaders were openly critical of Garvey. Their dislike may have come in part from jealousy. But they also believed that Garvey's movement was something of a circus and that his program was not sound.

Criticism from black leaders and complaints from some of those who lost money in his shipping company got Garvey into trouble with the federal government. In 1922, he was charged with using the mail to defraud while selling stock in the Black Star Line. He was convicted of the charge in 1923 and sentenced to five years in prison. He was able to remain free until 1925 while the case was appealed, but on February 8, 1925, he entered Atlanta prison to serve his sentence. President Coolidge commuted, or set aside, his sentence in 1927. But Garvey was deported from the United States as an undesirable alien. He went first to Jamaica and then to London. Although he tried, Garvey was not able to make the UNIA into a strong movement again. Garvey spent the rest of his life in London, where he died in 1940.

Although he did not achieve his program, Garvey made an important contribution to black Americans. As one historian wrote, he gave them a "psychological lift." He gave them a feeling of pride in being black and a feeling of personal worth. Even those who disagreed with him recognized that he was the leader of a real mass movement. Equally important, Garvey pointed the way for the black nationalists who were to appear later in American society.

Chapter 15

The Harlem Renaissance

Writers and artists were affected by the black nationalism of the 1920's. Many of the same forces that brought about the Garvey movement and black nationalism in politics and economics led to an outpouring of literary and artistic works. Black intellectuals and artists were drawn to New York City, and Harlem became the major center of this creative activity. For this reason, the cultural aspect of black nationalism was called the Harlem Renaissance. But it was also known as the Black Renaissance and the New Negro Movement.

THE HARLEM RENAISSANCE WAS PART OF ✓ A NEW LITERARY MOVEMENT

Several developments in American literature contributed to the black literary awakening of the 1920's. American literature began to come of age toward the end of the nineteenth century. Writers turned away from the shallowness and idealized version of life of the Victorian period. They began to write about reality, about the ugliness and hardships of real life. This became known as "realism" in literature. William Dean Howells and Henry James were important in this development. "Naturalism," which developed along with realism, was an effort to show society and the lives of men and women as truthfully as possible. This led writers to place growing emphasis on the lower classes in American society.

World War I caused important changes in outlook among American intellectuals. They seemed to lose faith in progress and to have serious doubts about traditional American values. The war caused them to deeply question whether the nation could ever attain real peace and democracy. Some felt that the Puritan tradition prevented Americans from expressing their emotional needs openly and honestly. Others felt that America's industrial economy placed too great an emphasis on money and possessions.

Although the writers of the 1920's were more concerned about the individual than about society, many wrote about America's social problems. Frank Tannenbaum studied conditions among Southern blacks. Other writers gave attention to labor, peace, and crime. Writers of fiction turned to the ugliness and tragedy in American life. Sinclair Lewis and Theodore Dreiser were representative of this group.

Some writers ran away from America's Puritanism and its Machine Age society. Paris was a favorite place of refuge for these disillusioned writers. Many also turned to subjects that provided escape. They concerned themselves with primitive, or uncorrupted, societies in Africa, Mexico, and other areas of the world. Some writers saw the Afro-American as primitive, free from the restricting Puritan values of white Americans, and free to live life to the fullest. These writers sought their escape from the Machine Age by studying and writing about Afro-American life.

WHITE WRITERS HELPED TO PREPARE THE WAY

A large number of books about blacks by white authors appeared during the 1920's. These works created an interest among white readers in work based on Afro-American life. In this way, they helped to prepare readers for the works of black intellectuals. The American public had not been accustomed to honest, serious treatments of black life. The black servant, clown, and minstrel comic were the stereotyped characters they had read about. But during the 1920's, white writers broke with this tradition. Even though their search for the primitive led to new stereotypes, their works were a major contribution in making black life a part of American literature.

Novelists began turning to black folk materials. Du Bois Heyward wrote about blacks in South Carolina in *Porgy* and *Mamba's Daughters*. Julia Peterkin, Sherwood Anderson, Conrad Aiken, and Waldo Frank were others who tried to deal realistically with black subjects. Carl Van Vechten probably made the most important direct contribution to the Harlem Renaissance.

Van Vechten brought black and white artists and intellectuals together in social gatherings. A number of the leading black figures of the Renaissance were among his friends. These included James Weldon Johnson, Countee Cullen, and Langston Hughes. Van Vechten took an interest in the works of individual black writers. He read their works and helped a number of them to find publishers. Historian Nathan Huggins, who has made a scholarly study of the movement, called Van Vechten "a kind of midwife to the Harlem Renaissance."

But blacks were not happy when Van Vechten's novel *Nigger Heaven* was published in 1926. The work was an example of novels which emphasized the primitive and exotic side of life in Harlem. Because it met the tastes of white readers, the book was a great success. W. E. B. Du Bois and other black critics felt the book was insulting to black Americans. They did not like the title, and they said that the novel was not a true picture of black life and feelings. But James Weldon Johnson defended Van Vechten's novel, and the novel did influence black writers. At least two of these black authors wrote similar books that sold well.

WRITERS OF THE RENAISSANCE BUILT ON THE BLACK PAST

The white contribution to the Harlem Renaissance must not be overemphasized. Racial pride and black nationalism were much more crucial to its development. The black intellectual became keenly aware of blackness. He turned away from white models and began to place a high value on those things in black life that had been looked down on before. Langston Hughes voiced this new outlook when he said: "We younger Negro artists who create now intend to express our individual dark-skinned selves without fear or shame. If white people are pleased we are glad. If they are not, it doesn't matter. We know we are beautiful. And ugly, too."

The interest of black intellectuals in subjects drawn from black life

161

did not begin with the Harlem Renaissance. Historians began studying the Afro-American past in the nineteenth century. The interest in black history was strong enough by 1916 to enable Carter G. Woodson to form the Association for the Study of Negro Life and History. Woodson also began publishing the *Journal of Negro History* and started a firm to publish books about black history. Du Bois also wrote numerous historical and sociological works.

A number of black creative artists helped to pave the way for the Renaissance. Some of them dealt with racial themes, but others avoided black subject matter. Paul Lawrence Dunbar, who wrote in the late nineteenth century, left a variety of works. Dunbar wrote novels and poetry in standard English and dialect. Although he differed from the writers of the 1920's in the way he treated black life, Dunbar had an influence on them. So did the novelist Charles Waddell Chestnutt. A number of poets began publishing before the Renaissance. These included James David Corrothers, Leslie Pinckney Hill, Fenton Johnson, Georgia Douglas Johnson, Alice Dunbar Nelson, and Angelina Weld Grimke. The poet and critic William Stanley Braithwaite of Boston had also received recognition before the Twenties.

Du Bois and James Weldon Johnson were two other important figures whose work began before the Renaissance. Du Bois showed literary talent in *The Souls of Black Folk,* a book of essays published in 1903. His novel *Quest of the Silver Fleece* appeared in 1911. Another book of essays and poetry, *Darkwater,* came out in 1920, and a second novel, *The Dark Princess,* appeared in 1928. Johnson began his career in New York City as a writer for musicals. In 1912, his novel *The Autobiography of an Ex-Coloured Man* was published anonymously. The work was printed again in 1927 with Johnson's name on it. A book of poems by Johnson dealing with black history, called *Fifty Years and Other Poems,* came out in 1917. He continued to write during the Renaissance. *God's Trombones,* a collection of black folk sermons, appeared in 1927. Johnson brought out a collection of black poetry, *The Book of American Negro Poetry,* in 1922. Johnson was also a critic of the Renaissance, and his book *Black Manhattan* dealt with the movement and the artists involved.

Alain Locke was another black intellectual who was a supporter, critic of, and a participant in, the Renaissance. Locke, who had a doctorate from Harvard and was the first black Rhodes scholar, was a professor of philosophy at Howard University. Locke edited a special issue of *The Survey Graphic* on Harlem in 1925. This journal, which was widely read by American intellectuals, brought the Renaissance to the attention of the educated public. This issue of *The Survey Graphic* was published in book form late in 1925, with the title *The New Negro: An Interpretation.*

MAGAZINES PUBLISHED THE WORKS OF YOUNG BLACK WRITERS

The NAACP and the National Urban League helped young writers by publishing their works in the organizations' magazines. Du Bois, as editor of *The Crisis,* invited young writers to send in poems and short stories. Jessie Redmond Fauset became literary editor of *The Crisis* in 1919. A poet and novelist herself, she worked closely with other young writers. The National Urban League began publishing *Opportunity* in 1923, with the University of Chicago trained sociologist Charles S. Johnson as editor. Most of the writers of the Renaissance wrote material for *Opportunity.* Johnson put together a collection of the works of black writers in *Ebony and Topaz.*

Both *The Crisis* and *Opportunity* sponsored literary contests. Cash prizes were awarded to winning authors. The leading writers of the Renaissance participated in these contests, and some of their best works first appeared in *The Crisis* or *Opportunity.* Several writers found employment on the staffs of the magazines. Eric Walrond and Countee Cullen both worked on *Opportunity* for a time.

CLAUDE MC KAY PUBLISHED PROTEST WORKS

Claude McKay has been credited with sounding the first note of the Renaissance and with setting the mood of the movement. McKay was born in Jamaica in 1889. He had published several books of verse before leaving Jamaica. McKay came to the United States in 1912, attended Tuskegee for a brief time, and then went to Kansas State University for two years. In 1915, he moved to New York City. His famous poem "If We Must Die" appeared in *The Liberator* in 1919. It was a bold work, calling upon blacks to meet violence with violence. Militance, protest, and racial pride were themes found in many of McKay's works. In his sonnet "White Houses," he wrote:

> Your door is shut against my tightened face,
> And I am sharp as steel with discontent
> But I possess the courage and the grace
> To bear my anger proudly and unbent.

McKay established his reputation as a poet in 1922 with *Harlem*

Shadows. This was a collection of his best poems. McKay left the United States in 1923, and he did not return until after the high point of the Renaissance. But he wrote two novels that were major works of the Renaissance. *Home to Harlem,* in 1928, treated lower-class life in Harlem. *Banjo,* which appeared in 1929, was set in Europe.

COUNTEE CULLEN'S WORKS WERE LYRICAL AND ROMANTIC

Countee Cullen was one of the young Renaissance writers. Born in New York City in 1903, he was educated at New York University and Harvard. His first collection of poems, *Color,* appeared in 1925. Then came *Copper Sun* and *The Ballad of the Brown Girl* in 1927. Cullen followed the style of John Keats, and much of his poetry was on non-racial subjects. Love, spring, youth, and death were his favorite subjects.

Although Cullen wanted to be judged as a poet, and not as a black poet, he could not escape his blackness. Some of his most moving verse dealt with racial themes. His poem "Heritage" treated the African background of black Americans, and "Shroud of Color" was a call for equal treatment of blacks. In his well-known poem "Yet Do I Marvel," Cullen expressed his bewilderment at being black and a poet:

Yet do I marvel at this curious thing:
To make a poet black, and bid him sing!

Cullen was a teacher in the New York City public schools from 1929 until his death in 1946. He published several works between 1927 and 1940. *Caroling Dusk,* a collection of poems by black poets, appeared in 1927. *The Black Christ,* a long poetic work, came out in 1929. His novel, *One Way to Heaven,* published in 1932, dealt with life in Harlem. He also wrote a book for children and other poetic works. However, critics believe that Cullen's best work was done during the Harlem Renaissance.

LANGSTON HUGHES USED SATIRE AND HUMOR

Langston Hughes was probably the best known of the Renaissance writers. He also was the most daring in using new literary forms and in celebrating blackness. Born in Joplin, Missouri, in 1902, Hughes lived with relatives in several places before finishing high school in Cleveland. Hughes was a free spirit who followed his youthful urges

164

Langston Hughes was one of the most talented and popular writers of the Harlem Renaissance.

to travel. Working as a seaman, he went to Europe and Africa. He continued his education at Columbia University and at Lincoln University in Pennsylvania.

His first published poem, "The Negro Speaks of Rivers," appeared in *The Crisis* in 1921. He produced two volumes of poetry during the Harlem Renaissance, *The Weary Blues* in 1926 and *Fine Clothes to the Jew* in 1927. Many of the poems used the rhythms and moods of jazz and the blues. Hughes also combined themes from the lives of lower-class blacks with protest. His "Brass Spittoons" dealt with the daily life of a bellhop. "To the Negro Washerwoman" celebrated the sacrifices a mother made to educate her children. His novel *Not Without Laughter* brought together the blues and spiritual traditions. Before his death in 1967, Hughes produced many works in fiction, drama, history, biography, autobiography, and children's literature. His humorous, biting, and moving stories about Jesse Simple were read by Americans everywhere.

OTHER IMPORTANT WRITERS APPEARED

McKay, Cullen, and Hughes were three of the leading writers of the Black Renaissance, but many others wrote important works. Jean Toomer drew upon black life for his work *Cane*, which combined narrative and poetry. Several writers emphasized life among middle-class blacks. Walter White, Jessie Redmond Fauset, and Nella Larsen used plots in their novels based on "passing" the color line and color differences among blacks.

Black writers outside New York City also produced important works. Among them were Jonathan Brooks in Mississippi, George Leonard Allen in North Carolina, and Frank Marshall Davis in Atlanta. Sterling Brown's writing career began during the Renaissance and continued long beyond it. Brown taught English at Howard University. His first collection of poems, *Southern Road,* did not appear until 1932. The same thing was true of Arna Bontemps, a poet and writer, most of whose major works appeared after the Renaissance.

BLACKS APPEARED IN MUSIC AND DRAMAS

In the theater, white playwrights wrote a number of plays dealing with black life. They gave black actors the opportunity to appear in major dramatic productions. Charles Gilpin became famous in 1920 for his role in Eugene O'Neill's *The Emperor Jones.* Another O'Neill play,

All God's Chillun Got Wings, brought Paul Robeson to the stage in 1924. A Southern playwright, Paul Green of the University of North Carolina, wrote a number of folk plays. His most outstanding play, *In Abraham's Bosom,* was produced in 1926. Jules Bledsoe and Rose McClendon played leading roles in this Pulitzer prizewinning play. Rose McClendon also had a role in *Porgy* by Du Bose and Dorothy Heyward. Richard B. Harrison gained fame for his role as "de Lawd" in *Green Pastures* by Marc Connelly, which opened in 1930.

Musical shows with black casts also became popular during the Twenties. *Shuffle Along,* a brilliant musical, opened in New York in 1921. This musical comedy ran for a year in New York City and for two more years in other cities. The success of *Shuffle Along* brought other black musicals into New York theaters. Ethel Waters, Adelaide Hall, Ada Ward, and Bill Robinson were stars in these shows.

Blacks also made contributions to serious music. J. Rosamond Johnson and Carl Diton wrote a variety of musical compositions. Harry T. Burleigh and R. Nathaniel Dett made lasting contributions in arranging Negro spirituals. A number of singers brought spirituals and other black music to large audiences. Paul Robeson, Lawrence Brown, Taylor Gordon, and Abbie Mitchell were singers with great talent. Roland Hayes, the tenor, and Marian Anderson, the contralto, began long and brilliant careers during the Twenties.

BLACK ARTISTS MADE CONTRIBUTIONS IN MANY FIELDS

Two major artists, Henry Ossawa Tanner in painting and Meta Warrick Fuller in sculpture, had established their reputations before the Renaissance began. Tanner went to Europe to study in 1891 and received acclaim for his painting "The Resurrection of Lazarus" in 1897. He lived in Paris during most of his career, devoting his paintings largely to religious subjects. Meta Fuller's sculpture was first shown in Paris, where it was exhibited in 1903. Her statues showed the artist's great feeling for human suffering. Both Tanner and Fuller continued to use conventional subjects and methods in their works.

During the Twenties, young sculptors and painters started to use African subject matter. They also turned to primitive forms. These artists tried to capture the spirit of black life in their works. Sculptor Richmond Barthé used a wide range of subjects, but he was representative of the new artists of the 1920's. In painting, Aaron Douglas was representative of this new trend.

JAZZ CREATED AN IMAGE OF HARLEM

Jazz gave Harlem its lively, exciting image during the Renaissance. In fact, this distinctly Afro-American music gave the 1920's a special flavor that caused the period to be called the Jazz Age. Jazz was not new in the Twenties, for it had long been a part of black life in the South. Jazzmen made their way to Northern cities before World War I. Chicago, St. Louis, and Kansas City became centers where jazz developed. Scott Joplin, William C. Handy, and others took this music to New York City. Black audiences crowded into theaters to hear such great jazz performers as Bubber Miley, Will Marion Cook, Will Vodery, and Jelly Roll Morton. Younger men like Fletcher Henderson, Duke Ellington, and Louis Armstrong also drew large crowds.

It was during the 1920's, though, that white Americans began to discover jazz. They flocked to the nightclubs and cabarets in Harlem to listen and sway to jazz music. To whites, jazz gave Harlem an exciting and exotic air. Of course, the black residents of Harlem knew the truth about life in their community. But they needed the money that whites brought to Harlem.

Jazz also moved downtown from Harlem and became a part of the Broadway musical theater. White audiences heard great jazz and blues musicians in these musicals, and they were introduced to such new dances as the Cakewalk, the Charleston, the Black Bottom, and the Lindy Hop. In addition, jazz musicians and blues singers began to move downtown to perform in New York City's nightclubs and bars. White musicians, too, began trying to master this great popular form of music known as jazz.

UNIT FIVE

FROM DEPRESSION TO WORLD WAR II

Chapter 16

The New Deal Years

The stock market crash in 1929 marked the beginning of many years of hard times known as the Great Depression. All Americans suffered during the Great Depression, but black Americans faced the greatest hardships and burdens. Banks closed, and those with savings accounts lost all their money. Factories, stores, and other businesses closed down or cut back their labor forces. As a result, many thousands of black workers lost their jobs in the industrial cities. At the same time, lack of markets for farm products and the increasing use of farm machines caused cutbacks in agriculture, driving farm workers into the cities. The majority of black families had to depend upon relief to stay alive. Then new hope came with President Franklin D. Roosevelt's New Deal. Although discrimination was present in the New Deal's relief, recovery, and reform programs, they helped Afro-Americans to make economic, political, and social gains.

BLACK UNEMPLOYMENT BECAME WIDESPREAD

By 1930, the black population of the United States was 11,891,143, or 9.7 percent of the total population. The great majority, 9,361,577, still lived in the South, but the percentage of the black population living in the South had dropped greatly since 1860. Blacks in the North and West numbered 2,529,566 in 1930. Most of these Northern and Western blacks lived in cities. Only about 300,000 Northern blacks lived in rural areas. There were 1,185,530 in New York City, Chicago, Philadelphia, and the areas around these cities. The rest lived in small industrial cities. Because these urban workers had been among the last to get jobs in industry, they were the first to lose their jobs. In fact, black workers began to feel the effects of hard times during the last years of the 1920's. When the Great Depression hit, suffering only became more widespread.

The years between 1930 and 1933 were a time of great hardship in the black community. The 1930 census gave some idea about how serious the situation had become. It showed that urban black workers were hit harder by unemployment than were white workers. A census report in 1931 revealed that in every city with a large black population, at least 25 percent of the black workers were without jobs. In Detroit, 60 percent of the men and 75 percent of the women were out of work. The National Urban League made three reports on black unemployment early in the Depression. The first appeared in the spring of 1930, and two more were issued in the spring and fall of 1931. All three reports showed that conditions were getting worse. In New York City, Cincinnati, St. Louis, Atlanta, Memphis, and other major cities, from 20 to 30 percent of black workers were unemployed. Many of these workers had been without jobs for a year or longer.

Other studies showed even higher percentages of unemployment among blacks in several other large cities. In Chicago, over 40 percent of the employable black men and over 55 percent of the women had no jobs. Between 1929 and 1932, unemployment among black workers in Philadelphia rose from nearly 16 percent to 56 percent. In 1934, 48 percent of Pittsburgh blacks were unemployed. By contrast, although millions of white workers also were without jobs, in most cities the percentage of white unemployment was only half as large as that among blacks.

The problem of jobs for blacks grew even more serious when whites began replacing blacks in many lines of work. In all sections of the country, unions, employers, and lawmaking bodies were helping to drive blacks out of types of work once considered black jobs. New laws on licenses were passed to push blacks out of barbering, plumbing, and other trades. Even in service fields, whites were taking over jobs as waiters, porters, elevator operators, and maids.

RELIEF PROGRAMS HELPED BLACKS

The high rate of unemployment made relief efforts especially important to blacks. During the years from 1929 until 1933, when Herbert Hoover was President, relief was largely a state and local matter. Blacks made up a large percentage of those seeking relief help. In Chicago, about 25 percent of the relief given in 1930 and early 1931 went to blacks. Chicago, New York City, Philadelphia, and Detroit had a total of 78,027 black families on relief in 1933. This number represented almost a third of all black families living in these cities. The situation was even worse in some other cities. In Pittsburgh and Cleveland, 43 percent of the black population was on relief in 1933. Akron, Ohio, led all cities, with 67 percent on relief.

Much discrimination was found in these relief programs. In some places, private groups that provided help did not give help to blacks. For example, only whites were served in some privately run "soup kitchens." In some cities, blacks also received less public assistance than whites did. In these cities, relief was given on the basis of the percentage of each race in the total population. Even though blacks had a larger percentage of the unemployed, they were a smaller percentage of the city population and therefore they received less aid for each unemployed family. Where public works were used as a form of work relief, such jobs usually went to white workers.

The suffering in black communities brought a significant change in some black churches. For the first time, many of them became actively involved in social welfare work. A few churches had engaged in such work in the 1920's, but the number increased greatly during the Great Depression. All over the country, black churches opened free kitchens and provided money and clothing to those in great need.

Under President Hoover, federal aid was given to farmers in the form of feed, seed, and fertilizer loans. The Reconstruction Finance Corporation (RFC) also made loans to farm owners. But the RFC made only large loans. The small farmers, both black and white, received little help from this agency. The loans for feed, seed, and fertilizer were of great help to black tenants and farm owners where the program was run fairly. In some places, black tenants received these loans and used them to pay cash for their supplies. The loan allowed them to end the season with rather small debts to pay off.

But in much of the South, the loan program was not run fairly. Reports of abuse of farm relief were common. Planters in some areas took the loan checks from their tenants, and then the planters loaned the tenants the money, giving it to them in small sums. These tenants had to pay the federal government 6 percent interest and also pay the planters from 8 to 10 percent interest—all for the same loan. Other planters took the loan money and bought seed, feed, and fertilizer at cash prices, then they sold them to the tenants at higher credit prices.

There were many other unfair practices in the farm relief program. Some planters used their tenants' names to get loans, and the tenants knew nothing about the loans. A few planters took the loan money and applied it to old debts they claimed the tenants owed, even though federal policies prohibited this. Black farm owners were not approved for loans in most black belt counties. Thus, they were forced to borrow money from local lenders at high rates of interest or sell their farms.

Similar abuses were reported in aid given to farmers by the Red Cross. Food and clothing provided by the Red Cross kept many farm families alive during the first winters of the Depression. This relief effort was run by local leaders, and this led to abuses. Blacks had almost no voice in determining which families received help. In some places, the planters refused to provide supplies for their tenants and forced them to seek relief from the Red Cross. A few cases were reported in which the planters charged their tenants for food and clothing furnished by the Red Cross.

BLACK AMERICANS BEGAN TO VOTE DEMOCRATIC

Although most black Americans were unhappy with President Hoover's policies, they were slow to leave the Republican Party. For sentimental reasons, many remained loyal to the party of Abraham Lincoln. Then, too, in many large cities, Republican bosses and their political machines controlled city governments. And black citizens often received offices and favors from them. Above all, black voters still did not trust the Democrats. At the national level, the Democratic Party was too Southern in its viewpoint. In many cities, the local Democratic Party was rather weak, and few blacks were attracted to it.

In 1932, the Democrats began trying to win black support. Robert Vann, the publisher of the Pittsburgh *Courier,* was active in the effort to win black voters away from the Republicans. He told his fellow blacks that the debt they owed to the party of Lincoln had been paid in full. He urged them to "go home and turn Lincoln's picture to the wall."

Nevertheless, most black Americans were not yet ready to forget Lincoln in 1932. They knew nothing about the Democratic candidate for President, Franklin D. Roosevelt. For all they knew, he might follow the same policies as Wilson. In addition, the Democratic candidate for Vice-President was John Nance Garner of Texas. Republicans spread the rumor that Roosevelt was a sick man, and that the Southerner Garner would soon be in the White House. In 1932, Roosevelt did not receive the support of a majority of black voters. He received only 23 percent of the black vote in Chicago, for example, and 36.7 percent in Detroit.

MORE BLACK VOTERS MOVED TOWARD THE DEMOCRATS

But, during his first term in office, President Franklin D. Roosevelt became more popular among black Americans. Although he did not speak out on many issues of special importance to them, black Americans began to hope that he would help them. Blacks waited to be shown whether or not they were included in the President's speeches about the need for justice and equality in America. Gradually, by small acts, Roosevelt convinced black people that he was concerned about them. He denounced lynching as murder and responded to the findings of a National Urban League study of economic conditions among blacks. Above all, Afro-Americans felt they were receiving sympathetic treatment from the Democratic administration. They considered the President's wife, Eleanor Roosevelt, a supporter and a special friend.

By 1936, the movement of black voters into the Democratic Party was well under way. Many black citizens attended Democratic rallies in cities across the country during the campaign of 1936. In the Presidential election, the Democrats made great gains in black support. For example, Roosevelt was supported by 49 percent of the black vote in Chicago and 63.5 percent in Detroit. This was only the beginning of the movement. Four years later, in 1940, President Roosevelt received 54 percent of the black vote in Chicago and 69.3 percent in Detroit.

THE NEW DEAL BROUGHT HOPE TO BLACK AMERICANS

In later years, Roosevelt was criticized by some historians for not speaking out about discrimination and segregation. They recognized but did not excuse his silence as due to political problems he faced. Namely, he needed white Southerners' support in order to succeed with his New Deal programs. In the 1930's, however, black people were more concerned about results than words. And black Americans had good reasons to support the New Deal. Roosevelt made it possible for significant changes to take place in America's racial situation.

Blacks soon realized that they had friends in the Roosevelt administration. Harold Ickes was one of these. Ickes, who had been president of the Chicago branch of the NAACP, was Roosevelt's Secretary of the Interior. The Secretary of the Interior took immediate steps to end discrimination in his department. He also suggested to the President in 1933 that someone be brought into the administration to look after the special interests of black Americans. Roosevelt asked Ickes to see that this was done. Ickes asked a white Georgian, Clark Foreman, to take on this responsibility. Foreman employed as his assistant a brilliant young black man, Robert C. Weaver. Foreman and Weaver did a good job of making the government officials who ran the New Deal programs more aware of the special problems of Afro-Americans. Other New Dealers who showed special concern for black needs included Daniel Roper, Secretary of Commerce; Harry L. Hopkins, administrator of the federal relief program; and Aubrey Williams, an assistant to Hopkins.

But Eleanor Roosevelt, the President's wife, became the person in the New Deal most admired by black Americans. Mrs. Roosevelt showed by word and deed that she believed in equality for all. She invited mixed groups of blacks and whites to the White House. She participated in interracial meetings and she spoke out for black causes. Mrs. Roosevelt saw to it that the President talked with black leaders when they wished to make personal appeals to him on important questions. In 1939, Mrs. Roosevelt earned the lasting affection of black Americans for her support of the talented singer Marian Anderson. The Daughters of the American Revolution refused to allow Marian Anderson to perform in Constitution Hall, a building in Washington, D.C., which they owned. Mrs. Roosevelt then helped to arrange an Easter morning concert by Marian Anderson at the Lincoln Memorial. She also withdrew as a member of the DAR.

EMPLOYMENT OF BLACKS IN GOVERNMENT INCREASED

Black citizens' support of the New Deal was based on more than a few friendly acts by New Dealers. During the 1930's, blacks made significant gains in participation in government and in federal employment. A number of talented men and women were brought into the government as advisers on racial matters. They made up what became known as the "black Cabinet." One of these "Cabinet" members was William H. Hastie, who served in the Interior Department. In 1937, Roosevelt appointed Hastie a federal judge in the Virgin Islands, and Hastie later became governor of the Virgin Islands. Other members of this group who participated in the federal government's affairs included Eugene K. Jones in the Department of Commerce, Mary McLeod Bethune with the National Youth Administration, Ira DeA. Reid with the Social Security Board, Lawrence A. Oxley in the Department of Labor, and Ambrose Caliver in the Office of Education.

Employment opportunities in the federal government increased on all levels. Black workers entered types of jobs that had never before been open to them. Professionally trained architects, lawyers, librarians, engineers, and others were employed. Lower-level white-collar jobs for stenographers, clerks, and secretaries also became available. The number of such jobs was not as great as black Americans wanted, but the policy of keeping blacks out of government jobs had ended.

By 1938, 82,000 black Americans had federal civil service jobs, or 9.8 percent of the total of all federal jobs. Most of the jobs were outside Washington as postal clerks, mail carriers, laborers, and janitors in federal office buildings and post offices throughout the country. And the great majority of the jobs in Washington, D.C., were also lower-level positions. This change in federal employment did not result in more jobs in the South, however. The increase in black employment came from more jobs in Washington.

NEW DEAL AGENCIES HELPED BLACK AMERICANS

The most important feature of the New Deal was the various agencies it set up to deal with the Depression. These federal agencies provided food, shelter, and jobs for Americans in need. Blacks were in great need of all of these. Among the agencies of particular importance to black Americans were the Federal Emergency Relief Administration (FERA), the National Recovery Administration (NRA), the Works Progress Administration (WPA), the Agricultural Adjustment Administration (AAA), the Public Works Administration (PWA), the Tennessee Valley Authority (TVA), the National Youth Administration (NYA), the Civilian Conservation Corps (CCC), and the Farm Security Administration (FSA).

Black Americans strongly supported President Franklin D. Roosevelt. This group of well-known officials who had important roles in the government during the New Deal was known as the "Black Cabinet."

Blacks received great help from these federal relief programs. Because they made up such a high percentage of the unemployed, blacks received a much larger share of direct relief than whites. Blacks did not face much discrimination in receiving food allowances, clothing, or other direct relief help, although blacks were usually kept out of the skilled jobs when work relief was provided. The housing programs also raised the standard of black life. Low-rent public housing was built to provide many families with decent homes for the first time.

A good deal of discrimination had to be overcome in several federal programs, however. The administrators of the NRA were involved in drawing up codes for American industries. These codes fixed the wages to be paid, the hours of work, prices of goods, and similar matters. When the code was being written, an attempt was made to allow employers to pay lower wages to black workers than to white workers. Black groups opposed this effort, and the final code required equal pay for all. Although many black workers were replaced with white workers as a result, a vital blow had been struck at the practice of lower wages for blacks.

The federal farm programs also led to unfair practices. The AAA program paid farmers to reduce the amount of crops they grew. As a result, the size of the cotton and tobacco crops were greatly reduced. The planters were supposed to pass on the payment they received for reducing their crops to their tenants when the tenants had helped cut back the amount grown. But many planters did not share this payment with their tenants. Others forced their tenants off the farm, and these tenants joined the jobless in the cities. The Farm Security Administration (FSA) had a better record, although it too failed to achieve all that was needed. This program bought poor land from small farmers in order to provide them with money to buy better land. Loans were made to allow poor farmers to develop their farms. Some 50,000 black farm families benefited from this program between 1937 and 1940.

Several New Deal programs were aimed at youth. Thousands of young people were able to stay in school by working in jobs under the National Youth Administration. This NYA work-study program paid students enough to buy the things they needed to remain in school. Black youth also entered Civilian Conservation Corps camps. There they worked and learned. These camps generally were segregated. And the number of black youths in these camps was based on the percentage of blacks in the total population. But on the whole, the youth programs had good records for fair treatment of black youth.

Other New Deal programs helped to raise the educational level of blacks. Many agencies had elementary instruction as a feature of their work. Adult education projects were started under the WPA, along with other projects involving professionally trained people and artists. The Public Works Administration (PWA) paid 55 percent of the cost of building new schools if the states and communities paid the balance. This program led to better school buildings in many Southern states, although most of these areas spent the greater part of this money on schools for white children.

DISCRIMINATION AND UNEMPLOYMENT CONTINUED

In spite of the gains they made, blacks remained concerned about discrimination in New Deal programs. This was especially true in the South, where local laws and customs were against equal treatment of blacks. Those in charge of New Deal programs often accepted this situation. Many New Deal projects were directed by local people who were particularly unfair in their treatment of blacks. In one city where relief money was divided according to population percentages, 15,000 black families received 45 percent of the funds and 5,000 white families received 55 percent. Blacks were kept out of skilled jobs, and they were paid less than the wages paid whites on similar projects. On projects in the North, blacks often were given only unskilled jobs.

Some rather strange things happened on some of these projects. Cities used federal funds to pave only those streets on which whites lived. Black schools were built without advice from black citizens. And planters and employers made deals with New Deal officials to keep black wage rates down.

The key to improving conditions among blacks was jobs. Blacks realized that much of the progress they had made had been wiped out by the Depression. During these years, they lost nearly 400,000 jobs in manufacturing, mining, and similar occupations. They lost another 100,000 jobs in the wholesale and retail trades. Also, the increasing use of machinery and the decline in cotton growing caused many farm workers to lose their jobs. In 1937, the percentage of black men and women in the North still unemployed was more than double that of white workers. The unemployment rate for blacks was nearly 39 percent and for whites 18 percent.

BLACK ORGANIZATIONS BEGAN CHANGES

The Depression caused black organizations to make important changes in their outlook. Both the National Urban League and the NAACP now placed their major emphasis on jobs. Both organizations also began working more closely with the masses of blacks. They realized the value of working together and of working through other organizations and groups. Younger black leaders, such as Ralph J. Bunche, were critical of the stress these groups had placed on strengthening black business and on noneconomic issues. They insisted that economic issues were basic to the black struggle.

Some still held to the view that blacks should develop separate businesses. W. E. B. Du Bois came out in favor of a separate black economy in 1934. But he believed it was only a temporary solution. Du Bois reasoned that segregation was a fact of life that blacks would have to live with for some time. For this reason, he favored building strong institutions in the black community. This view brought Du Bois into a serious conflict with the NAACP, and he was forced to give up his position with that organization.

The National Urban League began to focus its efforts in the local community to help both the unemployed and those who had jobs. Black professional and businessmen were organized into emergency advisory councils. The members of these councils appeared before relief groups to see that lower-class blacks received fair treatment. They also informed those who needed help of their rights under the new federal programs.

An important League program was the organization of Workers Councils. This was an attempt to prepare black workers to act in their own interest. Lester B. Granger, who had headed the League branch in Los Angeles, took charge of this program. Workers Councils were organized in most large American cities. Black workers were taught methods of union organizing and the value of belonging to unions. The councils hoped that these workers would join the trade union movements. This happened in a number of cities, but the Urban League did not actually promote union membership. Employers who supported the League did not favor this program. In one or two cities, League officials became involved in getting black workers into trade unions. But these efforts were not common.

The main attempt to bring black organizations together was through the National Negro Congress. In 1933, the NAACP brought together about twenty black and interracial organizations to form the Joint Committee on National Recovery. This group worked to promote black interests in the programs of the New Deal agencies. In 1935, the Joint Committee held a conference at Howard University, which began plans for the National Negro Congress. Although the NAACP did not favor this plan, the Congress was organized at a meeting in Chicago in 1936.

Young leaders, who felt that the older organizations were too conservative, were in the forefront of the movement. However, most black leaders endorsed the movement. Fraternal groups and other kinds of organizations joined the Congress. A. Philip Randolph became the first president. The NAACP did not support the Congress, because Communists were active in it. During the first year, the Communists remained in the background. Then, in 1939, they began attacking the non-Communist leaders. Randolph, Ralph Bunche, and other prominent blacks withdrew their support, and the National Negro Congress became a Communist-front group.

The Communists worked hard during the Depression to bring blacks into the American Communist Party. Their efforts to win black support received great publicity because of the Scottsboro Case. This case involved nine black youths charged with assaulting two white girls on a train in Alabama in 1931. The NAACP defended the boys but lost the case. The Communists then took over the court appeals of the case and carried on a worldwide effort to win support for the Scottsboro boys. The Communists collected large sums of money for the case, but they, too, lost the case on appeal.

By 1935, the American Communist Party's policy was to work with and influence liberal organizations. The NAACP and the National Urban League understood that the purpose of this attempt was to enable the Communists to control these organizations. As a result, these key black groups refused to work with the Communists. A few black Americans joined the Communist Party during the Depression, but the Communists were no more successful during the 1930's than they had been during the 1920's.

BLACKS WORKED TO OPEN UNIONS

The New Deal paved the way for more black participation in unions. The labor movement benefited from Section 7a of the National Industrial Recovery Act and from the Wagner Act. These laws gave workers the right to strike and to choose unions to represent them. Many tactics employers had used to weaken or destroy unions were now made illegal. The number of workers in unions increased greatly after the Congress of Industrial Organizations (CIO) was organized in 1935. Most of the CIO unions accepted black workers on an equal basis. By

1940, there were about 210,000 black members in the CIO.

The AFL began to change during the 1930's. Now it had to compete with the CIO for members, and the black workers in many industries were important in deciding which union would organize their factory. And within the AFL, A. Philip Randolph waged a constant struggle to end discrimination. His union, the Brotherhood of Sleeping Car Porters, was accepted as a full member of the AFL, and it was also recognized by the Pullman Company as the bargaining agent for all train porters.

BOYCOTTS WERE USED IN BLACK COMMUNITIES

The boycott became one of the favorite weapons used by black groups in search of jobs. Black boycotters, or pickets, urged customers not to buy in stores that discriminated against blacks. Boycotts soon became common in the black communities of Chicago, New York City, Washington, Richmond, and other cities. Without any national coordination, this movement spread across the country.

The use of boycotts to force white businesses in black communities to hire black workers began in Chicago, when publishers of the *Whip* took over the boycott campaign there in 1930. With the support of ministers and young people, more jobs were opened to black workers. In New York City, the Reverend John H. Johnson, vicar of St. Martin's Protestant Episcopal Chapel, was selected to head the movement in Harlem. A colorful figure dressed in cape, boots, and turban, who called himself Sufi Abdul Hamid, was involved in the movement both in Chicago and Harlem. The bitter struggle in Harlem gave rise to a riot in 1935. After the riot, new leaders came into the boycott movement. Among them was Adam Clayton Powell, Jr.

The boycott leadership varied from city to city. The NAACP organized a boycott of chain stores in Richmond, Virginia. In Washington, D.C., young black intellectuals, including William H. Hastie and John A. Davis, organized the New Negro Alliance. This organization won an important case before the Supreme Court, which ruled that citizens had a right to picket to end racial discrimination.

MANY CHANGES TOOK PLACE DURING THE THIRTIES

Under the shock of the Depression, some very basic changes in American society began to take place during the 1930's. Blacks became aware of their political strength in Northern cities and began to demand power and influence in return for their support. Interracial movements became more common, even in the South. Labor unions now were able to set up integrated locals in many Southern states. Here and there, the wall of Jim Crow began to crack. Black athletes became starring players on major college sports teams; but professional sports still refused to accept blacks.

New heroes also helped to relieve the bleakness of black lives somewhat during the Depression years by giving black Americans an opportunity to share in their accomplishments. At the Berlin Olympics in 1936, Jesse Owens won gold medals in several track events and set records in three events. Ralph Metcalfe, Archie Williams, and John Woodruff also won Olympic medals at Berlin. Joe Louis, the "Brown Bomber," was probably the most exciting athlete of the period. Louis became heavyweight boxing champion of the world in 1937, and kept his title for the next twelve years—longer than any other fighter had ever done. All blacks took pride in his accomplishments.

Chapter 17

Serving in the Armed Forces

The mood of black Americans was very different when World War II began than it had been during World War I. Blacks hated Hitler's Germany because it preached the belief in racial superiority. At the same time, they were also concerned about the racial situation in the United States. While most black Americans were willing to fight for their country, they were not willing to accept discrimination without protest. Black leaders did not ask black Americans to "close ranks" or to forget their own grievances. Instead, they urged blacks to demand equal treatment in the armed forces, and not just hope that racial progress would be achieved after the war.

SEGREGATION CONTINUED IN THE ARMY

The United States began preparing its defenses when war broke out in Europe in 1939. When a new draft law was debated in 1940, black Americans were concerned about how black soldiers would be treated in the armed forces. In 1940, only a few blacks were in the armed forces

—13,200 in the army and 4,000 in the navy. The Pittsburgh *Courier,* a leading black newspaper, set up the Committee on Participation of Negroes in the War to promote full involvement of blacks in the war effort. The committee obtained the help of Representative Hamilton Fish, a New York Republican. In Congress, Fish presented an amendment to the Selective Service Act banning discrimination in the drafting and training of soldiers. President Roosevelt signed the draft law on September 14, 1940. The committee hoped that the Fish amendment would end segregation in the armed services. Unfortunately, it failed to do so.

American military leaders were slow to accept change. They tried to keep the old patterns of segregation and discrimination. The Roosevelt administration wanted and needed black political support, however, and it was willing to listen to black demands. In addition, the government knew that black protest during this time of crisis would harm the United States and block its efforts to appeal to nonwhite peoples of the world for support. As a result, slow but important changes were made in the racial policies of the military services.

On September 27, 1940, three black leaders called on President Roosevelt. They were A. Philip Randolph of the Brotherhood of Sleeping Car Porters, Walter White of the NAACP, and T. Arnold Hill of the National Urban League. They urged Roosevelt to end segregation in the armed forces. Roosevelt told them that he would do what he could. When he talked to his civilian and military advisers, however, they sent him a memo saying that segregation had to be maintained. They said that segregation had worked in the past, and if it were ended now the nation's defense preparations would be hurt.

In October, the War Department explained its policies toward blacks in the army. The number of blacks accepted by the army was to be based on their percentage in the population, that is, about 10 percent. Black soldiers were to be placed in separate units. Only black medical officers and chaplains were to be assigned to black units that already had white officers. Black reaction to these policies was angry protest. And the Republican Party used the situation to try to win black votes during the Presidential election in November, 1940.

President Roosevelt took several actions to try to keep black political support. On October 25, 1940, Colonel Benjamin O. Davis was promoted to Brigadier General, at Roosevelt's personal request. Davis became the first black officer to hold this rank. At the same time, William H. Hastie was made Civilian Aide to the Secretary of War. Colonel Campbell Johnson was appointed an Executive Assistant to the Director of Selective Service. Several black colleges received ROTC units, or officer training units. These actions pleased black Americans, but they realized that the actions were taken partly for political reasons. They still wanted some basic changes in racial policies in the military services.

SOME BLACK GAINS WERE MADE

Soon after the Japanese attack at Pearl Harbor on December 7, 1941, brought the United States into World War II, a group of black editors made an appeal for integration in the military service. They suggested that a volunteer unit be formed that would accept men without regard to race, color, or religion. The government was not yet willing to agree to such a change. On the other hand, there was little discrimination in the operation of the draft law. Blacks played major roles in the Selective Service System that carried out the law. They were employed in clerical and white-collar jobs. They served on the various boards related to the draft, including many local draft boards. There were 1,800 black members of local draft boards by the summer of 1942.

The greatest change came in the training of officers. The need for black officers to lead the thousands of Afro-Americans entering the army caused a major change in policy. The army decided that black officers would be trained in the same schools and classes with white trainees. At Fort Benning, Georgia, and other officer training schools, blacks and whites lived, ate, and trained together. The problems that some warned would be created by integration did not develop. The new policy brought about a rapid increase in the number of black officers. Over 1,000 officers had completed their training by the end of 1942. The same practice was followed in training women as officers in the Women's Auxiliary Corps; but the women lived and ate separately.

ARMY ENLISTED MEN WERE SEGREGATED

Many problems existed in the training of enlisted men. The army maintained its policy of assigning black soldiers to separate units. Many of these units had white officers who were not happy about commanding black troops. Moreover, Northern blacks who were sent to training camps in the South deeply resented the Jim Crow practices they had to face.

Discrimination was common on military bases. Separate and inferior service clubs, theaters, and post exchanges were operated for

186

The army kept most military units segregated during World War II. But in some officer-training schools, black and white officers trained together. Black officers of the Women's Auxiliary Corps are shown here.

black soldiers. Buses into town were segregated. Some camp commanders would not allow the men to read black newspapers. Complaints about conditions caused the War Department to take action. In July, 1944, it ordered an end to discrimination in places of recreation and on buses. Nevertheless, many commanders ignored the order.

Fights between white and black soldiers were common. Black newspapers were filled with stories of black soldiers being beaten by local white police officers and white civilians. Discrimination was the cause of most of the clashes. A riot broke out in Alexandria, Louisiana, in January, 1942. The local police and state troopers shot thirty black soldiers before the riot ended. Serious disturbances also broke out at Fort Bragg, Fort Dix, and Camp Lee, following repeated attacks on black soldiers by groups of white soldiers. Over a hundred black officers were arrested at an Indiana base for trying to enter an officers club open to whites only. At a number of camps, black soldiers were arrested for refusing to do menial jobs that were assigned only to blacks.

THE NAVY SLOWLY BROKE WITH TRADITION
The navy moved faster than the other services in breaking with tradition. When the war began, blacks in the navy could serve only as messmen (cooks and kitchen helpers) in the Steward's Branch. Late in 1941, the navy stated that this policy would continue. Then, in April, 1942, Secretary of the Navy Frank Knox declared that blacks now would be accepted in all branches of the navy.

This change in navy policy came, in part, because of the heroic action of Dorie Miller at Pearl Harbor. Miller was a messman third class on the battleship *Arizona*. During the Japanese attack, Miller ran on deck during the bombing. He helped to move the ship's captain, who was badly wounded. Then he took over a machine gun he had not been trained to use and shot down at least four enemy planes. He was awarded the Navy Cross for his bravery. Miller continued to serve as a messman until he was killed in action in the Pacific in 1943.

The new policy announced by Knox was only a limited change. Although blacks were to be accepted in jobs other than messmen, they were not to serve at sea on combat ships. They were allowed to serve only on shore. Also, they were to be segregated in separate units. When this became known, black leaders began a vigorous protest. As a result, a special training camp was opened at the Great Lakes Naval Training Station in Illinois. By 1943, black sailors had been trained to do more than fifty different naval jobs.

Still, black sailors were unhappy about the limited number of jobs allowed them. Those not serving as messmen generally were assigned to handle ammunition or to load ships. Many showed their displeasure by going on hunger strikes, staging demonstrations, or failing to obey orders. In several such incidents, the men were discharged from the navy or sentenced to prison terms.

The cause of integration in the navy was helped greatly by a white officer, Lieutenant Christopher Smith Sargent, who served in the manpower policies section of the Bureau of Naval Personnel. His task was to help plan how to handle the large number of blacks entering the navy. Sargent set up a special programs unit to work on the problem. In February, 1944, the special unit was able to persuade the navy to staff two ships with black crews under white officers. Two months later, the navy commissioned twenty-two black officers.

The next step toward integration was taken in August, 1944. By then, James V. Forrestal, who was more sympathetic to integration than Knox, was Secretary of the Navy. Forrestal approved a plan to integrate the crews of twenty-five auxiliary ships. These integrated crews included as many as 10 percent blacks. The experiment worked well, and the navy began integrating the crews of all auxiliary ships. By 1945, the navy also had integrated all of its camps and schools.

Before completely ending segregation in the navy, Forrestal sent Lester Granger, Executive Secretary of the National Urban League, to study conditions. Granger visited naval bases all over the United States and in the Pacific. His report recommended ending all discrimination. On February 27, 1946, Secretary Forrestal issued an official order stating that "all restrictions governing the types of assignments for which Negro naval personnel are eligible are hereby lifted."

OTHER BRANCHES OF THE NAVY ACTED

The navy also ended discrimination in other naval branches. The Coast Guard began accepting blacks for general service in May, 1942. The Marine Corps, then a part of the navy, changed its policy, too. The Marine Corps had never allowed blacks to serve, but in June of 1942 it accepted black volunteers.

The Navy was slower in ending discrimination against black women. The WAVES, the women's naval reserve, formed in 1942, did not enlist black women until 1944. Even then, considerable pressure was required to bring this change. The Coast Guard's women reserve, the SPARS, was not opened to black women until October, 1944. The Marine Corps remained closed to black women throughout the war.

The Merchant Marine was not a part of the navy. But this civilian shipping operation was essential to winning the war. Men of many nations, including about 24,000 Afro-Americans, manned the merchant ships of the United States. These merchant seamen belonged to a labor union with a record of fair and equal treatment for all. The Merchant Marine was integrated from the beginning of the war. Four black captains commanded Liberty ships. Captain Hugh Mulzac sailed the S.S. *Booker T. Washington* across the dangerous waters of the Atlantic many times. Racial prejudice was absent, too, in the naming of ships. Twenty-two Liberty ships were named for black leaders, for seamen who had died in the merchant service, and for black colleges.

THE AIR CORPS REMAINED SEGREGATED

Before World War II, many military men believed that blacks lacked the ability to learn to fly planes. Under pressure from blacks and the White House, the army agreed in 1941 to train black pilots. But a policy of segregation was followed in the training program.

Tuskegee was selected as the place for the pilot training school. The school opened in July, 1941, with Captain Noel Parrish, a white Kentuckian, in charge of training. Parrish had faith that his students would become good pilots, and he set out to prove it. Among the first trainees to arrive was Benjamin O. Davis, Jr., a graduate of West Point. Young Davis was the son of General Davis and had been serving as an aide to his father.

The first five pilots completed their training on March 7, 1942. They were assigned to a new unit, the 99th Pursuit Squadron. By the end of 1942, forty-three pilots were in the squadron. Flight training continued, and a second black unit, the 332nd Fighter Group, was formed.

Discrimination remained a serious problem in the pilot training program. Colonel Frederick V. Kimble, the commander at Tuskegee, set up segregated living and eating facilities. This policy was protested by the men in training and by black Americans throughout the country. Conditions became so tense at Tuskegee that Kimble was forced to leave. Parrish replaced him as commander and began changing the rigid patterns of segregation. These changes helped to increase the morale of the men in training. But, even so, changes came so slowly that William H. Hastie resigned as aide to the Secretary of War in

1943. His resignation was a protest against segregation and discrimination in the Air Corps and the army.

In spite of the problems, more blacks participated in the armed services than ever before. About 1,000,000 black Americans entered the armed forces during the war. They served in branches of the service that had been closed to them before World War II. By January, 1942, over 100,000 black soldiers were serving in the army; by the fall of 1944, there were 701,678 in the army. In other branches of the service, by the fall of 1944, there were 165,000 blacks in the navy, 5,000 in the Coast Guard, and 17,000 in the Marine Corps.

BLACK AMERICANS FOUGHT IN EUROPE

A high percentage of black soldiers were sent overseas. As in World War I, a majority of the black soldiers were in the service branches of the army. They did heavy and difficult but very important construction work. They unloaded ships, carried ammunition, and transported supplies. A total of 124,514 black soldiers served in Europe in the Engineering Corps, the Transportation Corps, and similar units.

Many black combat units fought in Europe. Field artillery units, anti-aircraft battalions, tank battalions, and engineer combat battalions saw military action. The 761st Tank Battalion and the 614th Tank Destroyer Battalion were outstanding units in Europe. Blacks took part in the Allied invasion on France's Normandy coast on D-Day in June, 1944. The 969th Field Artillery Battalion was awarded a Distinguished Unit Citation for its part in the fighting at the battle of Bastogne in December, 1944.

The record of the 92nd Division, known as the "Buffalo" Division, was the subject of a good deal of controversy. The 92nd fought in the Mediterranean area. It was sent to Africa in June, 1944, and from there to Italy. The 92nd Division took part in the Allied offensive that pushed across the Arno River in September, 1944. Later in the year, the 92nd was forced out of several places it had captured, but it soon retook them. Then, in February, 1945, the division was badly beaten in the battle along the Cinquale Canal.

Truman K. Gibson, who had replaced Hastie as Civilian Aide to the Secretary of War, was sent to Italy to investigate. At a meeting with reporters, Gibson pointed out that "segregation as a policy would inevitably produce militarily unsound results." The actions of the 92nd Division during the fighting along the Cinquale Canal showed the results of the army's segregation policy. Gibson admitted what the newspapermen already knew, that some units of the 92nd Division had retreated in a "panicky fashion."

Gibson pointed out, however, that military authorities did not believe that any unit could operate efficiently when it had a large number of men of low literacy in it. Gibson explained to the reporters that a majority of the men in the 92nd Division made scores on the Army General Classification Test that placed them in the lowest literacy classes—Class IV and Class V. According to the official history of black soldiers in World War II by Ulysses Lee, in March, 1945, 75 percent of the men in the 92nd Division were in these lowest literacy classes.

Gibson also noted other effects on the 92nd Division of the Army's segregation policy. The men had received poor training in segregated camps in the United States. When the division arrived in Italy, black officers were discriminated against in promotions and in the use of officers' clubs. As a result, the morale of the officers and men was low. Then, too, since only black soldiers could be sent to the 92nd Division, no trained infantry replacements were available. When replacements were needed, untrained troops from service units had to be provided.

The newsmen reported only Gibson's criticisms of the 92nd. Some claimed that he told them that some units had "melted away" under fire, but Gibson denied that he said this. The part of Gibson's statement criticizing the division's actions received wide circulation in *The New York Times* and other leading American newspapers. These newspaper stories seemed to prove what many whites contended, namely, that blacks were unfit for combat. The black press was very critical of Gibson for allowing himself to be used by the white newspapermen to question the fitness of black soldiers. The *Chicago Defender* and several other black newspapers demanded that Gibson resign his position as Civilian Aide to the Secretary of War.

Later, two studies of the Cinquale Canal fighting were made. One was an official study by the Army War College made during the war. The other was made by a civilian after the war. The facts seemed to show that the 92nd Division was in an almost impossible military situation at Cinquale. And these same men fought well in other actions. Their courage was clearly proved by the more than 12,000 decorations men of the 92nd Division received.

Early in 1945, the army experimented with mixed units. The need for infantry replacements in Europe was great, and the army decided to accept black volunteers to serve in white units. But the black soldiers were not completely integrated into the units. They were formed into separate platoons. About 2,500 blacks saw action with the

First Army along the Rhine. The officers under whom they served found them to be good soldiers.

The two air units saw action in Europe. In April, 1943, the 99th Pursuit Squadron was sent to North Africa, where these airmen received further training from experienced combat pilots. Soon the squadron began serving as escorts to protect bombers on missions in the Mediterranean area and over Italy.

Colonel Benjamin O. Davis took command and trained the 332nd Fighter Group, which went overseas in January, 1944. It became a part of the 15th Air Force, which was bombing Germany, Austria, and Romania from bases in Italy. The 332nd was credited with destroying over 250 enemy planes. The Distinguished Flying Cross was awarded to over eighty pilots in the group. The 332nd also received the Distinguished Unit Citation for its action during a raid on Berlin on March 24, 1945.

BLACKS ALSO FOUGHT IN THE PACIFIC

Black soldiers also fought in the Pacific against the Japanese. About 200,000 black soldiers were serving in the Pacific area when the war ended in Europe in May, 1945. About 70,000 were sent to the Pacific from Europe. Many black soldiers in the Pacific were in the engineers units and other service units. They helped to build the Ledo Road, a vital military supply route that linked India and China. Those in the engineers units went ashore with the first invading troops to build airstrips and roads. Often they were under heavy enemy attack, and they had to fight to defend what they had built.

A number of black combat units engaged in action against the Japanese. The 24th Infantry helped to take the New Georgia Islands in May, 1942. The 93rd Division fought in the Solomons, the Treasury Islands, the Dutch East Indies, and the Philippines. Six other battalions of black combat troops served in the Pacific. About 12,500 blacks served in the fighting construction force known as the Seabees. They helped to build advanced bases, airstrips, and roads. Blacks in the Marine Corps also were sent to several areas in the Pacific.

Chapter 18

Black Americans on the Home Front

In January, 1942, an editorial in *The Crisis* proclaimed: "Now Is Not the Time to Be Silent. We must say all the things that cry aloud to be said—not later, but now." This editorial reflected the mood of black Americans during World War II. Black morale was low when war began in Europe in 1939. As the United States began its program of national defense, black Americans were not taken off relief rolls and given jobs in significant numbers. And segregation continued in the armed forces.

Afro-Americans became united in their determination to break down the barriers to their full participation in American life. They pledged to fight injustice at home, just as they were helping to fight it abroad. But large numbers of white Americans resisted basic changes in race relations and the caste system in the United States. All of this led to a tense racial situation, racial violence, and finally some important gains for black Americans on the home front.

BLACKS WERE NOT HIRED IN DEFENSE INDUSTRIES
The Great Depression ended for most white Americans in 1940. America's industries began expanding to meet the increased demand for products as the nation prepared its defenses. The drafting of men into the armed forces began to reduce the labor supply. The rapid industrial expansion brought a shortage of workers and caused wages to rise. Government joined industry in urging workers to take jobs in defense industries. Programs were started to train skilled workers. And still many worried that defense preparations would be slowed down by a shortage of workers.

At the very same time, black Americans continued to suffer economic hardships. The signs at factory gates reading "No Help Wanted" were replaced by signs saying "Help Wanted, White." In Illinois, for example, 95 out of 146 plants surveyed reported that they did not hire black workers. In some industries, all businesses followed white-only employment policies. This was especially true in the aircraft industry. One airplane company spokesman said that sometime in the future it probably would have "some jobs as janitors for Negroes." Between January and March, 1941, the aircraft industry hired 8,769 skilled and semi-skilled workers. Only thirteen of these jobs went to nonwhite workers. In the metal trades, 60,000 workers were hired, of whom only 500 were nonwhite.

Employers gave a number of reasons for their failure to hire more black workers. In some cases, the employers were prejudiced against blacks. Others said that they were afraid that black workers would be resented by white workers. Organized labor also had a role in job discrimination. Many of the AFL craft unions refused to accept black workers as members. In some trades, a worker had to be a union member to obtain a job.

The federal government made some efforts to encourage the use of black workers. The National Defense Advisory Commission (NDAC) was set up to oversee defense preparations. Robert C. Weaver, who served in the NDAC, was given the task of trying to get black workers hired in defense industries. The NDAC criticized industries with defense contracts for not hiring black workers, but the industries ignored these complaints and did nothing. The AFL and the CIO promised the Labor Division of NDAC to help end discrimination in defense industries. But little change resulted from this promise. And the NDAC had no power to enforce its orders against discrimination.

The Office of Production Management (OPM) took the place of

the NDAC in 1941. The OPM had two sections concerned with the hiring of workers from minority groups. The Labor Division of OPM contained branches on Negro Employment and Training and on Minority Groups. OPM called upon businesses and industries with defense contracts to make full use of black workers. A few opened more jobs to minority workers, but most employers ignored the appeal.

Discrimination was also practiced in training programs sponsored by the federal government. Although the National Defense Training Act of 1940 had a no-discrimination provision in it, blacks had trouble getting into the training program. They were not admitted to training programs in most Southern states. In the North, limited numbers received training. Those who received training still had trouble finding jobs. In 1941, the United States Employment Service reported that only one out of fifty black workers who completed training was able to find a job.

BLACK MORALE WAS LOW

The job situation, racial insults, and discrimination in the military services had a serious effect on black America's morale. Blacks were not excited by patriotic speeches and propaganda about the aims of the war. They reacted to statements about defending democracy in Europe and aiding peoples ruled by dictators with a feeling of frustration. Many remembered World War I and America's promise then to "make the world safe for democracy." Black hopes for a better life, raised by such promises, had ended when racism became even more oppressive after the war. Now black Americans again were being asked to join another struggle for freedom and democracy.

The great majority of Afro-Americans were willing to join in this struggle, but they were not willing to stop their fight for justice at home. They talked about winning a victory against injustice both abroad and at home. The black press reflected the mixed feelings of some Afro-Americans. George Schuyler of the Pittsburgh *Courier* stated that he could see little difference "between the 'democracies' and the 'dictatorships.' There is no difference between British rule in Africa and German rule in Austria."

The most common complaint was the absence of democracy at home for black Americans. *The Crisis* said that the "hysterical cries of the preachers of democracy in Europe leave us cold. We want democracy in Alabama and Arkansas, in Mississippi and Michigan, in the District of Columbia—*in the Senate of the United States.*" All of the leading black newspapers repeated this message over and over. Whites accused the newspapers of creating discontent among blacks. Some government officials wanted to charge some of these editors with disloyalty. Efforts also were made to keep some black editors from getting paper on which to print their newspapers. President Roosevelt put a stop to both of these moves.

What many white Americans did not understand was that the black press reflected the mood of the masses of black Americans. Discontent was widespread. This time it was not just black leaders and the middle class that were aroused. The lower classes were angry over job discrimination, segregation in the army, and acts of violence against black civilians and against men in uniform. A few refused to be drafted, declaring that they would not fight to defend a Jim Crow system. Some even joined pro-Japanese organizations that urged the unity of all nonwhite peoples.

But most black Americans supported their country while carrying on a militant fight to end racial discrimination. National and local groups put pressure on the federal government. In 1940, the Committee for Participation of Negroes in the National Defense called upon local blacks to make their voices heard. Over 5,000 people gathered in Kansas City to protest the hiring policy of defense factories and plants in that city. Black organizations called for special days of protest in early 1941. Mass protests were held in twenty-four states on January 26, 1941. The NAACP had designated this as National Defense Day.

These efforts brought no response from the government. But the black masses were now more united in their desire for action than they had ever been. They needed a leader who could express their discontent and organize their efforts. Meetings with government officials and letters and telegrams to Washington seemed to bring few results. Many black Americans called for more effective means of protest.

THE MARCH ON WASHINGTON MOVEMENT WAS FORMED
In January, 1941, A. Philip Randolph, whose union leadership had brought victory to the Brotherhood of Sleeping Car Porters, set forth a plan. Randolph called for a nationwide mass demonstration, a March on Washington. The march was to be a protest against keeping black people out of jobs in defense industries. At first, his proposal received little response. Black editors seemed doubtful that 10,000 black Americans would participate. The leaders of the older civil rights organizations, the NAACP and the National Urban League, were also slow in

giving support. Randolph's plan sounded almost impossible to carry out. It would take careful organization of a mass effort. How could so many people be brought to Washington, D.C., and housed and fed?

But in spite of the problems, the masses were ready for action. They were willing to support a demonstration that would be dramatic enough to force white citizens to realize the problems black Americans faced. The black press came to favor Randolph's plan and gave it publicity. Parades and mass meetings were held in major cities in support of the march. Still, the white press ignored the movement. Other pressures did move the Office of Production Management to send out a letter on April 11 urging that defense industries end discrimination against black workers. But this letter did not calm black discontent.

In May, 1941, Randolph issued his "Call to Negro America to March on Washington for Jobs and Equal Participation in National Defense on July 1, 1941." Randolph said that a "thundering march on Washington, ending in a monster and huge demonstration at Lincoln's Monument will shake up white America." He felt that it would also "shake up official Washington." The main purpose of the demonstration was stated in simple terms. It was a struggle for jobs.

Excitement increased after Randolph's call was sent out. During May and June, the black press was filled with news about the March on Washington. Local branches of the March on Washington Movement (MOWM) were formed throughout the country. The black newspapers began increasing their estimates of the number that would participate. One paper said that 50,000 were preparing to march; another pushed the number up to 100,000.

Black leaders were swept along in the excitement. Walter White of the NAACP was one of the first to join Randolph. Lester Granger of the National Urban League also became a part of the leadership group. The heads of several fraternal groups—Mary McLeod Bethune of the National Council of Negro Women and J. Finley Wilson of the Elks—began mobilizing members of their organizations. By the end of May, preparations were in high gear. The word was being spread through parades, posters, newspapers, and word of mouth. Plans also were being made for local marches in Chicago, Detroit, and Los Angeles a few days before the main march on Washington.

ROOSEVELT ACTED TO END JOB DISCRIMINATION

By June, 1941, the Roosevelt administration could no longer ignore the MOWM. Mayor Fiorello La Guardia of New York City was asked to look into the situation. He arranged a meeting between Randolph and White and representatives of the administration. In addition to La Guardia, Eleanor Roosevelt and Aubrey Williams of the National Youth Administration met with the MOWM leaders. The administration group asked Randolph to call off the march. He refused.

Other efforts were made to stop the march. Randolph was invited to Washington, D.C., to discuss the matter. Then, on June 15, President Roosevelt sent a public letter to the head of the Office of Production Management. The letter said that the government must see that industry opens "the doors of employment to all loyal and qualified workers regardless of race, creed, color, or national origin. But these were still only words. Nothing was said about setting up government machinery to insure that discrimination would be ended. Therefore, the preparations for the march continued with increased vigor.

Mrs. Roosevelt and Mayor La Guardia made several more attempts to get the leaders to call off the march, but the black leaders again refused to do so. The President met with them on June 18 and made a personal appeal, but even that did not change their minds. On June 24, La Guardia met with the leaders again. He showed them the draft of an executive order prohibiting discrimination in defense industries. The MOWM leaders insisted that the order also cover employment by government agencies. When this was agreed to, the leaders called off the march.

On June 25, 1941, President Roosevelt issued Executive Order 8802. The Executive Order declared that "it is the policy of the United States to encourage full participation in the national defense program by all citizens of the United States, regardless of race, creed, color, or national origin." Government departments, training programs, and defense contractors were ordered to take steps to end discrimination.

To carry out the order, the President set up a Committee on Fair Employment Practices. According to the order, the Committee was to investigate complaints and take the proper steps to correct grievances. The first Committee had four white and two black members. The members were: Mark Ethridge, publisher of the Louisville *Courier-Journal,* chairman; Daniel Sarnoff, president of the Radio Corporation of America; Philip Murray, president of the AFL; William Green, president of the CIO; Alderman Earl B. Dickerson of Chicago; and Milton P. Webster, vice-president of the Brotherhood of Sleeping Car Porters. Dickerson and Webster were the black members. Ethridge resigned as chairman in 1942 and was replaced by Malcolm S. MacLean, president of Hampton Institute.

JOB DISCRIMINATION CONTINUED ⌐

The creation of the Fair Employment Practices Committee (FEPC) marked the beginning of government concern about minority employment. The FEPC was in the Office of Production Management (OPM), but it was responsible to the President. Wherever the FEPC found discrimination, it recommended that the President take action. But the FEPC was not a strong agency. Its members served on a part-time, volunteer basis. The Committee lacked adequate funds to do an effective job. Its staff was too small to investigate the many complaints the FEPC received. Thus, it had to depend on the staff of the OPM to do some of its work.

Small changes and some progress did take place. The FEPC held hearings in Los Angeles, Chicago, New York, and Birmingham. A number of defense plants began to hire black workers. Some employed only a few "token" blacks in order to show that they were not practicing discrimination. In the federal government, a few departments began employing blacks for the first time.

Discrimination continued to be widespread after Executive Order 8802 was issued. The United States Employment Service made a study of the problem in 1942. Over half of the industries surveyed reported that they had no black workers and did not intend to hire any. Less than 25 percent of these industries hired workers without discrimination. Such studies showed that thousands of jobs remained closed to black Americans, even though there was a shortage of labor. Out of 282,245 job openings reported, 144,538 jobs were not open to black workers.

At the same time, the growing need for labor was forcing employers to employ minority group workers. But black workers were usually hired for menial jobs. Those who were qualified to do skilled work were employed as handymen, janitors, and porters. So, although conditions improved somewhat, blacks remained frustrated, bitter, and angry.

After the Japanese attack on Pearl Harbor in December, 1941, black leaders were reluctant to carry out the March on Washington. Lester Granger and Walter White withdrew their active support of the MOWM. Randolph carried on alone for a time. Large mass meetings were held at Madison Square Garden in New York City, and in Chicago. Others were scheduled for St. Louis and Washington. However, these activities did not lead to a stronger FEPC or to the ending of segregation in the armed forces. And as more jobs opened, it became harder to rally the masses. Randolph finally turned his attention to a campaign for a permanent FEPC. And the NAACP continued to fight for black equality by taking cases into the courts.

A NEW BLACK MIGRATION BEGAN

As the barriers to employment began to weaken in mid-1942, blacks began to move in search of better jobs. As during earlier migrations, many also moved in search of better social and political conditions. A new wave of migrants entered Chicago. They sought housing in the overcrowded South Side ghetto. As others came, black families spread into neighboring white areas. By 1944, about 277,000 blacks lived in Chicago, an estimated 70,000 of them arriving between 1940 and 1944.

In other cities, industries also attracted black workers. They went to Detroit, where jobs began to open in the automotive industry. The black population of Detroit jumped from 149,199 in 1940 to almost 250,000 in 1944. Migration also increased the black population of Philadelphia and the Camden, New Jersey, area.

Southern blacks also looked toward a new "Promised Land" during World War II. Many began to move to the West. Large numbers moved to California from Arkansas, Louisiana, Oklahoma, and Texas. By 1944, over 40,000 had moved to San Francisco alone. They took over the rundown houses in "Little Tokyo," left vacant when the Japanese-Americans were forced to leave. In smaller numbers, blacks also went to Oregon and Washington to work in the shipbuilding industry. An estimated 250,000 black Americans settled on the West Coast during the war.

No accurate count was made of the number of people who moved, but several estimates were made. The total white and black migration during the war years involved about 9,000,000 Americans. The number of blacks who changed homes was believed to be over 1,000,000. In 1947, the United States Census found that 22 percent of the nonwhite population had moved to a different county between 1940 and 1947. This report placed the number of nonwhite migrants between 1940 and 1947 at 3,156,000. Therefore, the estimate of 1,000,000 black migrants during the war may be far too small.

HOUSING WAS A CAUSE OF RACIAL TENSION

World War II brought a great increase in racial tension in the United States. Blacks became more militant and were determined to continue their struggle for equality. On the other hand, white people were determined to resist black advancement. Most white Americans did not understand the new mood of black Americans. At the beginning of the war, Southern spokesmen said that blacks had gained too much during World War I and had to be "kept in their place" this time.

A poll taken in 1942 showed there was little difference in white attitudes in the North and South. Most Northerners believed that there should be separate schools, separate eating places, and separate neighborhoods. Whites throughout the country believed that blacks were happy with things as they were. The war, white Americans felt, would bring no change in the treatment of blacks. In any case, those polled said that blacks, not whites, were responsible for inequality. They believed that blacks in America received as much as they deserved.

The strong white resistance to change had several effects. It was an important reason why the federal government did not do more to end discrimination. Yet white attitudes caused black bitterness and frustration to increase. These conditions made violence almost unavoidable.

Housing was a major cause of racial friction. The large migration to industrial cities helped cause a great shortage of housing. Because materials and labor were needed for the war effort, few new houses and apartments were being built. There was a great demand for all available housing. The federal government decided it had to provide shelter for war workers.

The plans for housing war workers were made before blacks became a significant part of the labor force in war production plants. Many problems arose in trying to provide suitable housing for black workers. Local agencies and neighborhoods often opposed government efforts to build homes outside existing black areas. Even temporary homes were opposed because whites feared that blacks might remain in the new areas after the war. The use of restrictive covenants to keep black Americans and other ethnic groups out of certain neighborhoods increased.

The housing situation differed somewhat from place to place. In the San Francisco area, property owners' groups used restrictive covenants against blacks and Chinese; but the government housing constructed at Marin City, near San Francisco, was rented on a nonsegregated basis. Restrictive covenants were widely used in Chicago. And serious incidents took place when blacks in the South tried to move into temporary housing outside the Black Belt.

The situation in Detroit was among the worst in the nation. Detroit's black ghetto, known as Paradise Valley, was greatly overcrowded, and housing there was very bad. A new housing project for war workers, named for the great black abolitionist Sojourner Truth, was completed in 1942. The new project was located outside Paradise Valley, and white groups were opposed to blacks living there. The housing authorities gave in to white pressures and announced that the name of the project would be changed and only whites would live there. The NAACP and many other groups protested this policy. Finally, the project's name was restored, and some of the units were opened to blacks.

The first black families who moved into the Sojourner Truth project were greeted by a white mob. Armed with rocks, sticks, and other weapons, the mob tried to drive the blacks out. When the police arrived, they did not try to break up the mob. Rather, they stopped blacks who tried to enter the area and searched them. Over a hundred blacks, but only about a half dozen whites, were arrested. The conflict continued for more than a month. Finally, on April 9, 1942, sixteen black families were escorted into the project by a force of local and state police. Racial tension continued to grow in Detroit.

RACIAL VIOLENCE BROKE OUT IN SEVERAL CITIES

Racial hostility broke into violence in several cities. In Los Angeles, the newspapers and some local officials helped to create hatred of Mexican-Americans. The press featured story after story accusing Mexican-Americans of being responsible for most of the crime in the city. The term "zoot suiter" was used to refer to Mexican youth, even though many other young Americans wore zoot suits during this period. (Zoot suits had long coats with wide, padded shoulders, and pants that were large at the knees and small, or pegged, at the bottom.)

The so-called "zoot suit riot" broke out in Los Angeles on the night of June 3, 1943. Mobs attacked a group of Mexican youths who had just left a meeting at a police station. Attacks continued during the nights of June 4, 5, and 6. On June 7, a mob of about a thousand soldiers and sailors set out to find zoot suiters. The mob attacked every Mexican and black youth they met. They wandered through the Mexican area and into the edges of the black areas, seeking victims. Violence spread to Pasadena, Long Beach, and San Diego. Mexican-Americans and black Americans were very bitter and angry at the police for being unable or unwilling to stop the mob attacks. When the violence finally ended, nothing was done to try to improve conditions or to prevent future riots.

THE DETROIT RIOT WAS THE MOST SERIOUS

The most destructive riot during World War II broke out in Detroit. Tensions had been building there for years. Blacks were bitter and frustrated over the housing situation. Jobs also were a major source of tension. White preachers of race hatred, such as Gerald L. K. Smith and Father Charles Coughlin, aroused the prejudices of the large number of Southern whites who had moved to Detroit to work. A number of strikes broke out in automobile plants over racial questions. White workers walked off the job at several plants when black workers were hired or promoted.

The dammed-up hatred broke into violence on June 20, 1943. That Sunday, serious trouble began at Belle Isle, a city-owned recreation park. Rumors began to spread wildly through the city. Whites were told a white woman had been assaulted on Belle Isle. A rumor spread among blacks that white sailors had thrown a black woman and her baby in the lake at Belle Isle.

White and black mobs quickly gathered and went into action. Whites roamed the streets destroying automobiles and beating blacks. Blacks attacked any whites they found in the black community. Later, blacks looted the stores along the main streets of the black area. White gangs gathered and dragged blacks from buses and streetcars. Many war workers, who were not aware of the trouble, were attacked while on their way home from work.

The police drove through the black area shooting those found in looted stores. A number of blacks, whom the police said were running away from stores, were shot in the back. Blacks who were watching the looting were sometimes clubbed by the police. Charges were made that the police held blacks while members of mobs beat them. In any case, the police did little to stop the white mobs.

On Monday evening, the mayor of Detroit admitted that the city police could not restore order. By that time, rioting had spread to 75 percent of the city. All public transportation had stopped, and the fire department was unable to control the fires. The hospitals were becoming overcrowded with the injured. Finally, the mayor asked for federal help. The following morning 6,000 federal troops entered the city. By that time, 34 people were dead and over 700 injured. Property losses were over $2 million. The war effort suffered greatly, too, for a hundred million man-hours had been lost in local war plants. Tensions remained high in Detroit, and the danger of renewed violence was great.

A short time after the trouble in Detroit, violence erupted in

The Detroit riot of 1943 was the worst wartime riot. White and black mobs attacked many innocent people, killing 34 persons and injuring more than 700 others.

Harlem. Even though New York City had a liberal, enlightened mayor, the people of Harlem shared the bitterness and frustrations of blacks in other cities. They had long protested against unemployment, bad housing, police brutality, the mistreatment of black soldiers, and many other problems blacks faced. Their anger burst into violence on Sunday night, August 1. A black soldier tried to defend a woman having trouble with a policeman at a Harlem hotel. A struggle took place, and the soldier reportedly took the policeman's night stick and struck him with it. The policeman drew his gun and shot the soldier, wounding him in the shoulder.

Word spread through Harlem that the police had killed a black soldier. The community rose in blind fury to strike back. They did not attack whites. Rather, they struck at white property, the symbol of their oppression. Blacks roamed up and down the main business street of Harlem breaking store windows. Later, poor blacks rushed in to loot the stores. Describing the scene, Walter White, of the NAACP, said that looters "passed like a cloud of locusts over the stores of Harlem."

The situation in New York City was handled far differently than that in Detroit. In New York City, the mayor, the police commissioner, and black leaders rushed to the riot scene. The mayor talked with black leaders before taking action. Black and white military policemen were used to work together to round up military personnel. Efforts were made to inform the people of Harlem that the black soldier had not been killed. Trucks with loudspeakers drove through Harlem to urge people to return to their homes. The police were given careful instructions on how to act before they were sent into the area. Still, the violence of this night, August 1, 1943, left 5 blacks dead, 500 injured, and about $5 million property damage.

BLACKS MADE GAINS IN EMPLOYMENT

In spite of the problems, black Americans made some solid gains in employment during World War II. Robert C. Weaver pointed out that blacks "secured more jobs at better wages and in more diversified occupational and industrial patterns than ever before." This progress fell far short of the complete integration of blacks in American industry. Yet, the gains made were significant. In the North, black chemists and engineers were accepted. Such business firms as Western Electric in New Jersey, General Electric in New York, Lockheed in California, and International Harvester in Illinois began fair employment policies early in the war period.

The Fair Employment Practices Committee (FEPC) contributed to black progress in jobs. The Committee's efforts helped to increase employment of blacks in clerical and professional jobs in the government. Many business firms changed their policies because of FEPC pressure. The Committee reported that it settled almost 5,000 cases involving discrimination. Even so, employers who were determined not to change ignored the Committee.

The labor shortage also played a major role in moving blacks into better jobs. The United States enjoyed full employment during most of the war. Many employers who may not have wanted to hire black workers had no choice. This situation also gave black workers the opportunity to obtain better jobs at higher pay. Even in the South, better jobs opened in industry. In some Southern areas work groups were integrated. This was especially true in shipbuilding firms in Georgia, Louisiana, and Virginia. And as jobs opened, the unions became more open. The CIO was particularly active in recruiting black workers. As union members, black workers had more security in their jobs. Between 1940 and 1944, the percentage of black males in skilled jobs increased from 4.4 to 7.3 percent of all skilled workers. In semi-skilled jobs, the percentage increased from 12 to 22.4 percent of the total.

UNIT SIX

THE POSTWAR YEARS, 1945 TO THE 1970's

Chapter 19

The Truman and Eisenhower Years

The period following World War II has been called a "second Reconstruction." During the years between 1945 and 1960, the federal government, for the first time since Reconstruction, became actively involved in protecting the rights of black Americans. The Supreme Court, the President, and finally Congress helped to bring significant progress toward full citizenship for Afro-Americans. Advances were made in politics, education, employment, housing, and other social and cultural areas.

During these postwar years, civil rights became one of the most significant issues in American life. A number of things helped to bring this about. By this time, black voters had become an important force, particularly in national elections. In addition, black Americans maintained the militant spirit they had displayed during the war and were determined to break down all barriers to full citizenship. Now the leading nation of the non-Communist world, the United States could no longer ignore the racial situation within its own borders. As former European colonies in Asia and Africa became independent nations after 1945, race relations in the United States became a matter of worldwide importance.

HARRY TRUMAN BECAME PRESIDENT

Shortly before World War II ended, the burden of the Presidency fell on Vice-President Harry Truman. On April 12, 1945, Franklin D. Roosevelt died at his cottage in Warm Springs, Georgia, where he had gone for a rest. The nation was shocked, and black Americans mourned the leader they had come to feel was their true friend. The sadness of black Americans was deepened by their uncertainty about the racial views of the new President.

Black delegates to the National Democratic Convention in 1944 had supported Henry A. Wallace for Vice-President. The dropping of Wallace and the selection of Truman as Roosevelt's running mate was viewed by many as a sellout to Southern racists. During the campaign, Republicans spread the rumor that Truman had been a member of the Ku Klux Klan. Truman assured black voters that he had "a record of fair play toward my Negro fellow-citizens that will stand examination." And investigations showed that he had considerable support among the black citizens of his home county in Missouri. Still, most black Americans agreed with the Pittsburgh *Courier* that Truman still needed "to demonstrate on a national scale his full position on the Negro question."

PRESIDENT TRUMAN MOVED SLOWLY ON CIVIL RIGHTS

When he became President, Truman knew that blacks and other liberal New Deal supporters feared that he would turn away from the reform policies of President Roosevelt. He was also aware of the importance of the black vote to the Democratic Party. Thus, the new President realized that he had to reassure black citizens and prove to them that he was not against civil rights. Truman invited black spokesmen to look into his record. In fact, he had been a strong advocate of equality of opportunity and equality before the law. In the Senate, he supported anti-lynching bills, efforts to end filibusters, and measures to prevent discrimination. But during his Senate years, Truman had not supported efforts to end segregation. It was not until after he became President that he came to realize that there could be no equality under segregation.

At first, Truman avoided taking strong actions on civil rights. He

210

wanted to keep the support of the South; therefore, he tried not to do anything that would offend Southerners. In addition, polls showed that the majority of white Americans everywhere were anti-civil rights. At first, the President hoped to satisfy black Americans with sympathetic statements and token actions. He spoke in favor of a permanent Fair Employment Practices Committee (FEPC) in 1945, and he asked for legislation to abolish the poll tax. Yet, he did not fight very hard to save the temporary FEPC when Congress ended it in 1945. And he failed to do anything to end voting discrimination.

Truman did make two appointments that were applauded by blacks. In October, 1945, Irvin C. Mollison was appointed a judge of the United States Customs Court. This was the first black appointment to a federal judgeship within the United States. The next year, Truman appointed William H. Hastie as Governor of the Virgin Islands.

THE UNITED NATIONS BROUGHT HOPE

Afro-Americans viewed the founding of the United Nations as one of the most significant events of the early Truman years. During the war, blacks became much more world-minded in their outlook. They came to see their condition in the United States as tied to the condition of minority and colonial peoples throughout the world. The establishment of the United Nations at the San Francisco Conference in 1945 brought them hope that liberation of oppressed peoples might be achieved by international agreement.

A number of black Americans attended the San Francisco Conference. The NAACP was invited to send representatives. Walter White and W. E. B. Du Bois attended as NAACP representatives and spoke out against colonialism. Ralph J. Bunche, who was Acting Chief of the Division of Dependent Territories in the State Department, served on the official staff at the conference. Among other blacks present were Dr. Mordecai Johnson of Howard University and Mary McLeod Bethune of the National Council of Negro Women. The major black newspapers sent reporters to cover the conference.

The hope for change was strengthened by the wording of the charter of the new organization. The United Nations pledged to work for international cooperation "in promoting and encouraging respect for human rights and for fundamental freedoms for all without distinction as to race, sex, language, or religion." Agencies of the United Nations wrote this principle into their purposes. In 1946, the Economic and Social Council provided for the establishment of a Commission on

Human Rights. The commission's aim was to protect minorities and to prevent "discrimination on grounds of race, sex, language, and religion." The Economic and Social Council also established UNESCO, a worldwide agency to develop education and scientific knowledge. Black sociologist Charles S. Johnson attended the first meeting of UNESCO in 1946 as a member of the United States National Commission.

In 1947, the NAACP and other organizations called upon the United Nations to take action on racial discrimination in the United States. W. E. B. Du Bois and historian Rayford Logan joined other black and white scholars in drawing up a formal statement. However, the United Nations took no action on this appeal.

The United States, like most other countries, strongly opposed action by the United Nations on matters it considered its own domestic responsibility. Yet President Truman was aware that peoples throughout the world were watching America's racial problem. The Soviet Union used American racial incidents in its propaganda campaign to win nonwhite peoples to Communism. In 1947, the President told a group of black reporters: "When we fail to live together in peace, the failure touches not us, as Americans alone, but the cause of democracy itself in the whole world. That we must never forget."

TRUMAN APPOINTED A COMMITTEE ON CIVIL RIGHTS
Even as the United Nations was being established, human rights violations in the United States grew more evident. Violence against black citizens increased greatly in 1946. Six persons were lynched, only one of whom had committed a serious offense. The National Guard had to restore order in Athens, Alabama, where a mob of 2,000 whites went on a rampage after a fight between two white men and a black man. A mob raided the black section of Columbia, Tennessee, following an incident between a black woman and her son and a white appliance repairman. In North Philadelphia, blacks and whites attacked each other with clubs, bricks, and bottles.

President Truman was greatly concerned about mob violence. He decided that a new policy on civil rights was needed. The federal government, he felt, should take a more active role in protecting the rights of black citizens. In the fall of 1946, after meeting with Walter White and other black leaders, Truman appointed the President's Committee on Civil Rights. The committee was instructed to study the ways the federal government was protecting civil rights and to recommend improvements. In 1947, the committee presented its report, *To Secure These Rights*. The report called for a broad program to end discrimination and segregation. It pointed out that moral, economic, and international considerations made it necessary for the government to act.

On February 2, 1948, President Truman sent a civil rights message to Congress. He requested legislation to begin carrying out the recommendations of the Committee on Civil Rights. Truman asked Congress to abolish the poll tax, to make lynching a federal crime, to end discrimination in employment, and to outlaw segregation of interstate passengers. He also asked that the civil rights section of the Department of Justice be expanded into a division. Blacks hailed the message as a great document, but the white South rose in bitter opposition to Truman's requests.

BLACK VOTERS SUPPORTED TRUMAN IN 1948

Civil rights became a major issue in the Presidential election of 1948. Truman's civil rights message was designed in part to keep black voters in the Democratic Party. Several of his advisers warned him that firm actions, not words, were needed. These advisers did not believe the South would leave the Democratic Party because the President supported civil rights. But the Southern reaction caused the President to try to play down civil rights as the Democratic National Convention drew near. In addition, Truman agreed to include the weak civil rights plank of 1944 in the 1948 Democratic platform. This caused other groups in the party to decide to act.

One group in the Democratic Party, the left wing, decided to leave the party. This group then formed the Progressive Party and nominated Henry A. Wallace for President. The Progressives made a very strong appeal for black support. Another group within the Democratic Party, the liberals, also were unwilling to accept the 1944 civil rights plank. And the liberals finally succeeded in getting a very strong civil rights platform plank adopted at the 1948 Democratic convention.

The Southern delegates then walked out of the Democratic convention. Later, they met in Birmingham and formed the States' Rights Democratic Party, better known as the "Dixiecrat" Party. J. Strom Thurmond of South Carolina and Fielding L. Wright of Mississippi were named as the Dixiecrat candidates. But the Dixiecrats did not seem to have overwhelming support in the South.

With the Democratic Party split on both the right and the left,

Thomas E. Dewey, the Republican candidate, was expected to win the election. It was clear that Truman needed solid black support if he was to have any chance to win. This situation caused the President to speed up his timetable on civil rights. On July 26, 1948, he issued two Executive Orders dealing with civil rights. The first of these, Executive Order 9980, required a policy of nondiscrimination in federal employment. This order created a Fair Practices Board in the Civil Service Commission to see that the policy was carried out. Executive Order 9981 called for desegregation of the armed forces.

On election day, the voters returned Truman to the White House. It was a close election, and many groups claimed to have been responsible for the victory. But it was generally agreed by those who studied the election that black voters made the real difference. A greater percentage of black Americans voted for Truman than had voted for Roosevelt. In the key states of California, Illinois, and Ohio, they provided the margin of victory.

THE ARMED FORCES WERE DESEGREGATED

The desegregation of the American military forces was a great landmark of the Truman and Eisenhower years. Segregation in the military forces long had caused resentment among blacks. Even before President Truman issued Executive Order 9981, his desegregation order, A. Philip Randolph had established the Committee Against Jim Crow in Military Service and Training. Randolph threatened that large numbers of black youth would choose prison rather than serve in segregated armed forces. Even after the President's order, Randolph continued his pressure for action, to make sure the order was not just a political move but would bring results.

Events proved that the President was sincere as he continued to press for desegregation. He appointed the Committee on Equality of Treatment and Opportunity in the Armed Services to work with the military forces. The Committee's work with the navy and air force was easy. The navy had changed from the most segregated of the services to the most integrated by the end of the war. In 1947, the air force was made a separate branch of armed services. When the President's order was issued, the air force, under Secretary of the Air Force Stuart Symington, was ready to begin integration. By November, 1949, the air force was able to report that its units were integrated.

The army posed the most difficult problem. Many civilian and military leaders of the army opposed desegregation. Two years after

214

the order, almost nothing had been done to achieve integration. A few commanders did begin desegregating, without approval from higher officials. But it probably would have taken a long time to complete desegregation in the army if the Korean War had not begun in June, 1950. When General Matthew Ridgeway replaced General Douglas MacArthur as American commander in the Far East, he asked permission to integrate all troops under his command. Integration was also being achieved among army units stationed in Europe.

Desegregation was completed after Dwight D. Eisenhower was elected President in 1952. The last all-black unit was disbanded by the end of 1954. Meanwhile, in 1953, President Eisenhower ordered an end to segregation in Veterans Administration Hospitals and in schools on military posts. In 1954, the navy desegregated restaurants, drinking fountains, and washrooms for civilians at the shipyard in Charleston, South Carolina. The same year, the air force promoted Benjamin O. Davis, Jr., to the rank of general.

PROGRESS WAS MADE IN POSTWAR EMPLOYMENT

Black people feared that they would have large-scale unemployment when World War II ended. Because black workers were among the last hired in most industries, they lacked seniority and they would be the first to lose their jobs. Many were in industries that had no important peacetime role, such as the production of ammunition and explosives. As American industry prepared for peace in late 1945, black workers did lose their jobs in greater numbers than white workers. The number of blacks in skilled jobs and in professional and managerial positions decreased. But fortunately, the nation's prosperity continued after the war and the United States had almost full employment. This meant that the major problem facing black workers now was not lack of jobs but discrimination in obtaining good jobs and advancement to higher level jobs.

The federal government became committed to fair employment during the war years, but it achieved uneven results. Civil rights groups believed that the most effective means of achieving fair employment would be a law of Congress containing strong enforcement powers. Many groups worked for such a law. The National Council for a Permanent FEPC had the support of church, labor, black, Jewish, fraternal, and professional groups. In 1950, the National Civil Rights Mobilization, composed of fifty-five organizations, urged Congress to act. The Leadership Conference on Civil Rights joined the fight in

1952. But Congress refused to pass a fair employment law.

In the absence of legislation, Presidents Truman and Eisenhower took steps to encourage fair employment practices. Truman's first move was to create the Fair Employment Board in the Civil Service Commission in 1948. Then, on December 3, 1951, he established the Government Contract Compliance Committee, whose duty was to see that private companies dealing with the government did not discriminate in employment. President Eisenhower replaced the Truman committee with a new Government Contract Committee in 1953. Eisenhower added to the authority and prestige of the committee by appointing Vice-President Richard M. Nixon as chairman. On January 18, 1955, Eisenhower set up a new committee to enforce fair employment in government agencies. His Committee on Government Employment Policy was responsible directly to the White House. These groups tried to accomplish their purpose through persuasion, and did achieve a great deal in this way.

Other efforts also were being made to improve employment conditions for black workers. Several states passed fair employment practices laws. New York began this trend in 1945, followed by New Jersey in the same year and by Massachusetts in 1946. Gradually, other states passed such laws. The NAACP and other organizations worked with industry and labor to secure the employment, training, and upgrading of black workers. The AFL-CIO announced a policy of nondiscrimination, but many unions continued to exclude black workers. Here and there, however, these efforts began to bring results. During the 1950's such corporations as Philco and the Fisher Body Division and the Electromotive Diesel Division of General Motors, as well as such industries as oil refining and brewing, were among those that began to employ black workers or to open skilled jobs to them.

GAINS WERE MADE IN VOTING

Voting and participation in political activities remained the key to the achievement of full citizenship by black Americans. But whites in the South were stubborn in their efforts to deny blacks the right to vote. The NAACP waged a long court battle to remove legal barriers to voting. The United States Supreme Court finally dealt a heavy blow to the white primary in 1944 with its decision in *Smith v. Allwright*. The Court ruled that primaries were not private activities. The right to vote in a primary, the Court said "is a right secured by the Constitution." Several states, including South Carolina, Alabama, and

Texas, then passed new laws to try to get around the Court's ruling. After years more of lawsuits and legal appeals, all-white primaries finally were declared unconstitutional in 1953.

In the meantime, the number of black voters in the South remained quite small. The Southern Regional Council found that in 1947 only 12 percent of the blacks of voting age in twelve Southern states were registered. In Alabama, Louisiana, and Mississippi, only 3 percent of the black citizens could vote. As late as 1956, only 19 percent of black residents of voting age in Alabama, Louisiana, Mississippi, and Georgia were registered, compared with 76 percent white residents of voting-age.

In 1957, Congress acted to protect the right to vote by passing a voting rights act. Under this law, the Department of Justice was able to bring suit to prevent anyone from denying a citizen the right to vote because of "race, color, or previous condition of servitude." In 1960, Congress strengthened the 1957 law. The Justice Department was given more power to investigate; the federal judges were given power to send in referees to register black voters where a pattern of discrimination existed.

Yet progress continued to be slow. Threats and terror were used to keep blacks from registering and voting. A number of blacks were lynched for trying to exercise their right to vote. In 1946, Macio Snipes, the only black person to vote in Taylor County, Georgia, was dragged from his home and shot. Such tactics increased during the 1950's. Because of the NAACP's involvement of voter registration drives, several NAACP officials lost their lives. In 1951, Harry Moore, the NAACP executive secretary for Florida, and his wife were killed when their home was bombed. George W. Lee, a black minister, was lynched in Belzoni, Mississippi, for leading a registration drive. An attempt was made on the life of Gus Courts, who had assisted Lee in the drive. Economic pressures were also used. Blacks who registered were fired from their jobs and denied credit at stores and banks.

Some gains in political representation were made during the 1940's and 1950's. The black voters of Harlem elected Adam Clayton Powell, Jr., to the House of Representatives in 1945. He joined William L. Dawson of Chicago to become the second black member of the House. In 1954, they added to their number Representative Charles C. Diggs of Detroit, Michigan. A fourth black Representative, Robert Nix, was elected in 1958 by the voters of Philadelphia, Pennsylvania. In 1946, thirty blacks were elected to state legislatures in ten states. The next year a Southern city, Winston-Salem, North Carolina, elected a black official to the city council. In 1953, Hulan Jack was elected to the important office of Borough President of Manhattan, in New York City. By 1959, the increase in the number of black voters in the South had begun to have an effect on Southern politics. Cities in Tennessee and North Carolina elected black members to their city councils. Black voters helped to elect moderate white officials in some places and helped to defeat strong segregationists in others.

HOUSING DISCRIMINATION REMAINED A PROBLEM

During the 1940's and 1950's, the black family seeking adequate housing still faced discrimination and sometimes violence. The federal government provided money for public housing and gave financial assistance to private housing. These programs were operated through private industry and by local public authorities. Federal officials were slow to take action against unfair housing practices. Blacks were often excluded from public housing. In addition, the Federal Housing Administration (FHA) approved private housing developments that excluded black families. In fact, for a time, the FHA required that housing developments be segregated.

The problem of discrimination in public housing had to be tackled city by city. The NAACP brought cases to court in a number of cities. In 1952, public housing was opened to black families through such NAACP legal action in Detroit; Long Branch, New Jersey; and in San Francisco, Sacramento, and Richmond, California. Two years later, other public housing projects were opened in San Francisco; in Camden and Elizabeth, New Jersey; and in Detroit and Hamtramck, Michigan. It was not until 1955 that the NAACP was able to get a general court order opening public housing in the cities of St. Louis and Detroit. Among the states, first Connecticut in 1949, then New York, New Jersey, Oregon, Washington, and Massachusetts in the 1950's, passed laws banning discrimination in public housing. New York and Oregon were the only states to make discrimination in private housing unlawful during this period.

Violence broke out in some places when black families moved into public housing projects. One of the worst outbreaks occurred in Chicago when several black families moved into the all-white Trumbull Park Homes in 1953. Mobs of whites hurled stones, garbage, and explosives at the apartments occupied by the black families. Police were on constant duty, but they made only half-hearted efforts to check the mobs. Four years later, when the police were withdrawn, black residents were still being subjected to mob attacks.

The Supreme Court ruled against the enforcement of racially restrictive covenants in 1948. The Court did not rule that such agreements were illegal, but it did destroy much of their effectiveness. The
Supreme Court decision in *Shelly v. Kraemer* was that state courts
could not enforce such covenants. And, in *Hurd v. Hodge,* the Court
ruled that covenants could not be enforced in federal courts. Nonethe-
less, blacks still faced violence when they moved into white neighborhoods. The governor of Illinois had to call out the National Guard in
1951 when Harvey E. Clark tried to move into an apartment in Cicero.
A mob of about 3,500 gathered, dumped the Clarks' furniture out the
window, and burned it.

THE COURTS RULED AGAINST SEGREGATED SCHOOLS

On May 17, 1954, the Supreme Court handed down its landmark ruling
that segregation in public education was unconstitutional. This was the
climax of a long legal battle fought in the courts by the NAACP. That
battle began at the university graduate school and professional school
level.

The first important ruling came in 1938, in the case of *Missouri ex
rel. Gaines v. Canada.* The Supreme Court held that Missouri had to
provide Lloyd Gaines facilities to study law about equal to those provided for whites. In response, Southern states began to establish makeshift graduate schools and departments at black state colleges. But
legal efforts to end segregation continued.

In 1949, Ada Lois Sipuel was admitted to the law school at the
University of Oklahoma. The Supreme Court had ruled in 1947 that
she had to be provided legal education at the same time that such education was provided other citizens of the state. She should not have to
wait until a new school was established for her. The 1950 ruling in
Sweatt v. Painter brought the end to segregation closer in graduate and
professional education. In that decision, the Supreme Court ruled that
a new law school established by the state of Texas for Heman Sweatt
was not equal to the University of Texas Law School. The new school
did not have the reputation, the distinguished graduates, and many
other things that make a desirable law school. This ruling practically
destroyed the doctrine of "separate but equal."

During the summer of 1950, the NAACP decided to begin a full-
scale attack on segregation in education. In 1952, NAACP lawyers
brought five school desegregation cases before the Supreme Court.

219

These cases involved segregation in South Carolina; Topeka, Kansas; Prince Edward County, Virginia; Delaware; and Washington, D.C. They were first argued in December, 1952, by a team of lawyers headed by Thurgood Marshall. The Court called for reargument and the presentation of more information.

Finally, on May 17, 1954, the Court handed down its historic decision. The five cases were treated together in the decision *Brown v. Board of Education*. The opinion was written by Chief Justice Earl Warren, whom President Eisenhower had appointed to the Court. The Court ruled, "We conclude that in the field of public education the doctrine of 'separate but equal' has no place. Separate educational facilities are inherently unequal."

SCHOOL DESEGREGATION MOVED SLOWLY

The Court asked for further arguments on how the decision should be carried out. The NAACP argued that the Court should require desegregation by September, 1955. On May 31, 1955, the Court set guidelines for school desegregation. It said that local boards were to draw up their own plans "with all deliberate speed." This left the question of time still open and undefined.

Some public school districts in Western and border states began desegregating in 1954. By the fall of 1955, 326 districts were at least partially integrated. But in the states of the Deep South, the ruling was completely ignored. Georgia, Virginia, Louisiana, Alabama, Mississippi, South Carolina, and North Carolina began a long campaign to preserve segregation. Racist groups were organized throughout the South to fight school desegregation. The most important such group was the White Citizens Councils. The Councils began in Mississippi in July, 1945, and spread throughout the Southern and border states.

Soon mob action became a part of the effort to block desegregation. A mob tried to stop desegregation of the high school in Clinton, Tennessee, in 1956. But a group of the town's leading citizens broke up the mob. Two years later, the high school was bombed. It was rebuilt and reopened on an integrated basis. In 1956, mob action also broke out in Mansfield, Texas, and Sturgis, Kentucky.

FEDERAL TROOPS WERE SENT TO LITTLE ROCK

The first major outbreak of violence came in 1957 when nine black students tried to enroll in Central High School in Little Rock, Arkansas. When the students tried to enter the school on September 3, they were turned away by National Guardsmen. Arkansas Governor Orval Faubus said that he posted the soldiers there "to preserve order." A federal judge ordered Faubus to stop interfering with desegregation. Faubus then removed the National Guard. When the black children returned to school on September 23, a mob of about 1,000 whites gathered and threatened to riot. The children were removed from the school at noon.

Daisy Bates, President of the Arkansas NAACP, asked President Eisenhower to see that the children were protected. Finally, President Eisenhower ordered 1,000 soldiers of the 101st Airborne Division to go to Little Rock. He also called the Arkansas National Guard into federal service. Order was restored, and the black children entered the school. But the soldiers remained on duty. The high schools in Little Rock were closed the following year. But, in 1959, they were reopened, with black children in attendance.

Public school desegregation progressed very slowly. Two North Carolina cities admitted a small number of black students to formerly all-white schools in 1957. Two years later, only thirty-four black children were enrolled in mixed schools in that state. In 1958 and 1959, blacks protested the slow pace of desegregation in Washington, D.C. A. Philip Randolph, Jackie Robinson, and Harry Belafonte led 10,000 black and white students in a Youth March for Integrated Schools in Washington, D.C., in 1958. The next year Roy Wilkins of the NAACP, Martin Luther King, Jr., and Daisy Bates joined Randolph, Robinson, and Belafonte to lead 26,000 students in a second march. By 1959, still no public schools had been desegregated in Alabama, Georgia, Louisiana, Mississippi, and South Carolina. Prince Edward County, Virginia, had abolished its public schools. Of the 3,000,000 black children of school age in seventeen border and Southern states, only 182,100 were in integrated classes.

SEGREGATION IN TRAVEL AND RECREATION DECREASED

Afro-Americans protested segregation in other areas such as travel, recreation, and places serving the public during the Truman and Eisenhower years. The NAACP continued to follow its strategy of leading the legal battle for full rights of citizenship. But during the 1950's, other groups began to use direct action as an effective method of black protest.

The Supreme Court struck a blow at segregation in public travel between the states (interstate travel) in 1947. It ruled that segregation on interstate buses was an unreasonable burden on interstate commerce. But this ruling did not lead immediately to the ending of segregation on buses and trains. Three years later, the Court did end segregation in dining cars on passenger trains. The NAACP continued the fight against segregated buses and trains in 1953 by appealing to the Interstate Commerce Commission (ICC). In 1955, the ICC ordered that segregation of interstate passengers in buses and waiting rooms must end by January 10, 1956. When the deadline arrived, several major railroads removed "white" and "colored" signs in their waiting rooms. But in many places, segregation continued. Segregation in air travel received a severe setback in 1956, however, when the Civil Aeronautics Board ruled that federal funds could not be used for segregated airports.

Discrimination in recreational facilities ended in a number of cities. Kansas City desegregated its swimming pools in 1952, and the city golf course was opened to black golfers in Louisville, Kentucky. By 1956, eleven Southern cities had begun operating some of their recreation facilities on a nondiscriminatory basis.

BLACKS BEGAN DIRECT ACTION EFFORTS

The first nationally significant direct action campaign began in 1955. This was the Montgomery bus boycott. On Thursday, December 1, 1955, Rosa Parks, a quiet, dignified seamstress boarded a city bus on her way home from work. The driver ordered her to give up her seat to a white passenger and move to the rear of the bus. When Rosa Parks refused to do so, the driver called the police, and she was arrested.

Word of her arrest spread through the black community. E. D. Nixon, a pullman porter and community leader, arranged for Rosa Parks' release from jail. Black women began to demand a boycott of the city buses. Nixon, attorney Fred Gray, and others set to work. Two Montgomery ministers, Martin Luther King, Jr., and Ralph D. Abernathy, agreed to cooperate. On Friday evening, a large group of black citizens met to make plans. They decided to call a boycott against the buses for Monday, December 5.

On Monday, the buses that served the black community were empty. That night another meeting was held to make further plans and to begin an organization. The Montgomery Improvement Association (MIA) was formed, and Martin Luther King, Jr., was elected its pres-

Rosa Parks, a seamstress, was arrested by Montgomery police when she refused to move to the rear of a bus. Her action soon led to the successful Montgomery bus boycott.

ident. The demands of the MIA were not drastic. It asked the bus line for courteous treatment of black citizens. It wanted seating to be on a first-come, first-served basis, with blacks sitting from the back toward the front and the whites from the front toward the back. The group also asked that black drivers be employed on routes with large numbers of black riders. The NAACP refused to join the campaign because the MIA did not demand an end to segregation.

The white citizens of Montgomery were surprised at the unity of the blacks. At first, they waited for the bus boycott to fail. The city officials and representatives of the bus company would not agree to the MIA demands. On January 10, Dr. King's home was bombed. And, as the bus company and local businessmen began to lose money, terror tactics increased. The MIA then changed its demands to include an end to all segregation on the buses. A lawsuit was filed, and NAACP attorney Robert Carter argued the case before a federal court on May 11, 1956. On June 4, the court ruled against segregation. An appeal was then made to the Supreme Court, which ruled that segregation on buses was unconstitutional. The city of Montgomery announced that it would obey the ruling. The boycott ended in success on December 2, 1956, some 381 days after it began.

The nonviolent direct action of Montgomery's black citizens inspired other blacks in the South. They, too, were tired of segregated travel and moving to the back of the bus. If the people of Montgomery could join together toward a common goal, so could they. A bus boycott began in Tallahassee, Florida, in May, 1956. The blacks of Birmingham, Alabama, also began to act against segregation on buses.

In January, 1957, a group of black ministers met in Atlanta and formed the Southern Christian Leadership Conference (SCLC). At a later meeting, the Montgomery boycott leader, Martin Luther King, Jr., was elected president, and Ralph D. Abernathy was elected treasurer of SCLC. The ministers felt that an organization was needed that would concentrate its efforts on the South. They did not intend to try to replace the NAACP or the National Urban League.

Another significant development was the Civil Rights Act of 1957. It was not a very strong law, but it was the first civil rights law passed by Congress since 1875. It showed that Congress finally realized its responsibility in the area of civil rights. The law provided for a Civil Rights Commission to gather information on the denial of voting rights. It created a Division of Civil Rights in the Department of Justice and gave the Justice Department the power to act to protect all citizens' voting rights.

PROGRESS WAS MADE IN OTHER AREAS

By 1959, a crack had appeared in the wall of segregation in many areas of American life. Professional organizations began to lower their bars against black members. The American Nurses Association began accepting black nurses in 1946. In 1950, the American Medical Association had a black delegate at its meeting. Black doctors were admitted as members of the Florida medical association. Lawyers, social workers, and librarians in the South began to accept black members here and there. But teachers' groups remained rigidly segregated.

The most publicized breakthrough was in sports. In baseball, Jackie Robinson, who had been an outstanding athlete at UCLA, joined the Brooklyn Dodgers in 1945. Two years later, the Dodgers brought Robinson into the major leagues, and he became the first black player on a major league baseball team. Soon, other teams followed the example of the Dodgers. Robinson received the National League's Most Valuable Player Award in 1949. Other outstanding black players who received this award or were batting or home run champions during the 1950's included Roy Campanella, Larry Doby, Willie Mays, Don Newcombe, Hank Aaron, and Ernie Banks.

Other sports also began to sign up black players. The Boston Celtics of the National Basketball Association signed Ed "Chuck" Cooper in 1950. Nat "Sweetwater" Clifton joined the New York Knickerbockers. By 1959, stars like Elgin Baylor and Wilt Chamberlain were adding excitement to professional basketball. The outstanding black star of professional football was Jimmy Brown of the Cleveland Browns. Brown broke nearly every ground-gaining record in the National Football League. Althea Gibson entered the National Tennis Championship in 1950, and the next year she became the Women's Singles tennis champion. Charles Sifford, the first black member of the Professional Golfers Association, won his first tournament in 1957.

Black athletes made valuable contributions on the American Olympic teams at London in 1948, Helsinki in 1952, and Melbourne in 1956. They won eight gold medals in 1948, eleven in 1952, and nine in 1956. Harrison Dillard, Mal Whitfield, Alice Coachman, Andrew Stanfield, Floyd Patterson, Mae Faggs, Charles Jenkins, and Ira Murchinson were among the first-place gold medal winners at these games.

Joe Louis had long been a household name among black Americans. He was a great boxing champion, and his rise from humble beginnings inspired many young blacks to follow this route to fame. Louis retired in 1949, after being heavyweight champion longer than any other fighter. During most of the 1950's other black prizefighters held the heavyweight championship. They included Ezzard Charles, Jersey Joe Walcott, and Floyd Patterson. Blacks also won boxing championships in other divisions. The best-known of these fighters were Sugar Ray Robinson, who won the welterweight and middleweight titles, and Archie Moore, who was light heavyweight champion for almost ten years.

BLACKS CONTRIBUTED TO AMERICA'S CULTURE ——

Signs of change in American life could also be seen on the stage and screen. A few black actors began appearing in Broadway productions. Ruby Dee made her first Broadway appearance in 1946 in *Jeb*. Two years later, Juanita Hall created a stir in her role as "Bloody Mary" in *South Pacific*. Pearl Bailey and Diahann Carroll had starring roles in the Broadway musical *House of Flowers* in 1954. Sammy Davis, Jr., was a great success in his first Broadway show, *Mr. Wonderful*, in 1956. And the next year, Lena Horne appeared in the musical *Jamaica*.

Works by black writers were produced on Broadway and in off-Broadway theaters. Langston Hughes wrote the lyrics for *Street Scene*, and Theodore Ward wrote *Our Lan'*. Both were performed on Broadway in 1947. Among the works by black playwrights produced on Broadway during the 1950's were *Take a Giant Step* by Louis Peterson, *Simply Heavenly* by Langston Hughes, and *A Raisin in the Sun* by Lorraine Hansberry.

Hollywood began making movies dealing with race relations. Four motion pictures, with sensitive treatments of this subject, came out in 1949. They were *Lost Boundaries, Home of the Brave, Pinky,* and *Intruder in the Dust*. All of them were rather remarkable productions for that time. But generally, Hollywood films continued to show black Americans only in roles that preserved racial stereotypes.

During the 1950's, popular music was dominated by black musicians. Jazz musicians like Charlie Parker, Thelonious Monk, Dizzy Gillespie, and Miles Davis helped to create "modern jazz." Gillespie helped to bring Afro-Cuban music into jazz. In 1950, Louis Armstrong was greeted by mobs of fans as he toured Europe. Sarah Vaughn's talent as a jazz and blues signer won the Downbeat Female Vocalist Award from 1946 to 1952. Ella Fitzgerald continued her distinctive and popular role as America's leading jazz singer. When rock-and-roll music became popular in the mid-1950's, white teenagers began discovering blues music.

Outstanding works in fiction and poetry were written by blacks during these years. The most outstanding name in poetry was that of Gwendolyn Brooks. She published her first collection of poems, *A Street in Bronzeville*, in 1945. *Annie Allen* won her the Pulitzer Prize in poetry in 1950. Miss Brooks' other works included a novel, *Maude Martha*.

Most black novelists used black themes, but some used other subjects. Frank Yerby's popular historical novel *The Foxes of Harrow* had little to do with black life. His other works followed the same pattern. Willard Motley's *Knock on Any Door* dealt with an Italian boy whose life in the slums led him into crime. His second novel, *We Fished All Night*, published in 1951, treated lower-class life in Chicago. Other black writers drew from their own experiences and wrote novels based on their lives. Two such works appeared in 1951. They were James Baldwin's *Go Tell It on the Mountain* and Owen Dodson's *Boy at the Window*. In 1954, John Oliver Killens drew upon his life in Georgia for his novel *Youngblood*.

Several other important works were published. Chester Himes' first novel, *If He Hollers Let Him Go*, appeared in 1945. *The Lonely Crusader* was published in 1947, and *Third Generation* appeared in 1954. Himes later wrote many more novels. And Ralph Ellison's outstanding novel, *The Invisible Man*, was published in 1952.

Chapter 20

The Civil Rights Movement

The Montgomery bus boycott gave the civil rights movement a new leader, the Reverend Martin Luther King, Jr. After Montgomery, nonviolent direct action became the main protest method of the civil rights movement. Thousands of Afro-Americans and white supporters of civil rights followed Dr. King into the streets and jails of many cities. But it was the young people who gave the "Negro Revolt" its great forward thrust. Black youth were impatient with slow racial progress and began calling for immediate equality and freedom. In many of their activities, they had the support of white students.

The heart of the movement was the masses of people—youth and adults, black and white—who staged nonviolent protests to break down segregation and to end discrimination. But when unrest moved into the Northern ghettos, nonviolence often gave way to rioting. The civil rights revolution also was helped by the election of President John F. Kennedy. Kennedy and his successor, President Lyndon B. Johnson, were strongly committed to the cause of equality. Under their leadership, Congress responded with far-reaching laws to fight discrimination.

THE CIVIL RIGHTS MOVEMENT
BEGAN WITH A SIT-IN

The great breakthrough in civil rights came in 1960. On February 1, four freshmen from the all-black Agricultural and Technical College sat down at an all-white Woolworth store lunch counter in Greensboro, North Carolina. They were not served, but they refused to move. When the manager closed the counter, the students took out their textbooks and began studying. This new method of nonviolent protest became known as a sit-in. When news of what was happening at the Greensboro lunch counter spread, other students joined in. Each day students returned and took seats at the counter.

White opposition to the sit-in was strong. The students soon realized that they needed help from adults. Therefore, a group of students called on Dr. George Simpkins, a respected black leader in Greensboro and president of the local branch of the NAACP. Because the NAACP had not yet decided its policy toward direct action, such as sit-ins, Simpkins called the New York City office of the Congress of Racial Equality (CORE).

CORE sent a representative to Greensboro. Founded in 1942 by James Farmer, CORE had pioneered the use of nonviolent direct action based on the ideas of Mohandas Gandhi in India. An interracial organization, CORE had been very active in attacking discrimination in Northern and border cities. But in 1960, this group was still not well known. The representative from CORE instructed the Greensboro students in nonviolent methods. The students practiced how to react to insults and even to physical attack without striking back or showing anger.

Within two weeks after the Greensboro sit-in began, the movement had spread to other cities. Students from Fisk University began a sit-in at the Woolworth lunch counter in Nashville, Tennessee. This protest developed into a full-scale boycott of local white stores. In Durham, North Carolina, white students from Duke University and black students from North Carolina College joined forces. They demanded integration of all facilities in local department stores and bus stations. Soon carefully planned sit-ins also were in progress in Atlanta, Georgia. Students from Clark, Morehouse, and Morris Brown Colleges, Atlanta University, and the Interdenominational Theological Center held these sit-ins. These students issued "An Appeal for Human Rights." They served notice that they did "not intend to wait placidly for those rights which are already legally and morally ours to be meted out to us one at a time."

SNCC HELPED DIRECT NEW STUDENT PROTESTS

As student protest spread across the South, the need for organized direction became clear. The Southern Christian Leadership Conference (SCLC) sponsored a student conference at Shaw University in Raleigh, North Carolina, from April 15 to 17, 1960. There were 212 student delegates, most of them from the South. Northern student representatives from CORE and SCLC, and other civil rights workers also attended.

The group decided to form the Student Non-Violent Coordinating Committee (SNCC). It was also decided that SNCC would maintain close ties with SCLC but would be a separate and independent organization. In May, 1960, another meeting was held in Atlanta. Marion Barry, a leader of the student movement at Fisk University, was chosen chairman of the temporary organization. Plans were made for an office and staff, and a drive to raise money. SNCC set as its purpose the coordinating of student protest activities throughout the South. Before the year ended, SNCC formally established itself as an organization.

The sit-in movement spread rapidly. The main target was segregated lunch counters, but in some places sit-ins were held in other places. Alabama State College students staged a sit-in at the courthouse in Montgomery. In Biloxi, Mississippi, blacks staged a "wade-in" at segregated beaches. In Atlanta and other places, "pray-ins" and "kneel-ins" took place at segregated churches. By late in 1961, about fifty towns and cities in the South had experienced sit-in demonstrations. Over 70,000 black and white students had been involved, and nearly 4,000 had been arrested.

The direct-action movement brought important results. Before the end of the first year, some eating places had been desegregated in more than 100 Southern and border cities. Late in 1960, four national chain stores announced that their lunch counters were to be open to all customers. This action integregated dining facilities in stores in 112 cities. But progress did not come easily. The demonstrators suffered insults and physical attacks. Riots broke out in Jacksonville, Florida, and other places. Many demonstrators were beaten and arrested. A number of those in the Mississippi "wade-in" were wounded. The home of the black attorney who defended the demonstrators in Nashville was bombed.

FREEDOM RIDERS HELPED END SEGREGATED TRAVEL

Even after the Supreme Court and the Interstate Commerce Commission ruled against segregation, seating on buses and in waiting rooms remained segregated in the South. Early in 1961, James Farmer of CORE made plans to test whether federal desegregation orders were being enforced. He advised President John F. Kennedy that a "freedom ride" was planned into the South and asked for protection. The NAACP promised its cooperation. Actually, this was not a new activity for Farmer, because he and other CORE members had taken a freedom ride in 1947 to test desegregation on interstate passenger trains.

On May 4, 1961, a group of seven black and six white "freedom riders" left Washington, D.C., headed for New Orleans. At bus stations in North and South Carolina, one or two of the riders were arrested. Serious trouble developed when they reached Anniston, Alabama. There a mob met one of the buses, cut its tires and set it on fire. Riders on the other freedom ride bus were beaten in Anniston and again in Birmingham. As a result, the freedom riders were forced to complete their trip to New Orleans by plane.

But by this time the freedom ride movement had attracted national attention. SNCC, SCLC, the Nashville Student Movement, and hundreds of individuals joined CORE in staging new rides. On May 20, 1960, serious disturbances broke out in Montgomery. A mob attacked riders arriving at the Greyhound station there. Several riders were badly injured. After the governor and local officials refused to protect the freedom riders, Attorney General Robert F. Kennedy sent federal marshals to Montgomery. In addition, groups of riders arriving in Jackson, Mississippi, were arrested. At least a dozen groups staged freedom rides before this kind of direct-action protest ended. But by then segregation had been all but eliminated in interstate travel.

A BROAD ATTACK ON DISCRIMINATION BEGAN
Between 1961 and 1964, demonstrations occurred in all parts of the South. Under Dr. King, SCLC began to play a leading role in the civil rights movement. Young ministers like Fred Shuttlesworth, C. T. Vivian, James Lawson, and James Bevel supported Dr. King. But SNCC provided the energy and idealism of thousands of students willing to make any sacrifice for the cause. James Forman, a 33-year-old former Chicago school teacher, and young John Lewis became the leaders of SNCC. Forman brought experience and maturity to the organization, but he matched his younger fellow members in dedication and willingness to give of himself for the cause.

The older organizations began to change to meet the demands of the changing racial situation. CORE became a more vital organization.

The attention it received because of the freedom rides caused its membership and financial support to increase. The National Urban League avoided direct-action campaigns, but under Whitney Young, Jr., it began adjusting its program to the new mood among black Americans. The NAACP, on the other hand, was more flexible. Its youth councils and local branches led demonstrations in a number of places. The NAACP also acted as service group for the direct-action organizations. It provided funds during emergencies and legal help where it was needed. Although there was some competition for funds and leadership among the organizations, they cooperated remarkably well during major campaigns.

The purpose and patterns of black demonstrations began to change in late 1961. After winning their goals in single-purpose programs such as desegregation of lunch counters, buses, or churches, the civil rights groups turned to the broader aim of complete desegregation and jobs. Black leaders learned that in most communities a rather small group of whites held the real power as decision makers. The white power group, which included many businessmen, usually wanted to preserve things as they were. The police and the government were instruments in maintaining the system. The purpose of black protests was to create a crisis so that white decision makers would be forced to recognize the need for change.

BLACK PROTESTS BROUGHT CHANGES IN THE SOUTH
It did not take much to create a crisis in most Southern communities. Groups of peaceful black citizens marching, singing, and demanding change were enough to arouse feelings of fear, anger, and violence among Southern police and those white citizens who strongly opposed equal rights for blacks. In many white communities in the South there were mass arrests, brutal attacks on demonstrators, bombings, and other violent acts.

This white response had several important results. Rather than stopping the demonstrations, white violence increased black anger and brought more blacks into the movement. Brutality against peaceful marchers also touched the conscience of the American nation and aroused world opinion to support the black struggle. Hundreds of white citizens joined blacks in demonstrations, went to jail with them, and contributed money to the struggle.

As nonviolent campaigns continued in a community, disorder often increased, business began to suffer, and economic development slowed down. Usually, at this point, local white leaders became more willing to negotiate with the black protesters. This pattern was repeated over and over in many Southern communities between 1961 and 1964. Albany, Georgia, was the scene of a massive protest effort from late 1961 to 1962. The Albany campaign was not a success. White opposition there was unyielding, and the civil rights organizations had not yet learned to resolve their own jealousies and to work together smoothly.

By 1963 civil rights groups had learned to work together effectively. Major demonstrations took place in Savannah, Georgia; in Cambridge, Maryland; in Jackson, Mississippi; and in Danville, Virginia. At the same time, other demonstrations on larger or smaller scales were going on in other towns and cities. Over 10,000 demonstrations took place in 1963 alone. Mass arrests were made in all of the cities where these demonstrations occurred. In Savannah, Georgia, black protesters demanded desegregation of movie theaters, restaurants, hotels, motels, and bowling alleys. Police used tear gas and fire hoses against the marchers, and many were arrested. By the end of the summer, businessmen and local leaders were willing to negotiate the black demands.

In 1963, Cambridge, Maryland, was the scene of violence between blacks and whites. The National Guard had to be called in to restore order, and soldiers remained in Cambridge for many months. Medgar Evers, Executive Secretary of the NAACP in Mississippi, led demonstrations at Jackson, Mississippi, in 1963. The police arrested about 700 marchers, including Evers and Roy Wilkins, the National Executive Secretary of the NAACP.

THE BIRMINGHAM PROTEST LED TO VIOLENCE
Police brutality against demonstrators occurred during the campaign in Birmingham, Alabama, where the forces of segregation had a strong champion in Police Chief Eugene "Bull" Connor. The "Birmingham project," under Martin Luther King's direction, began on April 3, 1963, with small groups staging sit-ins and picketing stores. Next, limited street demonstrations were held. The first large-scale street march was broken up by policemen with dogs. The police met each succeeding group of marchers with water hoses and attack dogs, and they forced the marchers back to the church from which they started.

A local judge ordered the demonstrations to stop. But Dr. King held another march on Good Friday, April 12. Connor and his police arrested Dr. King and fifty of his followers. The marches continued, and over a thousand demonstrators were arrested. The morale of the demonstrators started to decline. It seemed that the police would win. Then, on May 1, 1963, Dr. King reached a very difficult decision. He called upon the schoolchildren of Birmingham for help.

The young people of Birmingham responded eagerly. Wave after wave of students marched from the Sixteenth Street Baptist Church to face the police and firemen armed with their hoses, clubs, and dogs. Hundreds of teenagers and small children were knocked down by water from the high-pressure hoses, attacked by police dogs, and clubbed by policemen. Television cameras on the scene carried these events into millions of homes throughout the nation. Birmingham also became news around the world.

Finally, on May 7, a group of the city's top industrial, commercial, and professional leaders agreed to begin talking about black grievances. A few days later, it was announced that an agreement had been reached to begin desegregating some facilities. It was agreed that blacks were to be employed in downtown businesses and a biracial committee was to be set up. Some white citizens showed their displeasure with this agreement by bombing the home of the Reverend A. D. King, the brother of Martin Luther King, Jr. The A. G. Gaston Motel, where the Birmingham movement had its headquarters, was also bombed. At this point, anger caused thousands of blacks to end their nonviolence, and these rioters destroyed a nine-block area of the city.

Black youth came near to violence in Jackson, Mississippi, the next month. On June 12, Medgar Evers, the Executive Secretary of the NAACP in Mississippi, was shot from ambush and killed as he entered his home. Filled with anger and frustration, black youth poured into downtown Jackson on the day of the funeral. A minor conflict with police broke out, and widespread violence was only narrowly avoided.

THE MARCH ON WASHINGTON
HIGHLIGHTED THE DEMONSTRATIONS

The climax of the demonstrations in 1963 came on August 28 when over 200,000 people took part in the March on Washington. The march was a peaceful demonstration, with 30,000 white Americans and 170,000 black Americans singing "We Shall Overcome." The marchers carried banners and signs calling for decent housing and "Jobs and Freedom Now."

The man who put the march together was A. Philip Randolph, the grand old man of the black struggle. He was assisted in the planning by Bayard Rustin, the intellectual who had spent most of his life organizing demonstrations. The leaders of all the major civil rights organizations were involved. The "Big Five" leaders were Roy Wilkins of the NAACP, Martin Luther King, Jr., of SCLC, James Farmer of CORE, Whitney Young, Jr., of the National Urban League, and John Lewis of SNCC. These black leaders were on the Organizing Committee with four white leaders, Matthew Ahmann of the National Catholic Conference for Interracial Justice, Dr. Eugene Carson Blake of the World Council of Churches, Rabbi Joachim Prinz of the American Jewish Congress, and Walter P. Reuther of the United Automobile Workers.

On the day of the march, the crowd gathered on the grounds of the Washington Monument. They were entertained by many well-known black and white performers. The marchers then moved to the Lincoln Memorial for the main event of the day. In the march were distinguished black Americans and white Americans from many fields. Over seventy-five members of Congress attended to support the program. All the major civil rights leaders were there except James Farmer, who was in jail in Plaquemines, Louisiana, where he had been leading a demonstration.

Songs and speeches made up the main program. Joan Baez sang the anthem of the movement, "We Shall Overcome." Mahalia Jackson stirred the crowd with her powerful voice as she sang spirituals. The list of speakers was long. At last, Martin Luther King, Jr., rose to the strains of "The Battle Hymn of the Republic." The vast crowd and millions watching on television fell under his spell as he described his great dream for the nation. "I have a dream," he said, "that one day this nation will rise up and live out the true meaning of its creed: 'We hold these truths to be self-evident, that all men are created equal. . . .'" He dreamed of brotherhood in Georgia and an end to oppression in Mississippi. August 28, 1963, was, indeed, a day of hope.

BOTH PARTIES TRIED TO ATTRACT BLACK VOTERS

Both major political parties were aware of the militant concern of Afro-Americans over civil rights. The parties also knew that in a close election black voters held the balance of power in several important states. In the Presidential campaign of 1960, both parties tried to attract black votes. Their platforms contained strong statements on civil rights.

Senator John F. Kennedy, the Democratic nominee for President, criticized the Eisenhower record on civil rights. Vice-President Richard

The leaders of the major civil rights groups in the early 1960's were (left to right) John Lewis, Whitney Young, Jr., A. Philip Randolph, Martin Luther King, Jr., James Farmer, and Roy Wilkins.

M. Nixon, who was the Presidential candidate on the Republican ticket, defended that record. Senator Kennedy gained the upper hand when Martin Luther King, Jr., was sent to prison in October, 1960, for leading an earlier demonstration. Kennedy phoned Coretta King to express his concern about her husband. He also sent his brother, Robert F. Kennedy, to Georgia to talk to the judge who had sentenced Dr. King. It was not clear what role these actions played in obtaining Dr. King's release. But word of Kennedy's actions spread through black communities all over the nation. The Democrats made certain that it did.

On election day, blacks voted for John F. Kennedy because he seemed stronger on civil rights. About 70 percent of the black vote went to the Democrats. This vote made a great difference in several states. In Illinois, where Kennedy won by only 9,000 votes, he received 250,000 black votes. The story was similar in Michigan. Kennedy won Michigan by 67,000 votes, and he received about 250,000 black votes there. Black voters also kept South Carolina from going Republican. South Carolina's black voters cast 40,000 votes for the Democrats, and Kennedy carried the state by just 10,000 votes.

MORE BLACK OFFICIALS SERVED IN GOVERNMENT

After the election, Kennedy was slow in taking bold moves on civil rights. He hoped to advance the cause of civil rights without new legislation. The Department of Justice was instructed to take stronger action on voting rights. Kennedy also pressed for fair employment for blacks. He created the Committee on Equal Opportunity and appointed Vice-President Lyndon B. Johnson as chairman.

President Kennedy set an example of fair employment by appointing black officials to important positions in the federal government. Robert C. Weaver was appointed to head the Federal Housing and Home Finance Agency. Several blacks were appointed as federal judges. The famous NAACP lawyer Thurgood Marshall was made a judge on the United States Circuit Court of Appeals. James B. Parson became the first black federal District Court judge when he was appointed to the District Court of Northern Illinois. Wade McCree became a federal District Court judge in Michigan. Several blacks, including Marjorie Lawson, were appointed judges in Washington, D.C. Carl T. Rowan, a black journalist, became a Deputy Assistant Secretary of State and later Ambassador to Finland. Clifton R. Wharton was appointed Ambassador to Norway. Many other blacks received important appointments under President Kennedy.

STRONGER MEASURES WERE NEEDED

Afro-Americans pushed for stronger government action on voting and education. The Civil Rights Act of 1960, signed by President Eisenhower in May, 1960, gave federal judges the power to appoint referees to aid blacks in registering and voting. It was now a federal crime to use bombing and mob action to prevent carrying out court orders enforcing the law.

The new civil rights law did not bring much change in the South, however. The NAACP and other organizations therefore began campaigns to register voters throughout the South. White opposition remained strong. Local officials did nothing to stop threats against blacks who tried to register and vote. Southern judges refused to appoint voting referees, and the powers of the Justice Department were limited. The Kennedy administration brought more suits under the 1960 law than the Eisenhower administration had. But this was a slow process. And federal actions under the 1960 act did not solve the problem of the use of terror tactics against blacks. Even when whites were arrested for violence against blacks in the South, juries would not convict them.

Progress in school desegregation was also slow. But pressure continued on public schools and colleges. In 1960, a federal judge ordered desegregation of public schools in New Orleans. Federal marshals had to escort the first five black first-graders to school. White parents stoned blacks, fought with police, and boycotted the school. In other cities, integration proceeded more peacefully. In 1960, Houston, Texas, and Chapel Hill, Durham, and Raleigh in North Carolina, desegregated their schools. But only seventeen districts desegregated for the first time in 1960. South Carolina, Georgia, Alabama, and Mississippi still had not begun school desegregation.

By 1963, only 9.2 percent of all black students were attending integrated schools in the Southern and border states. In 1965, the federal government gave the school systems until the fall of 1967 to desegregate or face the loss of federal funds. All of the Southern states had some schools desegregated by 1966. Yet, in 1968, just 14 percent of the black students in eleven Southern states were in mixed schools. Hundreds of Southern cities still operated segregated schools.

Barriers to integration in higher education finally ended in Mississippi, Alabama, and South Carolina. In 1962, the University of Mississippi was ordered to admit James Meredith, a black student. Governor Ross Barnett pledged to disobey the court order. Then, at the last minute, he promised President Kennedy that he would make only token opposition and permit the university to be integrated. When Meredith went to the university in the company of United States marshals, rioting broke out. Two persons were killed and many injured. The President sent 12,000 troops to restore order. Meredith was admitted, but 300 soldiers remained on campus until July, 1963.

The President urged Governor George C. Wallace to help avoid violence when the University of Alabama was integrated. Wallace staged a brief protest by standing in the door of a university building. But two black students were admitted to the university in 1963 and protected by guardsmen.

South Carolina was the last state to end segregation in its colleges and universities. Desegregation in South Carolina ended, almost without incident, in 1963 when Clemson Agricultural College was ordered to admit Harvey Gantt.

GOVERNMENT ACTION IN CIVIL RIGHTS
INCREASED AFTER 1963

The demonstrations of 1963 caused President Kennedy to revise his views on civil rights. During his first years in office, he believed that he needed only to enforce the existing laws and take new actions in areas where the President was able to act on his own under executive powers. But in June, 1963, he made a television address to the nation calling for the most far-reaching civil rights legislation ever proposed.

During the summer of 1963, a bill was sent to Congress containing the President's recommendations. The March on Washington helped to emphasize the urgency of the situation. The civil rights movement had showed that it had large and influential support among Americans. Still, Congress continued to delay action on the bill. It seemed that a filibuster might kill the measure.

Soon after the March on Washington, other events caused Afro-Americans to lose some of their hope. In September, racism in Birmingham caused another event that sent a wave of shock across the nation. A bomb was thrown into the Sixteenth Street Baptist Church during Sunday School. Four children were killed, and twenty-one people were injured. In the November elections, many strong segregationists were elected to office in the South. The worst shock of all came on November 22, 1963—President Kennedy's death from an assassin's bullet during a visit to Dallas, Texas.

President Lyndon B. Johnson moved swiftly to assure black Americans that he was as deeply committed to civil rights as President Kennedy had been. In his first message to Congress, in January, 1964, he urged Congress to pass the civil rights bill. The President and civil rights groups continued to pressure Congress in the months that followed. Finally, in June of 1964, the Senate voted to limit debate, and the civil rights bill passed.

This Civil Rights Act of 1964 was the most sweeping civil rights measure ever to become law. The Attorney General received new powers to fight discrimination in education, voting, and the use of public facilities. Discrimination in public accommodations was made illegal, an Equal Employment Opportunity Commission was created, and federal funds were to be withheld from programs in which discrimination was practiced. Help was also provided to communities for resolving civil rights problems and for desegregating schools.

Opposition to the Civil Rights Act of 1964 developed immediately. Lester Maddox, who owned a restaurant and motel in Atlanta, created nationwide publicity by his efforts to keep black customers out of his restaurant. But the Supreme Court ruled that the law was constitutional. And many places of business all over the South began to comply with the law.

Everyone knew how blacks would vote in the election of 1964. The Republican Presidential candidate, Barry Goldwater, who had voted against the Civil Rights Act of 1964, tried to take advantage of white discontent, termed "white backlash." Governor George C. Wallace received an impressive number of "backlash" votes in the North during the Democratic Party primaries. Clearly, civil rights was a major political issue. Wallace finally withdrew as a third-party candidate to increase Senator Goldwater's chance of winning the election. Blacks were happy with President Johnson's record, and they believed his election was crucial to their cause. And black voters contributed heavily to the overwhelming victory won by President Johnson and Vice-President Hubert H. Humphrey in the 1964 election.

VOTER REGISTRATION EFFORTS INCREASED

Voter registration efforts were stepped up in the South in 1964. The NAACP, SCLC, CORE, and SNCC formed the Council of Federated Organizations (COFO) to carry on voter registration projects. COFO sent about 1,000 volunteers into Mississippi for the Mississippi Summer Project in 1964. These volunteers met bitter resistance. They were shot at, the buildings and churches they used were bombed and set afire, and many of them were arrested.

On March 15, 1965, President Johnson asked Congress for a

stronger law to protect voting rights. While the bill was before Congress, blacks continued to press for the right to vote, and white resistance hardened. On March 7, Dr. King and John Lewis of SNCC led a massive march in Selma, Alabama, to protest the intimidation of blacks trying to register. State police and sheriffs' deputies broke up the march with tear gas, clubs, and whips. Thousands of whites and blacks went to Selma for another march. A white minister, James J. Reeb, died from a beating he received from whites in Selma. On March 21, a second march from Selma to Montgomery began. President Johnson called the Alabama National Guard into federal service and ordered guardsmen to protect the marchers. The march ended with a rally at Montgomery attended by 40,000 people. A white participant, Viola Liuzzo of Detroit, was shot and killed by members of the Klan while driving back to Selma after the rally.

The events in Selma increased public support for the voting rights bill. Congress now passed the Voting Rights Act of 1965, and President Johnson signed it into law on August 6, 1965. The law provided for sending federal registration officials and election observers to counties where a pattern of discrimination existed. The use of literacy tests to discriminate was ended. The requirement of a poll tax in federal elections had already been eliminated by the Twenty-fourth Amendment to the Constitution ratified in 1964. The poll tax requirement in state elections was ruled unconstitutional by the Supreme Court soon after.

These new measures brought an increase in black registration. To keep their duties from being taken over by federal officials, many local officials began registering black voters. By 1966, almost 53 percent of voting-age blacks were registered in eleven Southern states. In 1968, 3,072,000 black citizens voted in the South.

THERE WAS ALSO BLACK UNREST IN THE NORTH

Unrest in the South served to point up the problems faced by black citizens in the North. Between 1950 and 1960, a total of 1,457,000 blacks moved out of the South. These migrants moved to the cities of the North and West, like those who had left the South before them. But conditions facing black newcomers in these cities were still extremely bad. White families began to move to the suburbs and left the decaying central cities to blacks. In spite of city and state laws, discrimination in housing continued. Blacks could buy and rent homes only in certain neighborhoods. Lending institutions, real estate brokers, and landlords made huge profits from blacks. They charged black families high rents and high prices for these homes, but nothing was done to keep up the property.

Other kinds of discrimination also continued in urban areas. Employment remained a problem. As industries moved their plants to the suburbs, many blacks lost their jobs. They could not buy or rent housing near the new plants. And often it was impossible to travel from the central city to suburban plants. Thus, unemployment was a continuing problem. In 1960, 10.7 percent of black male workers were unemployed compared with 4.8 percent of white male workers. Three years later, the percentages were 7.3 for blacks and 3.3 for whites. Even as blacks improved their employment status, the gap between the incomes of black families and white families remained great. In 1966, the median income of white families was $7,517 and black families $4,481. Two years later, the figure for whites had risen to $8,318 and for blacks to only $4,939. In 1968, an income of $3,335 was needed to support a nonfarm family of four above a poverty level. About 8.3 million nonwhite families in the United States lived below this poverty level.

School segregation also was a problem for Northern blacks. Although there were no laws requiring school segregation, separate schools did, in fact, exist. This *de facto* segregation was caused in part by segregated neighborhoods based on segregated housing patterns. In addition, school boards maintained segregation by drawing school boundaries in ways to keep black and white children in separate schools.

NORTHERN BLACKS PROTESTED SEGREGATED SCHOOLS

In 1960, black parents in New Rochelle, New York, called for an end to *de facto* segregation in the schools. The parents hired Paul Zuber, a black lawyer from New York City, to bring a court suit to end segregation. Zuber won the case in federal court, and New Rochelle was ordered to end *de facto* segregation.

Unrest over schools spread to other Northern cities. School boycotts became common after 1963. Boston, Chicago, Cleveland, and Cincinnati, among other cities, were the scene of boycotts in 1963 and 1964. Black parents waged a long, bitter struggle against the segregation policies of School Superintendent Benjamin C. Willis in Chicago. Northern whites supported these segregation policies by demanding to keep "neighborhood schools."

NORTHERN BLACKS TURNED TO VIOLENCE

Some Northern blacks followed the pattern of nonviolent protest used in the South. Dr. King went to Chicago in 1965, and at regular intervals after that, to work with black organizations in nonviolent demonstrations. Northern white leaders expressed great concern for bettering the conditions of black citizens. But usually they made small changes, while leaving the situation in housing, schools, and employment basically unchanged.

When the anger and frustrations of Northern blacks reached the breaking point, unlike Southern blacks they did not usually turn to nonviolent marches. Ghetto youth expressed their bitterness by destroying property belonging to white owners and clashing with the police. The police, even black policemen, represented the "enemy," because the police helped to maintain the system that black ghetto residents were struggling against.

The summer of 1964 was the first of a series of "long hot summers" during the 1960's. Rioting broke out in Harlem in July, 1964, and spread to Brooklyn. Riots also erupted in Rochester, New York; in Jersey City, Paterson, and Keansburg, New Jersey; in Dixmoor, Illinois; and in Philadelphia. During these outbreaks blacks broke into white-owned stores and looted them, and fought with the police.

Then, in 1965, the residents of Watts, a black suburb of Los Angeles, rioted. On August 11, a policeman tried to arrest Marquette Frye, an unemployed young black man, on a charge of driving while drunk. The resulting incident set off five days of rioting. Blacks burned buildings, looted, and attacked policemen. It took 13,000 National Guardsmen to restore order. When the rioting ended, 34 people were dead, 1,032 were injured, and about 4,000 had been arrested. About 200 businesses were totally destroyed, and three times that many were badly damaged. Property damage was estimated at $40 million.

During the next summer, more cities had racial disturbances. The National Guard had to help put down violence that erupted on the West Side of Chicago in July, 1966. About the same time, guardsmen had to be sent to Cleveland to restore order in the Hough section. Lesser disturbances broke out in Waukegan, Illinois; in Lansing and Benton Harbor, Michigan; in Omaha, Nebraska; in Brooklyn, New York; and in Dayton, Ohio. And rioting reached the Southern city of Atlanta during 1966.

American cities were hit by even worse racial disorders in 1967. More or less serious disturbances took place in nearly 150 cities. Tampa, Florida, and Atlanta, Georgia, had major riots. Minor disturbances broke out in other Southern cities. Most of the major riots, however, were in the North. Newark and several other New Jersey cities had widespread disorders. Major riots also broke out in Cincinnati and Detroit.

On July 27, President Johnson announced the creation of the National Advisory Commission on Civil Disorders. This commission was established to investigate the causes of racial disorders and to recommend ways of avoiding them. Governor Otto Kerner of Illinois was appointed chairman of the commission. The Kerner Commission issued its report on February 29, 1968. The commission said that white racism was a main cause of the riots. It recommended massive programs to create jobs; to reform the welfare system; to improve housing conditions; and to raise the quality of education. President Johnson made no comment on the report.

An era came to an end in 1968. Martin Luther King, Jr., went to Memphis to help support a strike by black sanitation workers. There, on April 4, he was shot and killed. His death touched off another wave of nationwide violence. Rioting broke out in 125 cities as black Americans expressed their rage and frustration over the loss of this great leader.

Chapter 21

The Challenge of Black Power

During the summer of 1966, the nation first heard the cry "black power." Since that time, black power has been an emotional issue in American life. Some Americans viewed it as a threat of violence, while others saw it as the first step toward true democracy and equality in America. Most black people agreed with the central idea of black power—that Afro-Americans needed to develop greater unity and racial pride. And most agreed with the idea that black people should have greater control over their own communities and the forces that affect their lives. The responses to black power varied greatly, but black power had a significant effect on the lives of black Americans in 1966 and in the years that followed.

STOKELY CARMICHAEL CALLED FOR BLACK POWER
During the summer of 1966, James Meredith, the first black student at the University of Mississippi, decided to undertake a "March Against

Fear." Meredith said that an "all-pervasive and overriding fear" filled the day-to-day life of black people in the United States. This was especially true of blacks in the South, particularly those in Mississippi. Meredith said that he had experienced this fear, and that he was determined to end it. To achieve this, he set out to walk from Memphis, Tennessee, to Jackson, Mississippi. He hoped that his walk through the heart of Mississippi would encourage the masses of black people in that state to register and vote.

On Sunday afternoon, June 5, Meredith set out from Memphis accompanied by a few friends. He had marched only about ten miles into Mississippi when a disturbed white citizen of Memphis shot him from ambush. At first, it was announced that Meredith had been killed. This news sent feelings of shock throughout the nation. Later reports lessened the shock when news came that Meredith was only slightly wounded.

The leaders of the major civil rights organizations rushed to Memphis to visit Meredith in the hospital. Three of them decided to continue the march. Martin Luther King, Jr., Floyd McKissick of CORE, and Stokely Carmichael of SNCC were joined by over 1,500 other marchers.

It became apparent to the marchers as they traveled through Mississippi that little had changed there. In Canton, they were denied the use of public property. State troopers used tear gas and rifle butts to force them to leave when they tried to stop on the grounds of a black public school. Martin Luther King, Jr., led a group to Philadelphia, Mississippi, in memory of Michael H. Schwerner, Andrew Goodman, and James E. Chaney, three young civil rights workers who had been murdered in Philadelphia in 1964. Dr. King and his followers were stoned and attacked by a mob. The local police did not interfere to try to prevent this violence until some of the marchers started to fight back.

It was not so much the violence against the marchers that captured the public's attention. Rather, it was the new term "black power" that caused widespread public excitement. In a speech at Greenwood, Mississippi, Stokely Carmichael, the young militant leader of SNCC, told a large mass meeting, "What we need is black power." A SNCC worker picked up the expression and led the crowd in chanting "black power" over and over again. As the march continued, the followers of Carmichael and of Floyd McKissick shouted this slogan from time to time. On June 17, television and other media spread the slogan "black power" across the nation.

246

BLACK POWER REFLECTED A NEW MOOD

Black power reflected the mood of black Americans in 1966. The civil rights movement was almost at a standstill after 1965. Important progress had been made in some areas, however. The Civil Rights Act of 1964 and the Voting Rights Act of 1965 had been passed. Although these acts were not fully enforced everywhere, important gains were made under them. Also, by 1965, all Americans were aware that serious problems existed in race relations in the nation. But contributions to civil rights groups began to fall off. Volunteers turned their energies to working in the poverty program and to protesting the war in Vietnam.

By 1966, only a relatively small number of black people had benefited from progress in civil rights. Thus, a few black children in the South were attending integrated schools, but the majority remained in the same inferior, segregated schools they had always attended. *De facto* segregation (segregation based on local practice but not on law) still prevailed in the schools of the North. In spite of federal and state measures to end discrimination in housing, the great majority of Northern blacks still lived in ghetto slums. Afro-Americans were not sharing in the nation's growing prosperity, and it seemed they were destined to remain poor and oppressed.

This situation caused a feeling of despair among black youth. The forgotten young people set off a wave of violence in the ghettos. They acted to draw attention to the terrible conditions of ghetto life by looting and burning. Many of these young people had never heard of Martin Luther King, Jr., and the nonviolent movement. When Dr. King went to Watts in Los Angeles to help restore order in August, 1965, most of the rioters did not know who he was. Standing amid the ruins of their community, one group of rioters declared that they had won a victory because they had drawn the nation's attention to their condition. The black riots caused civil rights leaders to realize that they had not reached the great mass of despairing black youth.

White resistance, or "white backlash" as it was called, also caused the civil rights movement to slow down. Harold Cruse, in his book *Crisis of the Negro Intellectual,* claimed that direct action was stopped by the white backlash. Cruse believed that the slogan "black power" was being used by CORE and SNCC to cover up defeat. He said that when the cry for black power began, social reality already had "forced so-called revolutionaries to put action aside and start thinking." And others agreed that black power brought a new direction for the civil rights movement. The idea of black power came as leaders were asking themselves, "Where do we go from here?" It caused a rethinking of the aims and goals of Afro-Americans.

THE SLOGAN CAUSED HEATED DISCUSSION

The call for black power caused anger and fear among many white Americans. To them, the new idea was associated with violence. Many believed that black power might lead to black supremacy, and they called it "racism in reverse." Such views were strengthened by the mass media. Reporters gave wide publicity to anything that Carmichael and other leaders said that seemed to connect black power with violence, even if this required that their statements be distorted. Liberal whites began to withdraw from the militant organizations that supported black power and to stop their contributions to those groups.

The more moderate civil rights leaders also were somewhat disturbed by the slogan. During Meredith's Mississippi march, Martin Luther King, Jr., expressed his opposition to black power. He said that he agreed with its positive aspects, but he felt that there were too many negative things connected with black power. Above all, Dr. King believed that it was self-defeating and showed an outlook of despair. He declared that the black power philosophy was "born out of the conviction that the Negro can't win. It was born from the wounds of despair and disappointment."

The NAACP and the National Urban League, too, expressed disapproval of black power. Roy Wilkins, in his keynote address to the NAACP convention on July 5, 1966, criticized black power. He said that before the appearance of black power the goals of the civil rights organizations had been the same. All of them had worked for "the inclusion of the American Negro, without racial discrimination, as a full-fledged equal in all phases of American citizenship." Wilkins believed that black power marked a turning away from nonviolence. He said that violence used in self-defense would lead to widespread violence against blacks. Wilkins also felt that black power meant separatism. The NAACP, Wilkins said, "will have none of this. It is the ranging of race against race on the irrelevant basis of skin color. It is the father of hatred and the mother of violence." The National Urban League was milder in its criticism. The League emphasized that it was still committed to an "interracial approach" to solving the problems of Afro-Americans. By 1968, Whitney Young, Jr., head of the National Urban League, was pointing to certain black power ideas that his organization could fully support.

SUPPORTERS EXPLAINED THE IDEAS OF BLACK POWER

Most black Americans understood that the supporters of black power were saying simply that black people "who were powerless before the continued injustices of the powerful need power." Almost from the beginning, most black Americans realized the positive and constructive aspects of black power.

One such group was the National Committee of Negro Churchmen, which met in New York City on July 22, 1966. This ministers' group said that black power was "an anguished and alarming cry" which showed that there were great problems in the life of the nation. They felt that black power "could serve a recreative role so desperately needed in America today." The committee saw black power as a means of moving blacks into the mainstream of American economic life.

The first stage in this movement, the committee said, would be the growth by black Americans into "responsible selfhood." To achieve this, they would have to overcome the results of centuries of racist repression and assert their own "inherent sense of worth and being." This was something each black person had to do individually as part of the community of black people.

Stokely Carmichael took the lead in explaining black power and in trying to convert it into a program for action. He called on black people to liberate themselves from the political, economic, and social forces that kept them second–class citizens. Thus, Carmichael urged blacks to organize themselves into strong political and social forces in order to gain control of the communities in which they lived. He did not favor alliances with whites to achieve this. Blacks, he felt, should organize and set their own goals. This meant a new role for white liberals. Carmichael urged whites to work in their own communities to fight racism and to build support for the black movement.

The black power advocates rejected integration as an immediate goal. Carmichael said that integration could be a long-range objective. But before blacks could achieve meaningful integration, he argued, they needed to "close ranks." That is, blacks needed to achieve group solidarity so that they could bargain effectively with other groups in American society. Carmichael believed that integration into American society as it existed was not enough. Black Americans, he felt, needed to help the nation to change its basic values. Racism and materialism had to be replaced by brotherhood and humanity as basic American values, Carmichael argued.

Charles Hamilton, a black political scientist, was one of the first scholarly advocates of black power. Hamilton and Carmichael together wrote a book titled *Black Power* in 1968, in which they defined black power as "a call for black people in this country to unite, to recognize their heritage, to build a sense of community. It is a call for black people to begin to define their own goals, to lead their own organizations, and to support those organizations. It is a call to reject the racist institutions and values of this society."

In other writings, Hamilton explained the relationship between the black community and the broader American society. Much of the black power philosophy dealt with development within the black community. Hamilton pointed out that "black people will need the help of whites at many places along the line." The black community lacked the technical and economic resources to pull itself up alone. American society as a whole would benefit by providing the resources to help the inner cities to become stable areas. Blacks also needed to become involved in decision making in all areas of American life on an equal basis. None of this would be easy to accomplish. Whites would feel threatened, and blacks would follow many paths in seeking political, economic, and social power.

BLACK POWER WAS INFLUENCED BY MALCOLM X ——
Many black thinkers had an influence on black power philosophy. The emphasis on building and supporting black businesses, which came to be called "black capitalism," owed much to the earlier teachings of Booker T. Washington and Marcus Garvey. W. E. B. Du Bois influenced the economic and political ideas associated with black power. The call for unity among black people throughout the world drew on ideas from Du Bois, Garvey, and other advocates of Pan-Africanism.

The most direct and immediate influence on black power thought came from Malcolm Little, who became famous as Malcolm X. As a child, Malcolm learned what racist violence was all about. The Klan burned his parents' home, and it was suspected that his father was killed because of his militant beliefs and actions. Malcolm grew up in the slums, where he learned to know poverty and despair. Like so many other youngsters of the slums, he turned to crime. Before he was 21 years old, he had been sentenced to ten years in prison.

In prison, Malcolm X changed the course of his life. There he began to read and study in order to improve his education. But even more important was his introduction to the beliefs of the Nation of Islam, or the Black Muslims, a growing religious movement among blacks. When he left prison in 1952, he began preparing to become

Malcolm X was one of the first militant spokesmen for black power. His ideas helped to shape the black power movement of the late 1960's.

a Black Muslim. Elijah Muhammad, the leader of the Nation of Islam, accepted Malcolm into the movement.

Malcolm X soon became the best known minister in the Black Muslim movement. He helped to build the Nation of Islam into a national movement. Malcolm spoke at colleges and schools throughout the country. He became a hero to militant youth. But his message was disturbing to white people and to many black people. Malcolm called for unity among Afro-Americans and for cooperation between black Americans and Africans. He believed that Pan-African unity was needed to provide the power for achieving political, economic, and social equality.

Malcolm X was often misunderstood. He was branded a separatist and an advocate of violence. While he was a member of the Black Muslims, he did reject white people, and he called for a separate state for blacks. Then in 1964, he broke with the Nation of Islam and became a member of the Moslem religion. He started two new organizations, the Muslim Mosque, Inc., and the Organization of Afro-American Unity.

Although Malcolm's views changed somewhat, he still did not think of integration as an immediate goal. He did not think immediate integration of blacks into American society was likely or necessary. As a first step toward equality, he called for black unity. To achieve unity, he believed that Afro-Americans first had to develop racial pride. Malcolm X said that white Americans needed to work within their own communities to combat racism there. He did not preach violence as a means of reaching the goals of black people. But he did advocate the use of violence in self-defense. Malcolm X spoke the language of the black urban masses, and they responded to him. His career was cut short when he was killed on February 21, 1965, but many of his ideas lived on in the black power philosophy.

BLACK PRIDE WAS SHOWN THROUGH SYMBOLS ⌐
Black power gave a great psychological boost to Afro-Americans. Black pride became a major force in the late 1960's. Blackness was no longer something to be ashamed of. Being black was to be gloried in and displayed proudly and with dignity. Many Afro-Americans insisted that they be called blacks, not Negroes or colored people. These latter terms were associated with the slave past, they argued, and did not reflect the new mood. Afro hair styles and clothes that reflected black Americans' pride in their African heritage also became popular.

Black pride went beyond symbols. Interest in learning about the history of black Americans increased. Students insisted that schools and colleges offer courses dealing with black life and culture. School systems began to revise their courses to include the role of Afro-Americans in American life. Major colleges and universities began to offer courses in black history and other subjects dealing with the black experience. Some set up new departments of black studies. Authors and publishers rushed to fill the demand for books and materials about black Americans.

BLACKS RESPONDED TO BLACK POWER IN MANY WAYS
A number of movements in the 1960's reflected the new mood of Afro-Americans. Several groups favored complete separation from American society. This was the view of the Nation of Islam, or the Black Muslims, which had begun during the 1930's as a small sect. By the 1960's, Elijah Muhammad had built the Muslims into a thriving religious and secular movement. Like the Garvey movement, the Black Muslims appealed mainly to lower-class blacks. The Muslims offered the black masses hope and a sense of worth. The Muslims demanded land within the United States to be used to establish a separate black nation. Elijah Muhammad preached that it was neither possible nor desirable to integrate with whites. He taught that "the white devils" were doomed and that the day of the black man was coming soon.

By the 1960's, the number of Muslims was estimated to be about 50,000 members. Black Muslims followed a strict discipline in morality, dress, and diet. The Muslims operated a number of business enterprises, including farms in the South, and hard work was emphasized. The Muslims seemed to be an extreme group to many whites, and the existence of the Muslims helped to increase white support for the civil rights movement. While many blacks sympathized with the Black Muslims, the great majority were not willing to turn from the goal of obtaining a fair share of what the United States provided for its citizens.

Other new groups appeared during the 1960's within the black movement. Members of one group, the Republic of New Africa, declared their independence of the United States. They asked for several states in the South in which to set up their republic, and they demanded reparation payments. A small group of black Jews obtained land in Liberia to establish a separate community, but they later moved to Israel.

The Black Panther Party, a revolutionary group, soon became the best known of the new groups. Huey P. Newton and Bobby G. Seale, two young black militants, founded the party in Oakland, California, late in 1966. The Panthers favored replacing capitalism with a socialist system. They had no objection to working with white radicals, so long as their white allies did not set the goals for blacks. In many ways, the Panthers were a stabilizing force in the ghettos. They sponsored a free breakfast program for ghetto children and free health clinics. They fought the use of drugs in black communities. But their open display of weapons and their use of revolutionary language made the Panthers a special target for law enforcement agencies, from city police to the Federal Bureau of Investigation. Many Panthers were sent to prison or lost their lives in clashes with the police.

The major civil rights organizations continued to push for integration. The National Urban League became more aggressive in its efforts to open more jobs. Businessmen, concerned about militant activities and boycotts, became more willing to listen to the League. And in response to black power, the League became more active in organizing black communities. It also emphasized job training for ghetto youth. The NAACP continued to press for civil rights legislation and for justice in the courts. The NAACP was deeply involved in political activities, and many of the gains in registration and election to office in the South came through the leadership of NAACP officials. The Southern Christian Leadership Conference (SCLC) began to try to mobilize the poor before Dr. King's death. Dr. King hoped to help black and white poor people to work together to solve their common grievances. His successor, Ralph D. Abernathy, continued this effort when he became head of SCLC. In May, 1968, he led the Poor People's March on Washington. Representatives of the nation's poor set up a camp site called Resurrection City in Washington, D.C. Over 50,000 people, about half of them white, participated in a Solidarity Day March on June 19. But the Poor People's March achieved few gains for the nation's poor.

SELF-HELP AGENCIES WERE ESTABLISHED
Numerous efforts were made by black Americans in the 1960's to establish self-help agencies and to gain greater control of their communities. Most of these self-help agencies received funds and aid from the federal government and from private industry. The anti-poverty program started by the Johnson administration helped to stimulate grass-roots activities in many black communities. President Johnson's

War on Poverty program failed to bring basic changes in the ghettos that blacks had hoped for. The program thus increased frustrations and made poor blacks more militant and willing to organize.

Most of the black self-help projects had practical purposes. The National Economic Growth and Reconstruction Organization (NEGRO) was organized in New York City in 1964 to increase business opportunities for blacks. It operated a hospital, a textile factory, and a construction company. By late 1967, it had assets of over $3 million and an annual payroll of over $1 million. Senator Robert F. Kennedy aided in forming two self-help community corporations in the Bedford-Stuyvesant section of Brooklyn in New York City. These projects received grants of funds from the Vincent Astor Foundation and the Ford Foundation, as well as from the federal government.

In Philadelphia, the Reverend Leon Sullivan formed the Opportunities Industrialization Center (OIC). This project enjoyed considerable success in training unemployed black workers and finding jobs for them. The OIC spread from Philadelphia to other cities. Churches and other black organizations operated similar projects.

Private corporations and business firms helped in the economic development of black communities. Several companies established black-operated factories and businesses in areas like Watts. Others opened job-training programs or hired large numbers of unskilled workers. Black businesses also received a boost when some corporations agreed to buy the products they produced and use them in making the corporations' products. The federal government also helped the growth of black businesses through the Small Business Administration, which furnished loans and advice to black businessmen.

CORE, which emphasized black economic development, helped to set up business cooperatives. It organized farmers' cooperatives in Louisiana and other Southern states. In Northern cities, CORE helped black businesses get started so that blacks could contribute more than labor to the economic system.

The Southern Christian Leadership Conference (SCLC) established Operation Breadbasket to increase economic opportunities in black communities. Under the direction of the Reverend Jesse Jackson, blacks in Chicago boycotted businesses that refused to hire or upgrade black workers. Businesses that sold inferior goods, refused to sell goods produced by black firms, or engaged in other unfair practices were forced by these boycotts to change their methods of operation. Jesse Jackson organized branches of Operation Breadbasket in cities across the country.

Clearly, self-help projects posed no threat to American capitalism. They also did not mark the beginning of a separate black economy. Such efforts brought a greater feeling of worth to many residents in black communities. These projects reached many who had not been affected by the civil rights movement before. But the economic gains of these projects were rather small. According to Bureau of the Census figures, 163,000 black businesses were in operation in 1969. They had annual sales of $4.5 billion. However, most black businessmen were limited to owning retail stores and firms that provided services. Gasoline stations, automobile sales, bars and restaurants, and food stores were the most common types of black businesses.

SUBSTANTIAL GAINS WERE MADE IN POLITICS

During the late 1960's, more blacks served in appointive and elective government offices than ever before. President Johnson appointed more blacks to high government positions than President Kennedy had. In 1964, Carl T. Rowan, who was then Ambassador to Finland, was named head of the United States Information Agency (USIA). As Director of the USIA, Rowan was the first Afro-American to sit on the National Security Council. The next year, Thurgood Marshall was appointed Solicitor General of the United States. And in 1967, Marshall became the first black Justice ever appointed to the United States Supreme Court.

Two important appointments were given to black women during 1965 and 1966. Patricia R. Harris became the first black woman to serve as an American ambassador when President Johnson appointed her Ambassador to Luxembourg. In 1966, Constance Baker Motley was the first black woman appointed as a federal court judge.

Black Americans received two other significant positions in the federal government in 1966. Robert C. Weaver became a member of the President's Cabinet when he was appointed Secretary of the new Department of Housing and Urban Development. And Andrew F. Brimmer was appointed a member of the Federal Reserve Board.

Black officials in prominent government positions received nationwide publicity, even though black officeholders still comprised a relatively small percentage of the total number of federal jobs. By 1968, 107 black Americans were serving in high positions on key governmental policy-making bodies. Seven blacks served as American ambassadors, eleven as federal judges, and many others as members of federal regulatory agencies. Ralph J. Bunche was Under Secretary General of the

United Nations, and eight black Americans served on the United States Mission to the United Nations.

The most significant gains came in elections to public offices. The registration drives in the South brought a great increase in black voters. In 1968, about 3.1 million Afro-Americans were eligible to vote in the South. Julian Bond was elected a member of the Georgia legislature in 1966, but he was denied his seat because of his opposition to the Vietnam War. Finally, the Supreme Court ruled that Georgia must allow him to serve as a duly elected member. Robert C. Clark was elected to the Mississippi legislature in 1967.

By 1969, about 400 Afro-Americans held local elective offices in Southern states. Although many of these were minor offices, these growing numbers reflected the great change taking place. Thirty blacks were members of state legislatures in Southern states at this time. Georgia had two state senators and twelve representatives. In several counties with black majorities, blacks held important offices. Charles Evers, the Executive Secretary of the NAACP in Mississippi, won the office of mayor in Fayette, Mississippi. In Greene County, Alabama, black majorities were elected to the school board and to the county commission. Voters in Macon County, Alabama, where Tuskegee is located, elected blacks to several offices, including that of sheriff. (Later, in 1972, Tuskegee elected a black mayor.)

The number of black office holders also increased in the North, where the support of white voters was needed for election to government offices. The highest elected black official was Republican Senator Edward W. Brooke of Massachusetts, who won his seat in the Senate in 1966. He became the first black member of the Senate since Reconstruction. After the 1968 election, nine blacks from Northern and Western states sat in the House of Representatives.

The use of black voters as a base for political power was demonstrated by the election of black mayors in several large cities. Richard Hatcher won office as mayor of Gary, Indiana, in 1967, with almost solid black support and some white support. Carl B. Stokes used the same strategy to become mayor of Cleveland, Ohio, in the same year. Flint, Michigan, and Springfield, Ohio, were among other Northern cities that elected black mayors in the mid-1960's.

BLACKS VIEWED THE ELECTION OF 1968 AS A SETBACK
During the election campaign of 1968, Republican Presidential candidate Richard M. Nixon appealed to white voters in "backlash" areas.

His emphasis on law and order gained him support in the South and among white voters in the suburbs and cities in the North. By 1968, the worst of the urban violence and rioting had come to an end. But many whites were still upset about the riots and the black power slogan. When Nixon won the election, most blacks expected a marked change to occur in the federal government's efforts on behalf of civil rights.

It seemed that black fears were justified as the new Nixon administration began its term of office. Members of the Nixon administration insisted that the President was completely committed to civil rights. Nixon aides talked about the importance of black capitalism and the need to support black businesses. James Farmer, the former head of CORE, was made Assistant Secretary of Health, Education, and Welfare. But the Republican Party's use of a much-talked-about "Southern strategy," or plan to gain white Southern support, led to a further slowdown in the already slow pace of desegregation in the South.

Evidence that such a "Southern strategy" existed was clear by mid-1969. Attorney General John N. Mitchell recommended a much weaker voting rights act to replace the 1965 law. The Attorney General and the Secretary of Health, Education, and Welfare announced that public school systems did not have to meet the deadlines set by the Johnson administration for desegregating their schools. The NAACP's Board of Directors asserted that "the abandonment of the firm and fixed deadline of September, 1969 . . . is a direct insult to our courts and has the distinct odor of political payoff." President Nixon also tried to appoint two Southern conservatives as Justices of the Supreme Court, but the Senate turned down these appointments.

BLACKS WERE DIVIDED OVER VIETNAM

Considerable opposition to the war in Vietnam had developed by 1968, but opinion was greatly divided. Opinion among black Americans was as divided as it was among white Americans. The militant groups generally held that the war was not an issue that should concern blacks. Some moderate blacks also felt that protesting the war would require time and energy that would be better used in the civil rights struggle. However, Martin Luther King, Jr., had been a leader of the antiwar movement before his death in April, 1968.

Blacks who opposed the war often did so for practical reasons. They stressed that the war was a terrible financial burden on the nation. The resources used to fight in Vietnam, they argued, could be used to rebuild America's cities and to fight poverty here at home. They were also concerned over the large numbers of young black soldiers who were dying in Vietnam. In 1966, for example, blacks made up 22 percent of the enlisted men serving in combat units in Vietnam. Blacks also made up 22 percent of those who were killed in the fighting.

Yet the door to opportunity seemed more open in the military service than in other areas of American life. By 1968, 321,000 blacks were serving in the armed forces. Their re-enlistment rate was three times greater than that of whites. A significant increase also occurred in the number of black students in the armed forces military academies. In September, 1968, Frederick E. Davison became the third black soldier in America's history to attain the rank of general.

BLACKS CONTINUED TO CONTRIBUTE IN MANY FIELDS

By the end of the 1960's, blacks were well established in major league football and basketball. By 1968, over half of the players in the National Basketball Association were blacks. The two professional football leagues had more than 25 percent black players, and the baseball leagues had over 30 percent. In 1966, a black umpire appeared in major league baseball, and Bill Russell became the first major league basketball coach the same year.

Blacks continued to play important roles in popular music during the 1960's. Chubby Checker started a new dance fad during the early 1960's by introducing "The Twist." "Soul" music became one of the most widely listened to types of popular music. James Brown was the leading "soul" singer of the period. In 1966, he ranked second in the Billboard Campus Popularity Poll. Aretha Franklin, the Supremes, Jimi Hendrix, Stevie Wonder, Diana Ross, Sammy Davis, Jr., and other singers enjoyed great success in popular music.

The black image in movies and on television improved. Sidney Poitier won an Academy Award in 1963 as the best actor for his role in *Lilies of the Field*. Major roles for blacks in motion pictures remained scarce until the late 1960's. But some of the most popular television shows included blacks in significant roles. Bill Cosby won Emmy awards in 1966, 1967, and 1968 for his role in the television series *I Spy*. By 1968, thirteen weekly series on the three major television networks were featuring or starring black actors and actresses.

259

Chapter 22

The 1970's: An Uncertain Future

To the casual onlooker, it may have seemed that much had changed in American race relations by the 1970's. But the careful observer would find that the change had been uneven. The civil rights and black power movements of the 1950's and 1960's brought slow reform, not revolutionary change. In politics and government, in the entertainment world, sports, and some other areas of American life, blacks were more visible than ever before. Rioting no longer seemed a major problem, and revolutionary talk was heard less often. Still, beneath this calm surface many of the old problems remained unsolved. And black militance remained a strong force in American life.

BLACK NATIONALISM WAS STRONGER BY THE 1970'S

As the 1970's began, it was not clear what methods and policies black leaders and organizations would use in their continuing efforts to end all forms of discrimination. It also was not clear how white Americans would respond to the continuing demand from blacks for an open society. The civil rights movement no longer was united on the methods to be used in achieving full citizenship. The search for identity by Afro-Americans had been impressively successful. Black people knew who they were and had effectively emphasized the symbols of black pride. More and more, blacks talked about controlling their communities and building effective black institutions. This was to some extent reflected in a growth in black nationalism, a turning inward. Several factors probably influenced this turning inward. The black power philosophy played an important role. White resistance to change, and the fear of many black Americans that the Nixon administration was not concerned enough about racial problems, were other significant forces.

BLACK LEADERSHIP CHANGED

It was apparent as the 1960's ended that black leadership was fragmented. Whites began to realize that no one leader or small group of leaders could speak for black people. The men who headed the older national organizations, such as Roy Wilkins and Whitney Young, Jr., until his death in 1971, remained influential. And there was also a growing group of younger political leaders who were responding to the needs of black Americans. At the same time, much of the action for change had moved into local communities and involved grass-root efforts.

Most of the new leaders were young, capable, and practical. Many of them were not known outside their own cities. Jesse Jackson was one who acquired a national reputation. His close relationship with Martin Luther King, Jr., and his successful efforts with Operation Breadbasket in Chicago brought him national attention. Jackson ran into problems with the leaders of the Southern Christian Leadership Conference in 1971, and he broke with the SCLC. Soon afterward, he started his own organization, People United to Save Humanity (PUSH).

Percy Green of St. Louis was less well known than Jackson. Green headed ACTION, which, like Operation Breadbasket, pressured businesses into hiring black workers in responsible positions. One of ACTION's major efforts was directed against the McDonnell-Douglas Corporation, an aircraft company. Green's group presented evidence to the Civil Rights Commission of unfair employment practices at McDonnell-Douglas. As a result, the Defense Department ordered the company to hire more black workers in order to keep its government contracts.

Another product of urban unrest and black militance was the National Welfare Rights Organization (NWRO). Founded in 1966, NWRO had chapters in every state by 1970. Its goals were the practical ones of obtaining more humane treatment for the nation's poor and an adequate income to raise the poor above the poverty level. Dr. George Wiley, a chemist from Cornell University, first headed NWRO; then Mrs. Johnnie Tillmon became executive director of NWRO. Other black women also were important leaders of the organization. In 1971, NWRO announced its income plan for a guaranteed annual income of $6,500 for every family. The following year, members of NWRO tried to get both major political parties to include this guarantee as a plank in their platforms.

Other new leaders urged separate development for black people. Leading advocates of a black nation within the American nation were Roy Innis of CORE and Nathan Hare, a black scholar. The best known of the militant groups, the Black Panther Party, began to change its emphasis in the early 1970's. Between 1966 and 1972, the Panthers had lost many members in clashes with law enforcement officials. In 1972, party leader Huey P. Newton began changing the image of the Panthers. They put their weapons away and began to avoid publicity. The Panthers turned their attention to what they called "survival" programs in black communities. They continued their free breakfast program for ghetto children. In addition, they began setting up free health clinics, distributing food and clothing, providing free ambulance service, free bus service for the families of prison inmates, and other services in ghetto communities.

MOST BLACKS NOW LIVED IN CITIES

By 1970, the great majority of blacks lived in cities. The 1970 census recorded a total of 22,673,000 black Americans. Of this total, 74 percent lived in metropolitan areas. Of those in metropolitan areas, 57.8 percent lived in central cities. There were over 8 million Afro-Americans living in the nation's fifteen largest cities. And nearly half of the black population was concentrated in fifty cities.

New York City, with 1.7 million, had the largest black population. Chicago ranked second with 1.1 million, and Detroit was third with over 660,000. Cities where blacks made up over 50 percent of the residents included Washington, D.C.; Compton, California; East St.

Louis, Illinois; Newark, New Jersey; Gary, Indiana; and Atlanta, Georgia. Several cities had more than 40 percent black residents in their total population. These included Baltimore, New Orleans, Savannah, Detroit, Richmond, and Jackson, Mississippi.

POVERTY AND JOB OPPORTUNITIES
REMAINED SERIOUS PROBLEMS

Poverty, low incomes, and unemployment were major problems among urban blacks. In late 1971, about 12 percent of urban blacks were out of work. The unemployment rate was even higher for black veterans returning from Vietnam. Some improvement in black economic status had taken place by 1970. Between 1965 and 1970, the economic gap between white and black families closed somewhat. During this period, the average white family's yearly income increased 40 percent to reach $10,236. The average black family's yearly income grew 60 percent and reached $6,279.

The average black family earned 61 percent as much money in 1971 as the average white family. In 1965, by contrast, it had earned 54 percent as much. Another indication of improvement was the fact that black families earning over $10,000 doubled between 1965 and 1970. A study in 1972 by the National Industrial Conference Board showed that in 1970, 28 percent of black families earned over $10,000, compared with 52 percent of white families.

Still, United States Census figures showed sharp differences between the percentages of whites and blacks below the poverty level. Government figures estimated that an income of $3,968 was necessary to support a nonfarm family of four at the poverty level. In 1970, the census found that nearly 17 million white persons and just over 7 million black persons lived below the poverty level. But in percentage terms, 9.5 percent of all white Americans had incomes at this level, compared with 32 percent of all black Americans.

The federal government did not make as strong efforts to enforce fair employment practices in the 1970's as in the 1960's. Two federal court decisions offered some hope for progress, however. A federal district court upheld the Philadelphia Plan, which required building contractors who wished to bid on federally financed construction projects costing over $500,000 to hire a fixed number of minority-group workers. By mid-1971, similar plans had been started in Washington, D.C., San Francisco, Seattle, and Atlanta. In another important ruling, the Supreme Court held that job tests could not be used unless they were related to ability to do a job.

Housing patterns in America's cities were both a cause and an effect of poverty. Nearly 80 percent of all new jobs now were in the suburbs located outside the cities. Industries followed the move of middle-class and working-class whites out of the central cities into the suburbs. Yet those blacks most in need of jobs were trapped in the central cities by discrimination and poverty. Housing decay in the central cities grew worse in spite of federal programs. And urban problems were given less emphasis during the first years of the Nixon administration.

The Federal Housing Administration (FHA) did not provide black families adequate housing assistance. For a time, it seemed that the federal government would help to open the suburbs to blacks and other low-income groups. But attempts to do this met strong opposition from suburban residents. A court suit brought by the federal government to overturn zoning regulations in Black Jack, Missouri, a suburb of St. Louis, dragged on for several years. In the meantime, other government programs to aid blacks in the central cities brought few results.

The FHA program to help black families buy homes in the cities often was used by housing speculators to benefit themselves at the expense of the poor. Speculators bought rundown houses at cheap prices, then did shoddy repair work on them. In some cases, FHA officials were influenced or even bribed to approve the sale of these houses at high prices on long-term loans. The poor family who bought such a home soon found that it needed costly repairs. Unable to pay for repairs, the family often had to move out. In city after city, such housing then became the property of the federal government. George Romney, President Nixon's Secretary of Housing and Urban Development, tried to reform the FHA program to end such dishonest practices. Meanwhile adequate housing for blacks in the central cities remained a serious national problem.

President Nixon, in June, 1971, issued a statement on housing discrimination. He pledged to enforce the Open Housing Act of 1968, which banned discrimination because of race or religion. At the same time, he reassured white residents in the suburbs by saying that he would not force economic integration, that is, the mixing of people of different income levels in the same neighborhoods. In other words, the federal government would not push for low and moderate income housing nor for public housing in suburban areas. This policy would not remove the barriers that trapped blacks in central cities and prevented them from leaving.

PRESIDENT NIXON MODIFIED
GOVERNMENT POLICIES

One of President Nixon's advisers urged him to follow a policy of "benign neglect," or a friendly hands-off policy on racial problems. The President never announced such a policy, and members of his administration insisted that President Nixon was committed to achieving results in this area. But many black citizens believed that the problems of black Americans were being ignored. Some black leaders charged that the policies of the Nixon administration were designed to turn back the clock in civil rights. In 1972, Vernon Jordan, Jr., the new Executive Secretary of the National Urban League, said that he feared that the "second Reconstruction" was ending. He charged that black people were "going out of style" and that their "aspirations and ideals" were being "shunted aside."

President Nixon's views on the use of federal power to end segregation helped to explain this gloomy outlook of many black Americans. The "second Reconstruction," like the first, was characterized by strong governmental action on behalf of civil rights. President Nixon's efforts to build up the Republican Party in the South, the so-called "Southern strategy," meant less emphasis on federal action. This was especially true in policies involving school desegregation. The President made it clear that he would not use strong measures to bring about desegregation. He favored leaving enforcement of desegregation largely to the courts and to local school boards. But the President did not mean that federal efforts to end segregation were to be halted. The Department of Health, Education, and Welfare and the Department of Justice continued to work with local and state officials to bring about school desegregation. And during the fall of 1970, the Nixon administration moved to desegregate more public schools in the South, and this effort met little open resistance.

SCHOOL BUSING BECAME A POLITICAL ISSUE

By 1971, opponents of school desegregation began to use the issue of busing as a means of fighting desegregation. Busing became a hotly contested issue in the North when federal courts began to order that school children be bused to end *de facto* segregation. In Pontiac, Michigan, school buses were destroyed. White parents formed the National Action Group (NAG) to protest busing. NAG staged a march on Washington. A Constitutional amendment was offered in Congress to prohibit busing to achieve racial balance in schools.

Governor George C. Wallace of Alabama made busing a hotly debated political issue during the Presidential primary campaigns of 1972. President Nixon took up the issue. He went on television to announce that he planned to ask Congress to pass a law to prevent the courts from ordering the use of busing to achieve desegregation. On March 24, 1972, Nixon asked Congress to halt all new busing orders until July 1, 1973. He also requested funds to be used in segregated inner-city schools to improve the quality of education in those schools.

Southern leaders were cool toward the President's proposals because they felt that these measures would aid Northern segregationists and have little effect in the South. Many Southern school systems were already using busing as a means of achieving desegregation. There was much confusion about the proposal. The Acting Attorney General told the House Judiciary Committee that President Nixon's proposals would permit the reopening of every school desegregation case in the country. At the same time, the Secretary of Health, Education, and Welfare stated that the proposals would permit the reopening of only a few cases.

The Department of Justice also began entering cases trying to keep courts from ordering school busing. The Department intervened in cases in Denver, Detroit, Richmond, and Nashville. It seemed to many black Americans that the very agency that had been given authority to protect the civil rights of blacks was now undermining those rights.

Protests came from within the Nixon administration. The Council of Black Appointees, composed of over forty government officials, sent the President a six-page report. A letter from Assistant Secretary of Housing and Urban Development Samuel C. Jackson was sent with the report. Jackson, one of the highest-ranking black officials in the administration, informed the President that his busing policies would increase distrust of the government in the black community. Jackson said that the activities of the Department of Justice had "already had a chilling effect on black people and others." In addition to this protest, 95 of the 148 lawyers in the Civil Rights Division of the Justice Department sent a letter to Congressional leaders opposing the President's proposed anti-busing legislation.

THE SUPREME COURT SHOWED SIGNS OF CHANGE

By 1972, the Supreme Court was giving indications of turning away from its strong support of civil rights. President Nixon had helped bring about this changing attitude on the part of the Court. In 1969, he appointed Warren Burger as Chief Justice of the Supreme Court. Then, after two Southern conservatives he wished to appoint to the Court were not approved by the Senate, Nixon selected as Justices Lewis F. Powell and William H. Rhenquist. Although the Senate approved these two Justices, blacks viewed them as less than strong supporters of civil rights.

Chief Justice Burger, in April, 1971, gave the first indication of a change in the Court's view concerning school desegregation. He stated that it was not necessary for every public school to have racial balance in order to meet the Court's desegregation guidelines. Chief Justice Burger declared: "The Constitutional command to desegregate schools does not mean that every school in every community must always reflect the racial composition of the school system as a whole." Some civil rights leaders believed this was a signal to Southern schools that they could slow down desegregation.

In 1971, the Supreme Court made its first anti-civil rights ruling in many years. The case involving swimming pools in Jackson, Mississippi, was a case that had begun many years earlier. In 1962, a federal court ordered the city of Jackson to desegregate all its public facilities. In order to avoid integrating the swimming pools, the city closed them. The Supreme Court ruled, five to four, that a city can close swimming pools to avoid complying with a court order to desegregate. In a strong dissent, Justice Thurgood Marshall said that the decision had "turned the clock back 17 years."

Then, in 1972, the Court upheld discrimination by private clubs. Justice Rhenquist, one of the new Nixon Justices, wrote the majority opinion. He said that so long as clubs announced that they were "not open to the public at large" they were free to practice discrimination and segregation.

In March, 1973, the Supreme Court handed down a decision that affected millions of black and white school children. The Court ruled that the use of the property tax to finance public schools was constitutional, despite the differences in wealth among communities in each state. Property taxes had long been used to support local schools, but in the early 1970's blacks and other minority groups argued that the result was that students from poor areas did not receive as good an education as students from wealthier communities. Again, Justice Marshall strongly dissented from the court's decision declaring that the decision was a "retreat from our historic commitment to equality of educational opportunity. . . ."

BLACKS MADE POLITICAL GAINS

Political participation continued to be an area of continuing progress for black Americans in the early 1970's. The elections of 1970 and 1971 brought new gains in office holding. Politics represented an area where black pride and black unity could bring practical results. The large concentration of blacks in urban areas formed political power bases. Political leaders began to emerge who were in step with the black mood of the 1970's and skillful enough to survive tough political battles.

At least 300 black candidates ran for national, state, and local offices in the November, 1970, elections. About 114 of them won offices. Maryland elected another black legislator, Parren Mitchell, to the United States House of Representatives. Ronald Dellums of California and George W. Collins of Illinois were other new members of the House. The voters of Harlem elected Charles B. Rangel to the House seat held for many years by Adam Clayton Powell, Jr. By 1971, a total of 14 blacks were now serving in the Congress, 13 in the House and 1 in the Senate. Progress in the South was particularly striking. As a result of state and local elections from 1968 to 1970, the number of black elected officials in the South rose from 385 in 1968 to 644 in 1970.

With the election of Kenneth Gibson as mayor of Newark, New Jersey, black mayors presided over 4 major cities and 77 smaller ones. Gibson joined Walter Washington of the District of Columbia, Carl B. Stokes of Cleveland, and Richard G. Hatcher of Gary as the chief executive of a large city. The elections of 1971 added, among others, black mayors in Englewood, New Jersey, and Kalamazoo, Michigan.

In 1971, black office holders in the South numbered 735. This number rose to 873 by early 1972. (A few individuals even held more than one office.) The largest group of office holders were city officials, who numbered 425. Also included were 6 state senators, 41 state representatives, 111 county officials, 117 law enforcement officials, and 176 members of school boards. One of the most publicized and exciting races of 1971 was Mayor Charles Evers' unsuccessful bid for the governorship of Mississippi.

Throughout the nation, the total of black elected officials exceeded 1,500 by 1971. Even so, this was less than 1 percent of all office holders in the nation. In some Northern and Western states, blacks now held positions of considerable political power. In Pennsylvania, K. Leroy Irvis was Democratic floor leader in the House of the state legislature. Assemblyman Willie L. Brown was chairman of the powerful ways and means committee of the California state legislature. In the Illinois state legislature, Cecil Partee served as President *pro tempore* of the Senate, and Corneal A. Davis was assistant Democratic minority leader in the House. California voters elected Wilson C. Riles as Superintendent of Public Instruction in a statewide election in 1970. These were only a few of the positions that served to give black Americans hope for progress through political participation during the 1970's.

A NEW POLITICAL STYLE DEVELOPED

Afro-Americans expected much of their political leaders. No longer could black politicians blindly follow the leaders of their political party. The voters back home were no longer satisfied with a few minor jobs. Black politicians were expected to speak out on the issues important to black people and to work for programs to advance black goals. Representative William Clay of St. Louis voiced the new political style when he said that blacks, like other groups, had to be practical and selfish in their own interest. They had to become a part of the give and take of politics and deal with anyone who could help them reach their goals.

In keeping with the new style in politics, the black members of the United States House of Representatives formed the Black Caucus. Representative Charles C. Diggs of Michigan was the first chairman of the group, then was succeeded by Representative Louis Stokes of Ohio in 1972. In 1971, the Black Caucus set up a staff, headed by Howard T. Robinson, to help it in its work. In 1972, August A. Adair, professor of government at Morgan State College, succeeded Robinson as staff director.

The Black Caucus engaged in a variety of activities. Its members discussed and made recommendations to have the group support or oppose bills before the House. The need for new legislation also became a regular subject for discussion. The Caucus gained considerable publicity on television, radio, and in the press by holding hearings on issues of concern to Afro-Americans. The Caucus held hearings, for example, on discrimination in the military services and on FBI investigations of black leaders.

In 1971, the Caucus sent President Nixon sixty proposals for improving the condition of minorities, and demanded that the President respond to the Caucus' recommendations by May 17, 1971, the seventeenth anniversary of the Supreme Court's school desegregation decision. The recommendations included requests for summer jobs for

The Black Caucus became an influential group in Congress in the 1970's. These Representatives skillfully supported programs to aid Afro-Americans.

black youth, funds for new jobs in public service in black communities, a guaranteed annual family income of $6,500, and improved enforcement of civil rights laws. Other proposals included an end to the war in Vietnam, home rule, or locally elected government, for the District of Columbia, and changes in American policies in African affairs.

President Nixon responded to the Caucus with a lengthy report. Nixon pledged that his administration would continue to press "for jobs, income and tangible benefits, the pledges that this society has made to the disadvantaged in the past decades." He did not agree that the massive programs recommended by the Caucus were needed. His welfare reform program included a guaranteed yearly family income of $2,400. Instead of the million summer jobs requested, the President promised about one-half million.

THE GARY CONVENTION
WAS A SIGNIFICANT EVENT

But the main political question of the early 1970's was the Presidential election of 1972. To prepare for the election, blacks held the National Black Political Convention in Gary, Indiana, on March 9–12, 1972. Representative Charles C. Diggs, Mayor Richard Hatcher, and Imamu A. Baraka (LeRoi Jones) of Newark helped organize the convention. Nearly 3,000 delegates and hundreds of observers attended the convention.

The Gary Convention was a very unusual event. Blacks of all political views gathered to try to agree on a set of principles to guide black people during the election year. Disagreement among the delegates was expected, but the amount of unity achieved was rather remarkable. Imamu A. Baraka, a black nationalist, emerged as the unifying force in the convention. The delegates passed eighty-eight recommendations on issues important to black Americans. This set of recommendations was called the National Black Agenda. It contained many of the issues that had been raised by the National Welfare Rights Organization, the Black Caucus, and other groups.

Two resolutions that were passed by the convention caused a great deal of controversy. Many blacks could not agree with a pro-Arab resolution that condemned Israel for its "expansionist policy." Even more controversial was the convention's actions concerning busing black students to achieve school desegregation. On the last day of the meeting, the convention passed a resolution favored by black nationalists which declared that "forced racial integration of schools" was unsound. The resolution stated that integration policies were "based on the false notion that black children are unable to learn unless they are in the same setting with white children." Instead of busing black children to achieve racial balance in schools, the resolution called for "quality education in the black community through community-controlled state school districts and a guaranteed equal share of all educational money."

Later, when reports in many newspapers and on television newscasts said that the convention's actions seemed to show that black Americans opposed busing, the steering committee of the Gary Convention amended the resolution. The amended resolution said that busing was not the "real issue in American education today." The steering committee called "the Nixon Administration and other forces" dishonest for making busing an issue. The committee's amended resolution pointed out that busing had, in fact, been used for many years in all sections of the country to maintain segregated schools.

This change in the resolution on busing still did not satisfy Roy Wilkins. In fact, the NAACP strongly opposed all of the more nationalistic recommendations and resolutions passed by the convention. As a result, Wilkins withdrew NAACP support from the convention. He said that the statement of policy adopted on busing gave "half-hearted or meaningless endorsement to busing while in fact calling for abandonment of the fight against segregation."

BLACKS PARTICIPATED IN THE 1972
PRESIDENTIAL CONVENTIONS

The Democratic National Convention met in Miami, Florida, during the summer of 1972 to name the party's candidates for President and Vice-President. Even before the convention met, it was clear that the Democratic Party was seriously split. Efforts to reform the party in order to give young people, women, and minority groups a larger role angered many older Democratic leaders. Many of these party leaders, along with some labor leaders and others, also were opposed to Senator George S. McGovern of South Dakota, who was the leading contender for the Democratic Presidential nomination.

Black political leaders played a greater role in the 1972 Democratic Convention than in any other national political convention in history. Late in 1971, the Democratic National Committee elected Patricia R. Harris, a black lawyer, as temporary chairman of the party's Credentials Committee for the 1972 convention. Patricia Harris had served as United States Ambassador to Luxembourg and as dean of the Howard University Law School. Another black woman, Yvonne Brathwaite Burke, who at that time was a member of the California state assembly, was named vice chairman of the Democratic National Convention. Newark's Mayor Kenneth A. Gibson served on the platform committee. During the convention, the Democratic National Committee elected Basil Paterson, a black politician from New York, as deputy chairman of the Democratic Party.

With black delegates making up about 15 percent of the members of the Democratic convention, all of the candidates were concerned about how these delegates would vote. Senator McGovern needed the support of many of the black delegates to win the nomination on the first ballot. Those opposed to Senator McGovern hoped to win some of his black support away from him. On the first day of the convention, the leading candidates spoke to a caucus of black delegates and alternate delegates. Among the candidates who spoke was Representative Shirley Chisholm of New York, the first black woman to seek the Democratic nomination for President. Representative Chisholm asked the black delegates to vote for her on the first ballot as a gesture of black unity. McGovern supporters successfully opposed this move. They feared that if black delegates voted for Shirley Chisholm, McGovern might not win on the first ballot, and this would aid the "stop-McGovern" delegates.

When the vote came, Senator McGovern received the Democratic Presidential nomination on the first ballot. Walter Fauntroy, the nonvoting member of the House of Representatives from Washington, D.C., and Representative William Clay of Missouri were able to keep the black delegates loyal to McGovern. McGovern had promised these black leaders more federal jobs for blacks if he became President. He also promised them funds for a black voter registration drive. But the convention delegates voted down the demand for a platform plank favoring a guaranteed annual income of $6,500 for every American family. Senator McGovern favored tax and welfare reform, as well as a guaranteed annual income lower than $6,500. But he changed his proposal for a guaranteed income several times during the election campaign.

The 1972 Republican National Convention was held shortly after the Democratic Convention. The Republicans were united, and they knew that they were meeting at Miami to nominate President Richard M. Nixon for a second term. The convention was planned carefully, and President Nixon and Vice-President Spiro Agnew won the nomination with little opposition. Black Republicans did not have important roles in the convention. But the number of black delegates at the 1972 Republican Party convention was much larger than at the convention in 1968. Black delegates made up 3.9 percent of the 1972 convention, compared with 1.9 percent in the 1968 convention.

. A number of well-known black Americans supported President Nixon for reelection. Before the convention, black Republicans sponsored a successful fund-raising event for the Nixon campaign. Former civil rights leader Floyd McKissick, actor and former football player Jim Brown, and Mrs. Betty Shabazz, widow of Malcolm X, were among those present. During the convention, entertainer Sammy Davis, Jr., appeared on stage with the President before a large audience of young Republicans. Other black entertainers who supported President Nixon included Lionel Hampton, Johnny Mathis, and James Brown.

BLACK AMERICANS MADE POLITICAL GAINS IN 1972

Black voters viewed the election results in 1972 with mixed emotions. They were not happy about President Nixon's landslide victory over Senator McGovern in which Nixon received over 60 percent of the popular vote. Black voters gave McGovern 87 percent of their votes. Now they feared that federal programs to aid black Americans might be reduced. Some black members of the Democratic Party believed that President Nixon's large popular vote might cause the Democratic Party to "move to the right" and stop seeking the support of black voters. Yvonne Brathwaite Burke of the Democratic National Committee said that she feared that white leaders of the Democratic Party "may start reading blacks out of the party."

In spite of these fears, black Americans had reason to take some satisfaction from the 1972 election results. A significant number of black politicians were elected to federal, state, and local offices. Three more black Representatives were elected to the House of Representatives, increasing the number of blacks in Congress to seventeen. The voters of Houston, Texas, elected Barbara Jordan to the House of Representatives. Yvonne Brathwaite Burke of Los Angeles, California, and the Reverend Andrew Young of Atlanta, Georgia, also won election to the House. About 100 black officials were elected to state and local offices in the South. This raised the number of black officeholders in the South to over 1,000.

It also was significant that the Democratic Party remained in control of both houses of Congress, since all black members of Congress, except Senator Edward Brooke, were Democrats. As a result, Representative Charles Diggs became chairman of the District of Columbia Committee of the House of Representatives. Other black members of the House received appointments to important committees. For example, Representatives Shirley Chisholm, William Clay, and Augustus Hawkins all served on the House Education and Labor Committee.

THE PATTERN OF THE 1970'S WAS NOT CLEAR

The picture of black life during the decade of the 1970's was slow to come into focus. Clearly, the great majority of black Americans still viewed full participation in American society as their ultimate goal. And considerable progress in this direction had been made. The first black American was elected to the New York Stock Exchange Board in 1972, and a number of blacks were serving on the boards of directors of major American business corporations by the 1970's. In sports, television, motion pictures, and the entertainment world, blacks continued to make considerable progress. The "Flip Wilson Show" and "Sanford and Son" were rated among the top shows on television. Actresses Cicely Tyson and Diana Ross, actor Paul Winfield, and playwright Lonne Elder III were nominated for Academy awards in 1973. In spite of racial incidents, the military services offered attractive careers to young black men and women. In 1973, the army had nine black generals and the air force had two; the navy had a black admiral.

Yet effective programs to deal with the problems of the cities, poverty, and housing continued to require massive action by the federal government. These programs were needed to help the millions of black Americans with incomes below or just above the poverty level. Most black Americans had little hope that the Nixon administration would take the needed action in these areas. They became even less hopeful when the President announced his budget recommendations to Congress in 1973. The President called for reduced spending on domestic programs, many of which affected the poor, the minorities, and the disadvantaged. These included job-training programs, summer youth employment services, regional medical programs, and mental health programs. President Nixon also announced that he planned to end the Office of Economic Opportunity as a separate federal agency.

Members of the Congressional Black Caucus declared that President Nixon's budget cuts were "repressive and inhumane." The President's supporters replied that the Nixon administration's policies were not discriminatory against blacks. They argued that the President was discontinuing only programs that had not worked well and at the same time strengthening programs that had been successful. They pointed to the increased federal support provided for black colleges and minority businesses as examples of programs that benefited from the President's new policies.

Even so, the serious problems of urban decay, poverty, and unemployment remained unsolved. No one could predict whether action would be taken to deal with these problems before the nation faced new urban crises. In the short run, some black Americans found hope in the fact that President Nixon believed in taking bold action when he was convinced of the need to do so. In the long run, they remembered that throughout history the American people have been able to bring about change rather rapidly when such change was in the best interest of the nation.

Books for Further Reading

Surveys of Black American History

*Bennett, Lerone, Jr., *Before the Mayflower: A History of the Negro in America, 1619–1964*, rev. ed. Baltimore, Maryland: Penguin Books, 1966.

*Franklin, John Hope, *From Slavery to Freedom: A History of Negro Americans*, 3d. ed. New York: Vintage Books, 1969.

*Logan, Rayford W., *The Negro in the United States: A Brief History*. New York: Van Nostrand, 1957.

*Meier, August and Elliott M. Rudwick, *From Plantation to Ghetto: An Interpretive History of American Negroes*, rev. ed. New York: Hill and Wang, 1970.

*Quarles, Benjamin, *The Negro in the Making of America*. New York: Collier Books, 1968.

UNIT ONE: The Years of Betrayal

*Hirshon, Stanley P., *Farewell to the Bloody Shirt: Northern Republicans and the Southern Negro, 1877–1893*. New York: Quadrangle Books, 1968.
    Recounts the Republican Party's loss of interest in the black American, and its consequences.

*Lewinson, Paul, *Race, Class and Party: A History of Negro Suffrage and White Politics in the South*. New York: Grosset and Dunlap, 1965.
    A study of the disfranchisement of Southern black voters between 1870 and 1900.

*Logan, Frenise A., *The Negro in North Carolina, 1876–1899*. Chapel Hill, North Carolina: University of North Carolina Press, 1964.

* Paperback edition.

The story of the black citizens of North Carolina following the end of Reconstruction.

*Logan, Rayford, *Betrayal of the Negro*. New York: Collier Books, 1965.
    Describes the erosion and destruction of black rights during the last quarter of the 1800's and the early 1900's.

*Redkey, Edwin S., *Black Exodus: Black Nationalist and Back-to-Africa Movements, 1890–1910*. New Haven, Connecticut: Yale University Press, 1969.
    The history of black emigrationists and early black nationalists.

*Smith, Samuel D., *The Negro in Congress 1870–1901*. Chapel Hill, North Carolina: University of North Carolina Press, 1940.
    A survey of the black members of Congress during the late nineteenth century.

*Tindall, George B., *South Carolina Negroes, 1877–1900*. Baton Rouge, Louisiana: Louisiana State University Press, 1966.
    An account of the loss of the vote and political rights among South Carolina blacks.

*Woodward, Vann C., *The Strange Career of Jim Crow*. New York: Oxford University Press, 1966.
    The development of the pattern and enforcement of Southern segregation.

Wynes, Charles, *Race Relations in Virginia, 1870–1920*. Charlottesville, Virginia: University of Virginia Press, 1961.
    A study of black Virginians and their situation following Reconstruction.

UNIT TWO: Accommodation and Protest

*Broderick, Frances L., *W. E. B. Du Bois: Negro Leader in the Time of Crisis*. Palto Alto, California: Stanford University Press, 1959.
    A biography of Du Bois based on his own writings and personal papers.

*Du Bois, W. E. B., *The Autobiography of W. E. B. Du Bois*. New York: International Publishers, 1968.
    Du Bois' own description of his life, written shortly before his death.

*Du Bois, W. E. B., *Souls of Black Folks*. New York: Fawcett, 1970. Du Bois' essays in which he stated his views and opposed Washington's philosophy.

Hughes, Langston, *Fight for Freedom: The Story of the NAACP*. New York: W. W. Norton, 1962.
An informal, interesting history of this famous black organization.

Kellogg, Charles F., *N.A.A.C.P.: A History of the National Association for the Advancement of Colored People, 1909–1920*, Vol. I. Baltimore, Maryland: Johns Hopkins University Press, 1967.
A scholarly history of the early years of the NAACP.

Meier, August, *Negro Thought in America 1880–1915: Racial Ideologies in the Age of Booker T. Washington*. Ann Arbor, Michigan: University of Michigan Press, 1963.
An analysis of the conflicting theories and ideas of Booker T. Washington, W. E. B. Du Bois, and others.

*Rudwick, Elliot M., *W. E. B. Du Bois: Propagandist of the Negro Protest*. New York: Atheneum, 1968.
A survey of Du Bois' life and thought.

*Spencer, Samuel R., *Booker T. Washington and the Negro's Place in American Life*. Boston: Atlantic–Little, Brown, 1955.
A careful study of Booker T. Washington and his influence on black America.

*Washington, Booker T., *Up From Slavery*. New York: Bantam Books, 1970.
Booker T. Washington's own life story.

UNIT THREE: Black Americans and Progressivism

*Bontemps, Arna and Jack Conroy, *Anyplace But Here*. New York: Hill and Wang, 1966.
Personal narratives which help explain the black migration to the North.

*Fox, Stephen R., *The Guardian of Boston: William Monroe Trotter*. New York: Atheneum, 1971.
The life of an important black leader of the early 1900's.

*Newby, Idus A., *Jim Crow's Defense: Anti-Negro Thought in America, 1900–1930*. Baton Rouge, Louisiana: University of Louisiana Press, 1965.
>Describes how deeply racism and prejudice affected American thought between 1900 and 1930.

*Osefsky, Gilbert, *Harlem: The Making of a Ghetto, 1890–1930*. New York: Harper Torchbook, 1966.
>The story of the evolution of Harlem as a black ghetto.

*Scheiner, Seth M., *Negro Mecca: A History of the Negro in New York City, 1865–1920*. New York: New York University Press, 1965.
>The history of black Americans in New York City from the Civil War to World War I.

*Spear, Allan H., *Black Chicago: The Making of a Negro Ghetto, 1890–1920*. Chicago: University of Chicago Press, 1969.
>Analyzes the development of the black ghetto in Chicago.

*Spero, Sterling D., and Abram L. Harris, *The Black Worker: The Negro and the Labor Movement*. New York: Atheneum, 1968.
>Discusses the problems ot black workers during the early twentieth century.

*Strickland, Arvarh E., *History of the Chicago Urban League*. Urbana, Illinois: University of Illinois Press, 1966.
>Describes the history and the development of the Urban League in Chicago.

UNIT FOUR: The Uncertain Years of the 1920's

*Bronz, Stephen H., *Roots of Negro Racial Consciousness, the 1920's: Three Harlem Renaissance Authors*. Roslyn Heights, New York: Libra Publishers, 1964.
>A study of the works of James Weldon Johnson, Countee Cullen, and Claude McKay.

*Cronon, E. David, *Black Moses: The Story of Marcus Garvey and the Universal Negro Improvement Association*, 2d. ed. Madison, Wisconsin: University of Wisconsin Press, 1969.
>An analysis of the black national movement headed by Garvey.

*Garvey, Amy Jacques, *Garvey and Garveyism*. New York: Macmillan, 1968.

An "insider's" view of Garvey and his movement, written by his wife.

Huggins, Nathan I., *Harlem Renaissance*. New York: Oxford University Press, 1971.
> The best general study of the Harlem Renaissance.

*Johnson, James Weldon, *Black Manhattan*. New York: Atheneum, 1968.
> The story of the Harlem Renaissance as told by one of its leaders.

*Meltzer, Milton and August Meier, *Time of Trial, Time of Hope: The Negro in America, 1919–1941*. Garden City, New York: Doubleday, 1966.
> A survey of black America between the two World Wars.

Rudwick, Elliott M., *A Race Riot at East St. Louis, July 2, 1917*. Carbondale, Illinois: Southern Illinois University Press, 1964.
> A detailed study of a race riot.

*Waskow, Arthur J., *From Race Riot to Sit-In; 1919 and the 1960's: A Study in the Connections between Conflict and Violence*. Garden City, New York: Doubleday, 1966.
> A comparison of the riots after World War I with the turmoil of the black power revolution of the 1960's.

UNIT FIVE: From Depression to World War II

Anderson, Marian, *My Lord What a Morning*. New York: Viking, 1956.
> The famous singer's autobiography.

*Carter, Dan L., *Scottsboro: A Tragedy of the American South*. New York: Oxford University Press, 1971.
> A study of the widely publicized Scottsboro case.

Dalfiune, Richard M., *Desegregation of the United States Armed Forces: Fighting on Two Fronts, 1939–1953*. Columbia, Missouri: University of Missouri Press, 1969.
> An account of the slow desegregation of the armed forces.

*Drake, St. Clair and Horace R. Cayton, *Black Metropolis: A Study of Negro Life in a Northern City*, 2 vols. New York: Harcourt Brace Jovanovich, 1970.
> A classic study of black life in Chicago.

*Garfinkel, Herbert, *When Negroes March: The March on Washington Movement in the Organization Politics for FEPC.* New York: Atheneum, 1969.
> The story of the proposed March on Washington during World War II.

*Green, Constance M., *The Secret City: A History of Race Relations in the Nation's Capital.* Princeton, New Jersey: Princeton University Press, 1967.
> Race relations in Washington, D.C., and the influx of black officials during the 1930's.

Lee, Ulysses, *The United States Army in World War II: The Employment of Negro Troops.* Washington, D.C.: Office of the Chief of Military History, United States Army, 1966.
> An official history of Negro fighting troops during World War II.

Robinson, Jackie (Charles Dexter, ed.), *Baseball Has Done It.* Philadelphia: Lippincott, 1964.
> Jackie Robinson's own story of his career as the first black baseball player in the major leagues.

Shogan, Robert and Tom Craig, *The Detroit Race Riot: A Study of Violence.* Philadelphia: Chilton Books, 1964.
> An analysis of the 1943 Detroit race riot.

*Sternsher, Bernard (ed.), *The Negro In Depression and War.* New York: Quadrangle Books, 1969.
> A collection of writings about black life during the 1930's and early 1940's.

*Wolters, Raymond, *Negroes and the Great Depression.* New York: Negro University Press, 1970.
> An account of Afro-American life during the Great Depression.

UNIT SIX: The Postwar Years, 1945 to the 1970's

Bates, Daisy, *The Long Shadow of Little Rock.* New York: David McKay, 1962.
> The story of the struggle for school desegregation by one of the leaders of the movement.

*Belfrage, Sally, *Freedom Summer.* New York: Viking, 1965.
> The personal story of one young participant in SNCC's summer voter registration drive in Mississippi.

*Bennett, Lerone, Jr., *What Manner of Man: A Biography of Martin Luther King, Jr.* Chicago: Johnson, 1964.
A balanced study of the life of Dr. King.

*Carmichael, Stokely S. and Charles V. Hamilton, *Black Power: The Politics of Liberation in America.* New York: Random House, 1968.
The book that helped define the concept of black power and its ideas.

*Edmonds, Helen G., *Black Faces in High Places: Negroes in Government.* New York: Harcourt Brace Jovanovich, 1971.
A comprehensive, up-to-date portrait of today's black leadership at all levels of government.

*Essien-Udom, E. U., *Black Nationalism: The Search for an Identity.* Chicago: University of Chicago Press, 1972.
A study of black nationalism and the Black Muslim movement.

*King, Martin Luther, Jr., *Stride Toward Freedom: The Montgomery Story.* New York: Harper Torchbook, 1958.
Dr. King's own story of the Montgomery bus boycott.

*Lewis, David, *King: A Critical Biography.* Baltimore, Maryland: Penguin Books, 1971.
A detailed study of the life and philosophy of Martin Luther King, Jr.

*Lincoln, Eric E., *The Black Muslims in America,* rev. ed. Boston: Beacon Press, 1973.
A basic, newly updated study of the Nation of Islam and its members.

*Malcolm X., *The Autobiography of Malcolm X.* New York: Grove, 1965.
The fascinating life story of this charismatic leader.

Muse, Benjamin, *Ten Years of Prelude: The Story of Integration Since the Supreme Court 1954 Decision.* New York: Viking, 1964.
A survey of school desegregation during the decade after the Court's decision.

Peck, James, *Freedom Ride.* New York: Simon and Schuster, 1962.
The story of CORE's freedom rides, written by one of the participants.

Report of the National Advisory Commission on Civil Disorders. New York: Bantam Books, 1968.

An official government study of the reasons for the ghetto riots of the 1960's.

Warren, Robert P., *Who Speaks For the Negro?* New York: Vintage, 1965.
    The philosophy of outstanding modern black leaders, including Dr. King, Malcolm X, James Farmer, and others.

*Zinn, Howard, *SNCC: The New Abolitionists, 1964–1965.* Boston: Beacon Press, 1966.
    An account of SNCC's goals, programs, and activities.

Index

Burger, Warren, 267
Burke, Yvonne B., 273, 274
businesses, black, 45, 140–42, 157–58, 180, 250, 255–56
busing, 265–66, 271–72

California: housing, 202, 218; office holders, black, 268–69; riots, 203, 243
Carmichael, Stokely, 246, 249–50
Chaney, James E., 246
Charleston (S. C.) riot, 126–27
Chestnutt, Charles W., 162
Chicago: migration to, 115, 116–19, 138, 201; Representative, black, 146, 217; school segregation, 242; violence, 131–33, 218–19
Chicago Defender, 115, 127–28
Chicago Whip, 148, 182
Chisholm, Shirley, 273, 276
Civil and Personal Liberty Leagues, 86
civil rights, 12–33, 150; accommodation, 35–45; backlash, 201–3, 213–15, 232–33, 238, 240, 247, 257–58; black power, 245–59; Congress and, 18–19, 215–17, 224, 239–41; Constitutional amendments, 13–21, 26, 30, 74, 76, 79–80, 94, 150–51, 241; Jim Crowism, 21–23, 42–44, 93–94; police brutality, 232–34; politics and, 2, 5, 7, 9–11, 78–96, 240, 256–58, 265–76; protest movements, 50–56, 93–94, 182, 198–99, 222–24, 228–48; "separate but equal" doctrine, 15, 21, 219–20; state vs. federal citizenship, 16–17; Supreme Court rulings on, 15–23, 96, 150–52, 182, 216–17, 219–22, 224, 240, 241, 263, 266–67; white supremacy, 24–33. *See also* Desegregation; Discrimination; Race relations; subjects
Civil Rights Acts: (1866–75) 12–15; (1957) 224; (1960) 238; (1964) 240, 247
Civil Rights Cases of 1883, 18–19
civil service, 92–95, 150, 175, 176; fair employment practices, 214,

216. *See also* Office holders, blacks
Clarke, Edward Y., 125
Clay, William, 269, 273, 276
Cobb, James A., 92, 94
Colored Farmers' Alliance, 7, 10
Commission on Interracial Cooperation, 148–49
Committee for Improving Industrial Conditions of the Negro, 58–60
Committee on Equal Opportunity, 237
Committee on Participation of Negroes in the War, 185
Committee on Urban Conditions Among Negroes in New York, 59–60
Communist Party, 144, 181
Congress: anti-lynching law, 144, 152–53; blacks in, 8–9, 146, 217, 257, 268–69, 273–75; civil rights, 18–19, 215–17, 224, 239
Congress of Industrial Organizations (CIO), 181–82, 195, 207. *See also* AFL-CIO
Congress of Racial Equality (CORE), 229–32, 240, 247, 255
Connor, Eugene "Bull," 233
Constitutional amendments, 13–21, 26, 30, 74, 76, 79–80, 94, 150–51, 241
Coolidge, Calvin, 144, 150, 158
Coughlin, Charles, 204
Council of Black Appointees, 266
Council of Federated Organizations, 240
Cox, Minnie, 83
Crisis, The, 73–74, 91, 95, 99, 149, 153, 163, 196
Cruikshank Case, 16–17, 20
Cullen, Countee, 161, 163, 164

Darrow, Clarence, 72, 152
Davis, Benjamin O., 185, 190
Davis, Benjamin O., Jr., 190, 193, 215
Davis, C. P., 127–28
Davis, John W., 145
Debs, Eugene V., 90
Democratic Party, 78–79, 86–96, 144–46, 210, 235–37, 272–76;

New Deal, 174–82; Populism, 8, 10–11; primaries, 32–33, 140–51; radicals, farmer, 3–7; split, 213–14, 272; white supremacy, 24–33. *See also* names, subjects
De Priest, Oscar, 146
desegregation, 265; housing, 151–52, 202–3, 218–19; professional organizations, 225; public facilities, 221–24, 229–31, 240, 267; schools, 219–21, 238–39, 258, 265–67, 271–72; sports, 225–26
Detroit: housing, 202–3, 218; race conflicts, 202–4; Representative, black, 217; school desegregation, 266
Diggs, Charles C., 217, 269, 271, 275
direct-action and non-violence, 229–43, 247–48
discrimination: business, 140; civil service, 92–95, 150; employment, 119–21, 138–39, 178, 180, 182, 195–201, 204, 206–7, 211, 241; farm relief, 173, 178; Great Migration and, 114–15, 119–22; housing, 151–52, 201–4, 218–19, 241–42, 264; military services, 99–105, 109–10, 184–93, 214–15; New Deal and, 174–75, 178, 179; public facilities, 14–15, 17–18, 20–21, 44, 213; war efforts and morale, 98–99, 196–97; women, 118. *See also* Civil rights; Desegregation; Race relations
Dixiecrats, 213
Du Bois, W. E. B., 46–53, 81, 114, 125, 158, 161, 250; author, 49–50, 162; economy, black, 180; NAACP, 70–73, 76, 91, 95, 149, 180; Niagara Movement, 53–56, 73, 84; politics, 87–96; race unity, 153–54; UN, 211–12; World War I, 98–99
Dunbar, Paul Laurence, 162
Dyer, L. C., 144, 146, 152–53

East St. Louis riot, 120–22
education, 15, 59, 74, 114; busing, 265–66, 271–72; desegregation, 219–21, 238–39, 258, 265–67,

271–72; Du Bois, and, 46–49, 52; New Deal, 178–79; segregation, *de facto*, 242, 247, 265–66; social work, 64–65; student protest movement, 229–32; Washington, Booker T., and, 37–45
Eisenhower, Dwight D., 214–16, 220, 221, 235–38
Elaine (Ark.) riot, 134–35
employment: discrimination, 119–21, 138–39, 178, 180, 182, 195–201, 204, 206–7, 213; fair employment practices, 199–201, 206–7, 211, 215–16, 237, 261–63; government (*see also* Officeholders, black), 92–95, 150, 175, 176, 214, 216; women, 57–58, 118–19. *See also* Labor
Enforcement Act (1870), 14, 16, 19
Europe, James R., 109
Evers, Charles, 257, 268
Evers, Medgar, 233, 234

Fair Employment Practices Committee, 199–201, 207, 211
Farmer, James, 229, 231, 235, 236, 258
Faubus, Orval, 221
Fauset, Jessie R., 163, 166
Federal Council of Churches, 149
Federal Housing Administration (FHA), 218, 264
Fish, Hamilton, 185
Fisk, University, 47–48, 64, 101, 229, 230
Florida: emigration, black, 116, 137; violence, 115
Forman, James, 231
Forrestal, James V., 189
Foster, Benjamin F., 8
freedom riders, 231
Fuller, Meta W., 167

Gaines, Lloyd, 219
Garvey, Marcus M., 154–58, 250
Georgia: civil rights protests, 233; emigration, black, 116, 137; office holders, black, 257; Populism, 8, 11; racism and violence,

PICTURE CREDITS

Page 6, Culver Pictures, Inc.; page 22, The Bettmann Archive; page 28, Culver Pictures, Inc.; page 39, Wide World Photos; page 51, Culver Pictures, Inc.; page 61, Schomburg Collection, New York Public Library; page 75, Schomburg Collection, New York Public Library; page 82, Brown Brothers; page 106, U.S. Signal Corps; page 117, Culver Pictures, Inc.; page 130, New York Public Library; page 143, Schomburg Collection, New York Public Library; page 155, Wide World Photos; page 165, Franklin Watts Publishers; page 177, Ebony Magazine, Johnson Publishing Company; page 187, Culver Pictures, Inc.; page 205, UPI; page 223, Wide World Photos; page 236, UPI; page 251, Wide World Photos; page 270, Ebony Magazine, Johnson Publishing Company.

A 3
B 4
C 5
D 6
E 7
F 8
G 9
H 0
I 1
J 2